THE POETICAL WORKS OF FEDERICO GARCÍA LORCA

Edited by Christopher Maurer

—

Volume III

SELECTED VERSE

Translated by Francisco Aragon, Catherine Brown,
Cola Franzen, Will Kirkland,
William Bryant Logan, Christopher Maurer,
Jerome Rothenberg, Greg Simon,
Alan S. Trueblood, John K.Walsh,
and Steven F. White

FEDERICO

GARCÍA LORCA

—

SELECTED

VERSE

—

Edited and with an introduction and notes
by Christopher Maurer

—

Translated by Francisco Aragon, Catherine Brown,
Cola Franzen, Will Kirkland,
William Bryant Logan, Christopher Maurer,
Jerome Rothenberg, Greg Simon,
Alan S. Trueblood, John K. Walsh,
and Steven F. White

—

Farrar Straus Giroux

New York

Farrar, Straus and Giroux
19 Union Square West, New York 10003

*The translations in this edition were made possible by the General
Book and Library Division of the Spanish Ministry of Culture
and also, in part, by a grant from the Wheatland Foundation,
New York*

Acknowledgments are made to And, Antaeus, The Berkeley Poetry
Review, The Chaminade Literary Review, Northwest Review, The
Paris Review, Poetry New York, Quarry West, Sequoia, Sulfur,
and Talus, *where some of the translations of these poems
originally appeared, in somewhat different form*

*Library of Congress Cataloging-in-Publication Data
García Lorca, Federico, 1898–1936.
[Poems. English. Selections]
Selected verse / Federico García Lorca ; edited and with an
introduction and notes by Christopher Maurer ; translated by
Francisco Aragon . . . [et al.]. — 1st ed.
p.   cm.
I. Maurer, Christopher.   II. Aragon, Francisco.   III. Title.
PQ6613.A763A6   1994   861'.62—dc20   94-14722   CIP*

ISBN 0-374-52352-5

18   17   16   15   14   13   12   11   10

Preface

This book contains poems from two previous volumes: *Poet in New York* (1989) and *Collected Poems* (1990). It draws on every book of poems which García Lorca published during his lifetime, and on his uncollected works.

With the exception of *Poem of the Deep Song*, the translations are those published in the two earlier volumes. The notes have been shortened and have been revised to include scholarship which has appeared over the past few years. The bibliography of English translations has been enlarged, in acknowledgment that translation is a provisional and a cumulative endeavor.

The "essential" Lorca is an elusive, and perhaps imaginary, figure, but this is the most complete anthology of his poems ever published in English.

C.M.

Contents

Introduction

Federico García Lorca was born in 1898—the year that Spain lost her colonies to the United States—in Fuente Vaqueros, an Andalusian village in the Vega, the verdant river plain that lies just to the west of Granada. His mother, Vicenta Lorca Romero, had worked briefly as a schoolteacher, and his father, Federico García Rodríguez, was a landowner whose fortunes rose with the boom of the sugar industry. When Federico was eleven years old, the family (including his younger siblings, Francisco, Conchita, and Isabel) established its home in the city of Granada, but continued to spend its summer vacations in the countryside. Later in life, even after he had lived for many years in Madrid and had traveled widely, García Lorca would insist on the importance of his rural upbringing: "I love the land. All my emotions tie me to it. The first memories I have are of the earth. The earth, the countryside, have wrought great things in my life" (*DS* 132). Both his poetry and his plays prove him a keen observer of nature and of the speech and customs of rural society. And few poets have ever had such a poignant sense of the beauty of their surroundings. Gerald Brenan (230) has recalled that in the 1920s Granada was

a quiet, sedate, self-contained country town, little troubled, except during the month of April, by tourists, and very different from the busy expanding place it is today. Its charm lay, of course, in its situation—the immense green plain, the snow-covered mountains, the elms and cypresses of the Alhambra hill, the streams of noisy, hurrying water. These made up something one could not expect to find anywhere else. But the city was also attractive for its own sake. Its streets and squares and vistas and public gardens might be too unobtrusive to catch the passing tourist's eye, but they had plenty in the way of character and variety to offer the resident. And then beyond them there was always the flat green countryside, with its great glittering olive trees and its clear racing streams bordered with blue iris and its groves of poplar poles by the river. There was a lyrical quality about the place, an elegance of site and detail, of tint and shape, that evoked Tuscany or Umbria rather than the harsh and tawny lion-skin of Spain.

García Lorca wrote several lectures in which he ponders the peculiar, somewhat feminine, character of Granada: her air, "so beautiful that it is almost thought" (*DS* 54); her crystalline water, which descends from the sierra and "lies down to die" in the reflecting pools of the Alhambra (*HCS* n.p.); her long and memorable sunsets; her fondness for tiny things; her contemplative way of life (in contrast to Seville, city of Don Juan); and her landlocked situation: the Mediterranean is thirty miles away, and, unlike Seville, Granada "has no outlet except her high natural port of stars" (*OC* III:249).

Throughout his adolescence, until 1916 or 1917, Federico felt a greater affinity for music than for literature. He was fascinated as a child with the theater, but he also received thorough training as a classical pianist, and his first sense of artistic wonder arose not from his reading but from the piano repertoire of Beethoven, Chopin, Debussy, and others, and, in the early 1920s, after he had become a close friend of the composer Manuel de Falla, from Spanish folk music. Not only did Lorca compose his own piano music (a few specimens are extant); his earliest prose pieces—"Nocturne," "Waltz by Chopin," "Ballade," "Sonata," etc.— are an attempt to turn musical forms to literary use. It has often been noticed that not until the death of his piano teacher in 1916 did Lorca take his first steps as a writer.

Until 1919, Lorca's intellectual milieu—a rich one, by provincial standards—was the circle of talented adolescents who gathered daily in a nook called El Rinconcillo in the Café Alameda in Granada. In that year, one of his professors at the University of Granada, Don Fernando de los Ríos, a leader of the Spanish Socialist Party, persuaded Federico's parents to allow their twenty-year-old son to enroll in the Residencia de Estudiantes in Madrid, an educational institution modeled on Oxford and Cambridge and designed to nurture a cultural elite to steer Spanish society toward liberal ideals. The move to Madrid widened Lorca's horizons, bringing him into contact with intellectual modernity. A lecture society, founded in 1924, gave Lorca and the other Residentes the chance to hear a number of foreign scholars, writers, and musicians: Claudel, Valéry, Cendrars, Max Jacob, Marinetti, Madame Curie, H. G. Wells, Le Corbusier, Chesterton, Wanda Landowska, Ravel, Milhaud, Poulenc, etc. In Madrid, Lorca came under the protection of the great Spanish poet Juan Ramón Jiménez and the playwrights Eduardo Marquina and Gregorio Martínez Sierra, and met many of the leading figures of his own cultural generation. Three of his closest friends in the 1920s were the poet Rafael Alberti, the painter Salvador Dalí, and the filmmaker Luis Buñuel. With Dalí the friendship was exceptionally close. The painter invited him to visit his family in Cadaqués during Holy Week of 1925—Lorca's first trip to Catalonia—and two years later Lorca and Dalí collaborated on the Barcelona production of Lorca's historical drama *Mariana Pineda*. The surviving correspondence between them and Lorca's "Ode to Salvador Dalí" show how deeply they loved one another, and how profoundly that friendship influenced their art:

> . . . *I sing a common thought*
> *that joins us in the dark and golden hours.*
> *The light that blinds our eyes is not art.*
> *Rather it is love, friendship, crossed swords.*

During his years at the Residencia, Lorca worked sporadically on degrees in philosophy and letters and law. His real passion, of course, lay in poetry, in theater, and in music, and by 1927 he had assembled five of his major books: *Book of Poems* (written 1918–20), *Poem of the Deep Song* (mostly 1921), *Suites* (1921–23), *Songs* (1921–26), and *The Gypsy Ballads* (1921–27).

The first of them, *Book of Poems*, published in 1921, contains verses selected with the help of Federico's brother Francisco from among all that he had written since 1918. Some of these poems concern religious faith, a subject to which Lorca had devoted hundreds of pages of his earliest prose. Others dwell on the poet's longing to be at peace with nature, his loneliness, or his sense of estrangement from his own childhood. In sentimental verses reminiscent of the early Jiménez, Rubén Darío, and minor poets of Hispanic *modernismo*, he regrets that reason and rhetoric—the rhetoric of literature—have replaced the poetic faith which allows children to commune with the world of nature.

There is an ache in the flesh of my heart,
in the flesh of my soul.
                    And when I speak
my words bob in the air
like corks on water.

Poem of the Deep Song, Lorca's second book, was written at a time when he and Falla were organizing Spain's first amateur festival of *cante jondo* (a type of popular Andalusian music also known as flamenco), in order to save it from commercial adulteration. Here, as in *Suites*, Lorca is exploring the possibilities of the sequence—the "suite"—of short poems, and the quasi-musical concept of the theme and variations. In these poems, Lorca's subject matter is so "typically" Andalusian, so vulnerable to the dangers of "local color," that Lorca tells a friend he "deserves a smile" for his "daring" (*E*: I:48–49). The brevity and intensity of the *cante jondo* lyrics had been a revelation to him: "It is wondrous and strange how in just three or four lines the anonymous popular poet can condense all the highest moments in human life." Those brief poems, he wrote in 1922, were an inspiration to all poets "who to some degree are concerned with pruning and caring for the overluxuriant lyric tree left to us by the Romantics and Post-Romantics" (*DS* 30–31). Lorca was aware that a new era had begun in Spanish poetry: the poets of the Hispanic world had discovered the short poem (*cante jondo* lyrics, and, more important, haiku) and, like the English and American Imagists, the central importance of the metaphor.

Suites—a collection which Lorca never finished and which was not published until 1983, almost half a century after his death—grew from the same structural idea as *Poem of the Deep Song*: the poetic sequence. By 1923, when this cycle came to a close, Lorca was becoming a master of brevity and of poetic irony, and had proven—to himself, at least— that he could tackle any subject, from Andalusian folk music to the mysteries of time or of personal identity. In the most ambitious of his

Suites, "In the Garden of the Lunar Grapefruits," the twenty-five-year-old poet discovers one of the central themes of his work, the elegiac notion of lost possibility. If *Book of Poems* mourned the loss of *what once was*—the poet's childhood—the "Lunar Grapefruit" poems commemorate *what might have been*. In the summer of 1923 Lorca explained excitedly to a friend: "My *garden* is the garden of possibilities, the garden of what is not, but could (and at times *should*) have been, the garden of theories that passed invisibly by and children who have not been born" (*E* I:69–70).

Written somewhat later, *Songs* is a collection of short lyrical poems thematically related to the *Suites* (in fact, much material from the unpublished *Suites* appears to have been "recycled" into *Songs*). Here Lorca's poetic sequences are much looser. Hoping to show "all the strings of [his] lyre," he divided the collection into chapters: "Andalusian Songs," "Songs for Children," "Games," "Three Portraits with Shading," erotic poems, etc. As in his earlier books, quite a few of the "songs" draw on the structural elements of Spanish folk music (e.g., the use of assonant rhyme and parallelism). In his conversations with Manuel de Falla about *cante jondo*, Lorca had given much thought to how "learned" poetry like his own might best draw on folk poetry. The path he chose, under Falla's guidance and the inspiration, at times, of French and Russian composers and the Ballets Russes, was one of suggestive stylization, rather than quotation or pastiche. "Nothing but the quintessence and this or that trill for its coloristic effect ought to be drawn straight from the people. We should never want to copy their ineffable modulations; we can do nothing but blur them. Simply because of education" (*DS* 33).

Another collection—soon to become Lorca's best-known work—was taking shape as he worked on *Songs: The Gypsy Ballads* (the full Spanish title is *Primer romancero gitano: First Gypsy Ballad Book*). One of the traditional poetic genres that most interested Lorca was the narrative verse form known as the *romance*: the octosyllabic ballad, with feminine rhyme in its even-numbered lines, sung by the Spanish people since the Middle Ages. During Lorca's lifetime, "traditional" ballads were still heard in the Spanish countryside, and philologists like Ramón Menéndez Pidal, whom Lorca helped to gather southern versions, were laboring to record and analyze them. Lorca's "Ballad Book" is a highly stylized imitation of these traditional poems and of popular ballads about crimes and miracles sung by the blind in village squares. He describes it as a great vision—a reredos, or "carved altarpiece"—of Andalusia, "with its gypsies, horses, archangels, planets, its Jewish and Roman breezes, rivers, crimes, the vulgar note of the smugglers and the celestial note of the naked children of Córdoba. A book that hardly expresses visible Andalusia at all, but where hidden Andalusia trembles" (*DS* 105). Stylistically, what interests him is the possibility of fusing narration—the traditional ballads are mostly narrative poems—and lyricism (see, for example, "Sleepwalking Ballad"). Metaphor plays a negligible role in the traditional ballad, but acquires supreme importance in Lorca's collection, thanks, in part, to his admiration for the Baroque poet Luis de Góngora, whom he studies in one of his finest lectures (*DS*, 59–85). By the time he finished the *Ballads*, Lorca was able to emulate many of the qualities of Spanish traditional verse, both lyrical and narrative. Without resorting to direct imitation, he had drawn characters from traditional children's songs; had captured the brevity and intensity of the lyrics of *cante jondo*; and had tried to imbue his own poetry with the sense of mystery—the feeling of fragmentation, of a "story only half told"— which one finds in traditional lullabies and ballads. Brevity, simplicity, a sense of mystery, and the conviction that only metaphor, not merely sentiment, makes poetry last: these were some of the elements of Lorca's early poetics.

The success of *The Gypsy Ballads* in July 1928 brought Lorca fame as a poet throughout the Hispanic world. Only later did he attract the same sort of recognition as a playwright. During the 1920s he worked incessantly on puppet plays and short dialogues, a historical drama in verse (*Mariana Pineda*), and on farces like *The Shoemaker's Prodigious Wife* and *The Love of Don Perlimplín for Belisa in Their Garden*. Both in his poetry and in many of his plays, Lorca had searched for some of the essential elements of Andalusian culture: *cante jondo*, the gypsies, the peculiar admixture of Semitic, Christian, classical, and pre-classical civilizations. Avoiding the pitfalls of "local color" and the merely "picturesque," he had tried to connect Andalusian culture to its pre-Hispanic or non-Andalusian roots: the music of *cante jondo*, for example, had been brought by the gypsies to Spain from India.

With the success of the *Gypsy Ballads*, a painful estrangement from Salvador Dalí, and a failed love affair with Emilio Aladrén, a sculptor whom he met in Madrid in 1925, Lorca grew listless and depressed. By 1927 he was complaining bitterly to friends that he was being pigeonholed as a "gypsy poet." "This gypsy myth of mine annoys me a little," he wrote bitterly to his friend the poet Jorge Guillén. "The gypsies are a theme. And nothing more. I could just as well be a poet of sewing needles or hydraulic landscapes. Besides, this gypsyism gives me the appearance of an uncultured, ignorant and *primitive poet* that you know very well I'm not. I don't want to be typecast" (*Selected Letters*, 94). Fleeing that image, Lorca left Spain. Fernando de los Ríos, the family friend who had helped him enroll at the Residencia de Estudiantes a decade earlier, was about to depart for New York on a lecture tour, and Federico's parents allowed the poet to accompany him. The two of them departed in June 1929 on the SS *Olympic*, sister ship of the *Titanic*. With generous financial support from his parents, the thirty-one-year-old Lorca enrolled in English classes at Columbia University, and lived in Manhattan, with a brief sojourn in Eden Mills, Vermont, from June 1929 to March 1930. As at the Residencia, his studies were infinitely less important to him than his writing. While in New York and during an additional three months in Cuba, Lorca worked on his theater, delivered a series of lectures, went to plays and concerts, walked the streets of New York and Havana, and composed the difficult poems that would be published posthumously in 1942 as *Poet in New York*. One decisive part of his experience in the New World was the Wall Street crash of 1929, described in a moving letter to his family (*PNY* 247–51).

Written in 1929–32 and gathered into a book toward the end of Lorca's life, *Poet in New York* is a sharp departure from all his earlier works. In it, one finds an anguish that is both personal and societal. An intensely lonely poetic "narrator" with the qualities of biblical prophet and priest raises his voice in condemnation of urban capitalist society and all that it entails: an anthropocentric worldview; the degradation of nature; indifference to suffering; the materialistic corruption of love and religion; and the alienation of social groups, particularly the blacks. By the time he returned to Spain, Lorca had proven to himself that he could write long, memorable poems in free verse on the most unpoetic of subjects (the title *Poet in New York* was meant to sound paradoxical). In offering his own dark vision of urban modernity, he had defied those who considered him a minor, Andalusian "folk poet."

In April 1931, less than a year after Lorca's return to Spain, the country entered a new period in its history. Miguel Primo de Rivera, the dictator who had governed since 1923, was ousted from power in 1930; the Bourbon monarch Alfonso XIII abdicated; and the Second Republic came into being. During the final half decade of his life, Lorca contributed enthusiastically, as lecturer and as man of the theater, to the cultural program of the Republic. One of his major projects was directing La Barraca, a university theater group which traveled through the Spanish countryside giving free performances of the classical theater (Cervantes, Lope de Vega, Calderón, etc.). With a portable stage and a minimum of equipment, La Barraca performed in town squares before audiences who had never seen any theater at all. "Outside of Madrid," the poet remarked to an American journalist, "the theatre, which is in its very essence a part of the life of the people, is almost dead, and the people suffer accordingly, as they would if they had lost eyes or ears or a sense of taste. We are going to give it back to them" (*OC* II:507).

Lorca's own theater was deeply affected, not only by the experience he was acquiring as a stage director, but by social concerns present in even his earliest writing but heightened by his visit to New York and his travels through the Spanish countryside. By February 1935, after the premiere of *Yerma* in Madrid, Lorca had declared himself an ardent advocate of the theater of social action. "The theater is a school of weeping and laughter, a free tribunal where men can question norms that are outmoded or mistaken and explain with living example eternal norms of the human heart" (*DS* 124). His three most important plays from the 1930s—*Blood Wedding, Yerma, The House of Bernarda Alba*—rebelled, in one form or another, against Spanish bourgeois society. For one thing,

Lorca was calling on the Spanish and European theater to rediscover its roots, and one of those roots lay in Greek tragedy. In the three plays just mentioned, the theatrical form—poetic tragedy—seemed, itself, a protest against the prosaic, realist conventions of the bourgeois theater; for example, the popular middle-class drawing-room comedies of Jacinto Benavente. In his travels with La Barraca, in his support for other amateur theater groups, and in the presentation of his own works, Lorca searched for "alternative" audiences or did his best to provoke middle-class ones. In his own works, he was exploring a number of controversial issues, including homoeroticism, the class system, and the societal role of women.

It has often been noticed that in the last five years of his life, from the declaration of the Second Republic to the outbreak of the Spanish Civil War in 1936, Lorca wrote far less poetry than he had in the past. It would be fairer to say that his poetry had found a new, more public venue: the stage. "Theater," he remarked in 1936, is simply "poetry that rises from the book and becomes human enough to talk and shout, weep and despair" (*OC* II:673). For the Lorca of the 1930s, all theater worthy of the name questions social norms, and there can be no more effective agent of change than poetry.

Meanwhile, his lyrical poetry grew more intense. *The Tamarit Divan* (or *The Divan of the Tamarit*), written in 1931–34 and published posthumously, is a collection of twenty poems in which Lorca pays distant homage to the love poetry of the Arabs. In its "casidas" and "ghazals" (the names of verse forms of classical Arabic poetry), the poet reckons gravely with a love affair which has come to an end and which reminds him only of death. Eros and Thanatos are drawn together here, as they are in all of Lorca's work:

There is no one who can kiss
without feeling the smile of those without faces;
there is no one who can touch
an infant and forget the immobile skulls of horses.

Under the "lukewarm roses" of the nuptial bed, "the dead are moaning, awaiting their turn." Only death can still the poet's longing:

Everything else all passes away.
Now blush without number. Perpetual star.
Everything else is something else: sad wind
while the leaves flee, whirling in flocks.

Lorca wrote these verses in April 1934, aboard the *Conte Biancamano*, on his return voyage to Spain from Buenos Aires, where he had given a series of lectures and directed the Argentine premiere of *Blood Wedding*. To huge, admiring audiences in Buenos Aires and Montevideo he had delivered a stirring speech on artistic inspiration, "Play and Theory of the Duende" (*DS*, 42–53), suggesting that great art—art with *duende*—can occur only when the creator is acutely aware of death. In his lecture on "The Poetic Image of Don Luis de Góngora," given years earlier in 1926–27, Lorca had admired the calm, rational way the Baroque poet "reined in" his imagination and chose his deathless metaphors. Góngora's lesson for modern poets lay in his clarity, his faith in analogy and myth, his sense of poetic proportion and equilibrium. The lecture on *duende* acknowledges three other, very different elements in the process of artistic creation: demonic irrationality, closeness to nature, and, above all, an awareness of death:

The duende does not come at all unless he sees that death is possible. The duende must know beforehand that he can serenade death's house and rock those branches we all wear, branches that do not have, will never have, any consolation. // With idea, sound, or gesture, the duende enjoys fighting the creator on the very rim of the well. Angel and muse escape with violin and compass; the duende wounds. In the healing of that wound, which never closes, lie the invented, strangest qualities of a man's work. (DS, 49–50).

That lecture, Lorca's final attempt at a theory of artistic inspiration, throws much light on his later verse.

Written in the same period as the *duende* lecture and the *Divan*, but published in Galician rather than Spanish, Lorca's next work, *Six Galician Poems*, pays homage to another of Spain's non-Castilian literary traditions. Galicia—the hilly, rainy farming region in northwestern Spain, whose spiritual capital is the medieval cathedral town of Santiago de Compostela, had been the home of an important school of medieval lyric poetry: the so-called Portuguese/Galician lyric. A great Galician poet, Rosalía de Castro, whom Lorca deeply admired, had emerged in the nineteenth century, and in the 1920s and 1930s, Galicia was in the midst of a linguistic and literary Renaissance. Lorca's interest in Galicia was heightened by his trip to Buenos Aires, a city with a large population of Galician immigrants.

The contemplation of death returns to the fore in *Lament for Ignacio Sánchez Mejías* (written in 1934, published in 1935), one of the greatest elegies ever written by a European poet, and the greatest one in Spanish since Jorge Manrique's fifteenth-century "Verses for the Death of His Father." In it Lorca commemorates a beloved friend, a *torero* gored to death in a provincial bullring. One striking thing about this poem is the "totality" of its vision, from the metonymical description of the goring itself, where the sensorial phenomena of the accident crowd in upon the poet, chaotically, "at exactly five in the afternoon," to his restrained meditation on death and his angry refusal of consolation.

Lorca's return to "classical" forms of theater—the tragedy, *commedia dell'arte*, the puppet play—coincided, near the end of his life, with his renewed interest in one of the classical forms of poetry: the sonnet. Young Spanish poets, he remarked in 1936, were crusading for a return to "traditional forms, after a wide-ranging, sunny stroll through the freedom of meter and rhyme" (*OC* II:676). In the final few years of his life, he worked on a little anthology entitled *Sonnets of Dark Love: dark* love because some of these poems, eleven of which are extant, were inspired by a young engineering student—secretary of La Barraca—with whom he had fallen in love in 1933, Rafael Rodríguez Rapún. This is Lorca's last major poetic work (it, too, was published posthumously), and like all his previous ones, it alludes to an earlier poetic style. In his *Poem of the Deep Song*, Lorca had acknowleged the *cante jondo* lyric, and in *Songs* and *Suites*, other forms of traditional song, including children's songs and the lullaby. The *Gypsy Ballads* drew on the most popular of all Spanish verse forms, and in his Galician poems Lorca had imitated the parallelism of medieval lyric. In the *Lament*, we find not only the style of the ballad (the second section is written in octosyllables) but also, somewhat more vaguely, that of the Catholic liturgy. In the *Sonnets* he returns to a classical genre—the cycle of love sonnets—and draws boldly on the imagery of the sixteenth-century mystical poet San Juan de la Cruz, who had described the "dark night of the soul" in preparation for its encounter with God.

Lorca once remarked to a friend, apropos of the death of Sánchez Mejías, that it had been "an apprenticeship" for his own. Death came to him violently, in August 1936, in the early days of the Spanish Civil War, during the Fascist uprising in Granada. Aware that war was imminent and that his liberal views made him suspect to the right-wing movement that was rising in arms against the Republic, Lorca had fled from Madrid to the apparent safety of his family home. After a period in hiding at the house of a friend, he was arrested and, by order of one of Franco's generals, driven into the countryside and executed. His body was buried in an unmarked grave near the hamlet of Víznar.

In 1935, less than a year before his death, while working on *The House of Bernarda Alba*, Federico García Lorca had begged indulgence for his inexperience as a playwright: "I still haven't reached . . . maturity . . . I still consider myself a true novice, and I'm still learning my profession . . . One has to ascend one step at a time . . . [No one should] demand of my nature, my spiritual and intellectual development, something that no author can give until much later . . . My work has barely begun" (Ucelay, 57–58). "Barely begun," his work was at an end. In the twenty years since he had taken up his pen, García Lorca had produced at least nine books of poetry, music, innumerable drawings, several volumes of charming lectures and letters, and had given new direction to the Spanish theater. For decades, his work would be read in the *shadow* of his death. Poems and plays seemed to foretell his early end and even its violence: an attempt, perhaps, on the part of his readers to endow a "senseless" act, a "terrible mistake" with some sort of meaning. Faithful to his own vision of social justice, he had always taken pains to distance himself from the partisan violence around him.

Some have argued that a poet's death is his "last creative act"; that even a random, "senseless" death is the peculiar act of closure which gives form, and therefore meaning, to his life's work. "For a Romantic," Nadezhda Mandelstam (428–29) once wrote, "death is an undeserved outrage against his person. But for someone who has found his place in life—a life replete with meaning—death is simply his last creative act. I believe that the cleansing power of lyric verse flows from the poet's acceptance of life with its sorrow and misfortunes, from his certainty that through ordinary everyday existence one achieves awareness of another life, thus coming to know the Creator through what He has created." Whether or not Lorca ever accepted his fate is an unanswerable, though not an idle, question. But few readers of his poems would doubt that he has deepened their own sense of the pain and beauty of life, "with its sorrows and misfortunes." His poetry touches wistfully, elegiacally, occasionally with anger, on the principal themes of human existence: the otherness of nature, the limitations of language and reason, the demons of personal identity and artistic creation, sex, childhood and death.

Always, no matter what he is writing about, he is a writer of elegy. Typically, he draws on an "absent" style—on "dead poets," *cante jondo*, Góngora—to evoke an absent object. Reading forwards or backwards, from his final pages to the very earliest ones he wrote, or vice versa, it seems that the theme of his entire oeuvre is *the impossible*: the melancholy conviction that all of us have certain indefinable longings which cannot be satisfied by anything around us. Robert Bly (101) got it right: Lorca is a poet of desire. He is always saying "what he wants, what he desires, what barren women desire, what water desires, what gypsies desire, what a bull desires just before he dies, what brothers and sisters desire." Lorca's powers of metaphor push desire even further, into the world of plants and rocks and insects. In his poems, all of life is riven by some sort of longing and want.

In his work, one finds different figures of desire: the sexual urge; longing for marriage or maternity; the yearning for social justice; the drive toward personal fulfillment of one sort or another; and, above all, the yearning of the poet, through language, to capture reality. "The poet," Lorca wrote in 1928, "is in a sad state of 'wanting and not being able.'

He hears the flow of great rivers, passing by in silence, with no one else to hear their music. On his brow he feels the coolness of the reeds, swaying in their No Man's Land. He wants to feel the dialogue of the winds that tremble in the moss . . . He wants to penetrate the music of the sap running in the dark silence of huge treetrunks . . . He wants to press his ear to the sleeping girl and understand the Morse code of her heart . . . He wants . . . But he cannot. (C II:16)

In Lorca, poetic activity, metaphor itself, is *the* figure of desire. As the poet Michael Heller (33) wrote, apropos of *cante jondo*, "any trope of language leads always to a beautiful and terrifying indeterminacy." Poetry like Lorca's exists to remind us of its limitations and of the inability of reason and language to fully "capture" reality or experience. What is most memorable in Lorca's poetry and theater is that desire is never fully defined, only gestured at, and therefore unable *ever* to be satisfied. Before desire is defined, it is somehow cancelled: by madness, despair or melancholy, by societal indifference, by language, or, more neatly, by death. A poem from *Songs*, written when Lorca was twenty-three, is emblematic:

RIDER'S SONG

Córdoba,
distant and lonely.

Black pony, large moon,
in my saddlebag olives.
Well as I know the roads,
I shall never reach Córdoba.

Over the plain, through the wind,
black pony, red moon.
Death keeps a watch on me
from Córdoba's towers.

Oh, such a long way to go!
And, oh, my spirited pony!
Ah, but death awaits me
before I ever reach Córdoba.

Córdoba.
Distant and lonely.

(trans. Alan S. Trueblood)

Mysterious and fragmentary as any traditional ballad, the poem offers no explanation of why the rider wants to reach Córdoba, why he is certain he will never do so. Córdoba itself seems indefinable and a little arbitrary. It is, simply, the *desideratum* that creates a poetic field of force. It is, in abstract terms, the unknown, the absent, the impossible, clothed in sound. In any case, desire is defeated, its object recedes beyond the horizon, the rider's voice—brave voice—expires in a final sigh of resignation. "Rider's Song" is an emblem of Lorca's own broken journey, toward a destination no critic, no reader, no poet will ever define.

Christopher Maurer

Vanderbilt University
Nashville, Tennessee

Selected Poems

De

LIBRO DE
POEMAS

From

BOOK OF POEMS

Translated by

Catherine Brown

[*Girl with Hoop Skirt and Ring, 1924*]

Veleta
Julio de 1920
(Fuente Vaqueros, Granada)

Viento del Sur.
Moreno, ardiente,
llegas sobre mi carne,
trayéndome semilla
de brillantes
miradas, empapado
de azahares.

Pones roja la luna
y sollozantes
10   los álamos cautivos, pero vienes
¡demasiado tarde!
¡Ya he enrollado la noche de mi cuento
en el estante!

Sin ningún viento,
¡hazme caso!
Gira, corazón;
gira, corazón.

Aire del Norte,
¡oso blanco del viento!,
20   llegas sobre mi carne
tembloroso de auroras
boreales,
con tu capa de espectros
capitanes,
y riyéndote a gritos
del Dante.
¡Oh pulidor de estrellas!
Pero vienes
demasiado tarde.
30   Mi almario está musgoso
y he perdido la llave.

Sin ningún viento,
¡hazme caso!
Gira, corazón;
gira, corazón.

Brisas gnomos y vientos
de ninguna parte,

Weathervane
July 1920
(Fuente Vaqueros, Granada)

    South wind.
Dark and burning,
soaked with orange blossoms,
you come over my flesh,
bringing me seed
of brilliant gazes.

    You turn the moon red,
make captive poplars moan,
but you've come
10   too late!
I've already scrolled up the night
of my tale on the shelf!

    Without any wind
—Look sharp!—
Turn, heart.
Turn, my heart.

    Northern air,
white bear of the wind!
You come over my flesh
20   shivering with boreal
auroras,
with your cape of phantom
captains,
laughing aloud at Dante.
Oh polisher of stars!
But you've come
too late.
My case is musty
and I've lost the key.

30   Without any wind
—Look sharp!—
Turn, heart.
Turn, my heart.

    Gnome breezes and winds
from nowhere.
Mosquitoes of the rose
with pyramid petals.

5

mosquitos de la rosa
de pétalos pirámides,
40 alisios destetados
entre los rudos árboles,
flautas en la tormenta,
¡dejadme!
Tiene recias cadenas
mi recuerdo,
y está cautiva el ave
que dibuja con trinos
la tarde.

Las cosas que se van no vuelven nunca,
50 todo el mundo lo sabe,
y entre el claro gentío de los vientos
es inútil quejarse.
¿Verdad, chopo, maestro de la brisa?
¡Es inútil quejarse!

Sin ningún viento,
¡hazme caso!
Gira, corazón;
gira, corazón.

Corazón nuevo
Junio de 1918
(Granada)

Mi corazón, como una sierpe,
se ha desprendido de su piel,
y aquí la miro entre mis dedos,
llena de heridas y de miel.

Los pensamientos que anidaron
en tus arrugas ¿dónde están?
¿Dónde las rosas que aromaron
a Jesucristo y a Satán?

¡Pobre envoltura que ha oprimido
10 a mi fantástico lucero!
Gris pergamino dolorido
de lo que quise y ya no quiero.

Yo veo en ti fetos de ciencias,
momias de versos y esqueletos

Trade winds weaned
among rough trees,
40 flutes in the storm,
begone!
My memory is chained;
captive the bird
that sketches the evening
in song.

    Things that go away never return—
everybody knows that.
And in the bright crowd of the winds
there's no use complaining!
50 Am I right, poplar, teacher of the breeze?
There's no use complaining!

    Without any wind
—Look sharp!—
Turn, heart.
Turn, my heart.

New Heart
June 1918
(Granada)

    Like a snake, my heart
has shed its skin.
I hold it here in my hand,
full of honey and wounds.

    The thoughts that nested
in your folds, where are they now?
Where the roses that perfumed
both Jesus Christ and Satan?

    Poor wrapper that damped
10 my fantastical star,
parchment gray and mournful
of what I loved once but love no more!

    I see fetal sciences in you,
mummified poems, and bones

de mis antiguas inocencias
y mis románticos secretos.

¿Te colgaré sobre los muros
de mi museo sentimental,
junto a los gélidos y oscuros
20   lirios durmientes de mi mal?

¿O te pondré sobre los pinos
—libro doliente de mi amor—
para que sepas de los trinos
que da a la aurora el ruiseñor?

¡Cigarra!
3 de agosto de 1918
(Fuente Vaqueros, Granada)

A María Luisa

¡Cigarra!
¡Dichosa tú!
Que sobre lecho de tierra
mueres borracha de luz.

Tú sabes de las campiñas
el secreto de la vida,
y el cuento del hada vieja
que nacer hierba sentía
en ti quedóse guardado.

10   ¡Cigarra!
¡Dichosa tú!
Pues mueres bajo la sangre
de un corazón todo azul.

La luz es Dios que desciende,
y el sol,
brecha por donde se filtra.

¡Cigarra!
¡Dichosa tú!
Pues sientes en la agonía
20   todo el peso del azul.

Todo lo vivo que pasa
por las puertas de la muerte

of my romantic secrets
and old innocence.

    Shall I hang you on the wall
of my emotional museum,
beside my dark, chill,
20   sleeping irises of evil?

    Or shall I spread you over the pines
—suffering book of my love—
so you can learn about the song
the nightingale offers the dawn?

Cicada!
August 3, 1918
(Fuente Vaqueros, Granada)

To María Luisa

    Cicada!
Oh happy cicada!
On a bed of earth you die,
drunk with light.

    You know from the fields
the secret of life;
you keep the tale
of that old fairy
who could hear the grass be born.

10   Cicada!
Oh happy cicada!
For you die under blood
of a deep blue heart.

    The light is God descending,
and the sun
the chink it filters through.

    Cicada!
Oh happy cicada!
For you feel in your throes
20   all the weight of the blue.

    Everything alive that passes
through death's doors

9

va con la cabeza baja
y un aire blanco durmiente.
Con habla de pensamiento.
Sin sonidos . . .
Tristemente,
cubierto con el silencio
que es el manto de la muerte.

30   Mas tú, cigarra encantada,
derramando son te mueres
y quedas trasfigurada
en sonido y luz celeste.

    ¡Cigarra!
¡Dichosa tú!
Pues te envuelve con su manto
el propio Espíritu Santo,
que es la luz.

    ¡Cigarra!
40 Estrella sonora
sobre los campos dormidos,
vieja amiga de las ranas
y de los oscuros grillos,
tienes sepulcros de oro
en los rayos tremolinos
del sol que dulce te hiere
en la fuerza del Estío,
y el sol se lleva tu alma
para hacerla luz.

50   Sea mi corazón cigarra
sobre los campos divinos.
Que muera cantando lento
por el cielo azul herido
y cuando esté ya expirando
una mujer que adivino
lo derrame con sus manos
por el polvo.

    Y mi sangre sobre el campo
sea rosado y dulce limo
60 donde claven sus azadas
los cansados campesinos.

    ¡Cigarra!
¡Dichosa tú!

goes head down, with
a white somnolent air.
With speech only thought.
Soundless . . . sadly,
cloaked with silence,
the mantle of death.

   But you, cicada,
30 die enchanted, spilling music,
transfigured in sound
and heavenly light.

   Cicada!
Oh happy cicada!
You are wrapped in the mantle
of the Holy Spirit,
who is light itself.

   Cicada!
Sonorous star
40 over sleeping fields,
old friend of the frogs
and the shadowy crickets,
you have golden tombs
in turbulent sunbeams
that wound you, sweet
in the vigor of Summer.
The sun carries off your soul
to make it into light.

50   Let my heart be a cicada
over heavenly fields.
Let it die singing slow,
by the blue sky wounded.
And, as it fades,
let this woman I foresee
scatter it through the dust
with her hands.

   And let my blood on the field
make sweet and rosy mud
where weary peasants
60 sink their hoes.

   Cicada!
Oh happy cicada!

Pues te hieren las espadas invisibles
del azul.

Árboles
1919

 ¡Árboles!
¿Habéis sido flechas
caídas del azul?
¿Qué terribles guerreros os lanzaron?
¿Han sido las estrellas?

 Vuestras músicas vienen del alma de los pájaros,
de los ojos de Dios,
de la pasión perfecta.
¡Árboles!
10 ¿Conocerán vuestras raíces toscas
mi corazón en tierra?

Hora de estrellas
1920

 El silencio redondo de la noche
sobre el pentágrama
del infinito.

 Yo me salgo desnudo a la calle,
maduro de versos
perdidos.
Lo negro, acribillado
por el canto del grillo,
tiene ese fuego fatuo,
10 muerto,
del sonido.
Esa luz musical
que percibe
el espíritu.

 Los esqueletos de mil mariposas
duermen en mi recinto.

 Hay una juventud de brisas locas
sobre el río.

For you are wounded by invisible swords
from the blue.

Trees
1919

    Trees!
Were you once arrows
fallen from blue?
What terrible warriors
cast you down? The stars?

    Your music springs from the soul of birds,
from the eyes of God,
from perfect passion.
Trees!
10 Will your tough roots know
my heart in the soil?

Hour of Stars
1920

    The round silence of night,
one note on the stave
of the infinite.

    Ripe with lost poems,
I step naked into the street.
The blackness riddled
by the singing of crickets:
sound,
that dead
10 will-o'-the-wisp,
that musical light
perceived
by the spirit.

    A thousand butterfly skeletons
sleep within my walls.

    A wild crowd of young breezes
over the river.

El camino

No conseguirá nunca
tu lanza
herir al horizonte.
La montaña
es un escudo
que lo guarda.

No sueñes con la sangre de la luna
y descansa.
Pero deja, camino,
10   que mis plantas
exploren la caricia
de la rociada.

¡Quiromántico enorme!
¿Conocerás las almas
por el débil tatuaje
que olvidan en tu espalda?
Si eres un Flammarion
de las pisadas,
¡cómo debes amar
20   a los asnos que pasan
acariciando con ternura humilde
tu carne desgarrada!
Ellos solos meditan dónde puede
llegar tu enorme lanza.
Ellos solos, que son
los Buddhas de la Fauna,
cuando viejos y heridos deletrean
tu libro sin palabras.

¡Cuánta melancolía
30   tienes entre las casas
del poblado!
¡Qué clara
es tu virtud! Aguantas
cuatro carros dormidos,
dos acacias,
y un pozo del antaño
que no tiene agua.

Dando vueltas al mundo,
no encontrarás posada.
40   No tendrás camposanto

The Road

Your lance
will never wound
the horizon.
The mountain
is a shield
that guards it.

Do not dream
of the blood of the moon,
just rest.
10 But, oh road, let
the soles of my feet
be caressed by the dew.

Enormous palmist!
Perhaps you read souls
in the faint tattoos
they leave forgotten on your back?
If you are a Flammarion
of footprints,
how you must love
20 the passing donkeys
who, with humble tenderness,
caress your riven flesh!
They alone consider
the aim of your enormous lance.
Buddhas among fauna,
they alone,
when old and wounded,
spell out
your wordless book.

30 How melancholy you are
among the village houses!
How bright your virtue!
You patiently support
four sleeping wagons,
two acacias,
and an ancient well
that has no water.

In all your travels
round the world,
40 you find no shelter,

ni mortaja,
ni el aire del amor renovará
tu sustancia.

Pero sal de los campos
y en la negra distancia
de lo eterno, si tallas
la sombra con tu lima
blanca, ¡oh, camino!,
¡pasarás por el puente
50   de Santa Clara!

El concierto interrumpido
1920

A Adolfo Salazar

Ha roto la armonía
de la noche profunda
el calderón helado y soñoliento
de la media luna.

Las acequias protestan sordamente,
arropadas con juncias,
y las ranas, muecines de la sombra,
se han quedado mudas.

En la vieja taberna del poblado
10   cesó la triste música,
y ha puesto la sordina a su aristón
la estrella más antigua.

El viento se ha sentado en los torcales
de la montaña oscura,
y un chopo solitario—el Pitágoras
de la casta llanura—
quiere dar, con su mano centenaria,
un cachete a luna.

Cantos nuevos
Agosto de 1920
(Vega de Zujaira)

Dice la tarde:
        «¡Tengo sed de sombra!»

no cemetery, no shroud;
nor will the air of love
renew your being.

But come out of the fields
and if, in the black distance
of the eternal, you carve
the shadow with your
white file, oh road!
you'll go over the bridge
50   of Santa Clara.

The Interrupted Concert
1920

To Adolfo Salazar

The half moon, a fermata
somnolent and frozen,
marks a pause and splits
the midnight harmony.

Blanketed in sedge,
the ditches protest mutely,
and frogs, the muezzins of shadow,
have fallen silent.

In the old town tavern
10   the sad music stopped,
and the oldest of stars
has damped its hurdy-gurdy.

The wind has settled
in dark mountain hollows,
and a solitary poplar,
Pythagoras of chaste plains,
wants to lift up its hundred-year-old hand
and slap the moon in the face.

New Songs
August 1920
(Vega de Zujaira)

The afternoon says:
                    "I'm thirsty for shadow!"

17   *from* BOOK OF POEMS

Dice la luna: «Yo, sed de luceros».
La fuente cristalina pide labios
y suspiros el viento.

Yo tengo sed de aromas y de risas.
Sed de cantares nuevos
sin lunas y sin lirios,
y sin amores muertos.

Un cantar de mañana que estremezca
10   a los remansos quietos
del porvenir. Y llene de esperanza
sus ondas y sus cienos.

Un cantar luminoso y reposado,
pleno de pensamiento,
virginal de tristezas y de angustias
y virginal de ensueños.

Cantar sin carne lírica que llene
de risas el silencio.
(Una bandada de palomas ciegas
20   lanzadas al misterio.)

Cantar que vaya al alma de las cosas
y al alma de los vientos
y que descanse al fin en la alegría
del corazón eterno.

Se ha puesto el sol
Agosto de 1920

Se ha puesto el sol.
                Los árboles
meditan como estatuas.
Ya está el trigo segado.
¡Qué tristeza
de las norias paradas!

Un perro campesino
quiere comerse a Venus, y le ladra.
Brilla sobre su campo de pre-beso,
como una gran manzana.

And the moon: "I want stars."
The crystal fountain asks for lips,
the wind, for sighs.

I'm thirsty for scents and for laughter.
Thirsty for new songs
without irises or moons,
without dead loves.

10   A morning song that can shiver
quiet backwaters
of the future and fill
their waves and silt with hope.

A luminous and tranquil song
full of thought,
virgin to sadness and anguish,
virgin to reverie.

A song skinned of lyric, filling
silence with laughter.
20   (A flock of blind doves
tossed into mystery.)

A song to go to the soul of things
and to the soul of winds,
resting at last in the bliss
of the eternal heart.

The Sun Has Set
August 1920

The sun has set,
               and trees,
like statues, meditate.
The wheat has all been cut.
What sadness
in the quiet waterwheels!

A country dog
hungers for Venus
and barks at her.
She shines above her pre-kiss field
10   like a great apple.

10   Los mosquitos—pegasos del rocío—
vuelan, el aire en calma.
La Penélope inmensa de la luz
teje una noche clara.

«Hijas mías, dormid, que viene el lobo»,
las ovejitas balan.
«¿Ha llegado el otoño, compañeras?»,
dice una flor ajada.

¡Ya vendrán los pastores con sus nidos
por la sierra lejana!
20   Ya jugarán las niñas en la puerta
de la vieja posada,
y habrá coplas de amor
que ya se saben
de memoria las casas.

El lagarto viejo
26 de julio de 1920
(Vega de Zujaira)

En la agostada senda
he visto al buen lagarto
(gota de cocodrilo)
meditando.
Con su verde levita
de abate del diablo,
su talante correcto
y su cuello planchado,
tiene un aire muy triste
10   de viejo catedrático.
¡Esos ojos marchitos
de artista fracasado
cómo miran la tarde
desmayada!

¿Es este su paseo
crepuscular, amigo?
Usad bastón, ya estáis
muy viejo, Don Lagarto,
y los niños del pueblo
20   pueden daros un susto.
¿Qué buscáis en la senda,

Mosquitoes—Pegasuses of the dew—
wheel in the still air.
Light, that vast Penelope,
weaves a brilliant night.

"Sleep, my daughters,
for the wolf is coming,"
bleat the little sheep.
"Is it autumn yet, my friends?"
asks a crumpled flower.

20   Now shepherds will come with their nests
across the mountains, far away!
Now little girls will play
in the old inn's door,
and the houses will hear
love songs they've long known
by heart.

The Old Lizard
July 26, 1920
(Vega de Zujaira)

In the sunbaked path
I've seen the good lizard
(drop of crocodile)
meditating.
Like a diabolical abbot
with his green waistcoat,
his perfect demeanor,
and his ironed collar;
melancholy, like
10   an old professor.
Those wilted eyes
of an artist manqué—
how they observe
the fainting afternoon!

Is this your evening
stroll, my friend?
You should use a cane;
you're getting on now,
Mr. Lizard,
20   and the village children
could give you a scare.

filósofo cegato,
si el fantasma indeciso
de la tarde agosteña
ha roto el horizonte?

    ¿Buscáis la azul limosna
del cielo moribundo?
¿Un céntimo de estrella?
¿O acaso
30 estudiasteis un libro
de Lamartine, y os gustan
los trinos platerescos
de los pájaros?

    (Miras al sol poniente,
y tus ojos relucen,
¡oh dragón de las ranas!,
con un fulgor humano.
Las góndolas sin remos
de las ideas, cruzan
40 el agua tenebrosa
de tus iris quemados.)

    ¿Venís quizá en la busca
de la bella lagarta,
verde como los trigos
de Mayo,
como las cabelleras
de las fuentes dormidas,
que os despreciaba, y luego
se fue de vuestro campo?
50 ¡Oh dulce idilio roto
sobre la fresca juncia!
¡Pero vivir! ¡qué diantre!
Me habéis sido simpático.
El lema de «me opongo
a la serpiente» triunfa
en esa gran papada
de arzobispo cristiano.

    Ya se ha disuelto el sol
en la copa del monte,
60 y enturbian el camino
los rebaños.
Es hora de marcharse,
dejad la angosta senda

Myopic philosopher,
what do you seek
along the path,
if the hesitant specter
of an August afternoon
has broken the horizon?

   Are you begging azure alms
from this dying sky?
A star-penny?
Maybe you studied
a book by Lamartine
and you just enjoy
the plateresque twitter of birds?

   (Looking at the setting sun,
your eyes gleam
—oh dragon of the frogs!—
with a human brilliance.
Oarless gondolas
of ideas ply murky water
in your burnt pupils.)

   Maybe you're looking
for the pretty lizardess,
green like May wheat
or the hair of dormant fountains,
who spurned you
and left your field?
Oh sweet idyll, broken
on the cool sedge!
But that's life! What the hell!
You've been good to me.
The motto "I'm against
the serpent" triumphs
in that double chin, big
as a Christian archbishop's.

   The sun has dissolved now
on the crest of the hill,
and returning flocks
stir up the dust.
It's time to go.
Leave this narrow path,
leave off your meditation.
You'll have time later

y no continuéis
meditando,
que lugar tendréis luego
de mirar las estrellas
cuando os coman sin prisa
los gusanos.

    ¡Volved a vuestra casa
bajo el pueblo de grillos!
¡Buenas noches, amigo
Don Lagarto!

    Ya está el campo sin gente,
los montes apagados
y el camino desierto.
Sólo de cuando en cuando
canta un cuco en la umbría
de los álamos.

to look at the stars
as the worms consume you
slowly.

    Back to your house
under the cricket village!
Good night, Mr. Lizard,
friend!

    Not a soul in the fields now:
extinguished the mountains,
deserted the path.
From time to time
in the shadow of poplars
a cuckoo sings.

De

POEMA DEL
CANTE JONDO

From

POEM OF

THE DEEP SONG

Translated by

Cola Franzen

[*Float of the Virgin of Sorrows, 1924*]

De *Poema de la Siguiriya Gitana*

A Carlos Morla Vicuña

Paisaje

El campo
de olivos
se abre y se cierra
como un abanico.
Sobre el olivar
hay un cielo hundido
y una lluvia oscura
de luceros fríos.
Tiembla junco y penumbra
10 a la orilla del río.
Se riza el aire gris.
Los olivos
están cargados
de gritos.
Una bandada
de pájaros cautivos,
que mueven sus larguísimas
colas en lo sombrío.

La guitarra

Empieza el llanto
de la guitarra.
Se rompen las copas
de la madrugada.
Empieza el llanto
de la guitarra.
Es inútil
callarla.
Es imposible
10 callarla.
Llora monótona
como llora el agua,
como llora el viento
sobre la nevada.
Es imposible
callarla.
Llora por cosas
lejanas.

From *Poem of the Gypsy* Siguiriya

For Carlos Morla Vicuña

Landscape

The field
of olive trees
opens and closes
like a fan.
Above the olive grove
a foundering sky
and a dark rain
of cold stars.
Bulrush and penumbra tremble
10   at the river's edge.
The gray air ripples.
The olive trees
are laden
with cries.
A flock
of captive birds
moving their long long
tails in the gloom.

The Guitar

The weeping of the guitar
begins.
The goblets of dawn
are smashed.
The weeping of the guitar
begins.
Useless
to silence it.
Impossible
10   to silence it.
It weeps monotonously
as water weeps
as the wind weeps
over snowfields.
Impossible
to silence it.
It weeps for distant
things.

29

Arena del Sur caliente
20 que pide camelias blancas.
Llora flecha sin blanco,
la tarde sin mañana
y el primer pájaro muerto
sobre la rama.
¡Oh guitarra!
Corazón malherido
por cinco espadas.

El grito

La elipse de un grito
va de monte
a monte.

Desde los olivos,
será un arco iris negro
sobre la noche azul.

¡Ay!

Como un arco de viola,
el grito ha hecho vibrar
10 largas cuerdas del viento.

¡Ay!

(Las gentes de las cuevas
asoman sus velones.)

¡Ay!

El silencio

Oye, hijo mío, el silencio.
Es un silencio ondulado,
un silencio,
donde resbalan valles y ecos
y que inclina las frentes
hacia el suelo.

Hot southern sands
20 yearning for white camellias.
Weeps arrow without target
evening without morning
and the first dead bird
on the branch.
Oh, guitar!
Heart mortally wounded
by five swords.

The Cry

The arc of a cry
travels from hill
to hill.

From the olive trees
a black rainbow
over the blue night.

     Ay!

Like the bow of a viola
the cry has set the wind's
10 long strings to vibrating.

     Ay!

(The people of the caves
bring out their oil lamps.)

     Ay!

The Silence

Listen, my child, to the silence.
An undulating silence,
a silence
that turns valleys and echoes slippery,
bends foreheads
toward the ground.

El paso de la Siguiriya

Entre mariposas negras,
va una muchacha morena
junto a una blanca serpiente
de niebla.

Tierra de luz,
cielo de tierra.

Va encadenada al temblor
de un ritmo que nunca llega;
tiene el corazón de plata
y un puñal en la diestra.

¿Adónde vas, Siguiriya,
con un ritmo sin cabeza?
¿Qué luna recogerá
tu dolor de cal y adelfa?

Tierra de luz,
cielo de tierra.

Después de pasar

Los niños miran
un punto lejano.

Los candiles se apagan.
Unas muchachas ciegas
preguntan a la luna,
y por el aire ascienden
espirales de llanto.

Las montañas miran
un punto lejano.

Y después

Los laberintos
que crea el tiempo,
se desvanecen.

(Sólo queda
el desierto.)

The Passage of the Siguiriya

Among black butterflies
goes a dark girl
beside a white serpent
of mist.

Earth of light,
sky of earth.

She goes chained to the tremor
of a rhythm that never arrives;
she has a heart of silver,
in her right hand a dagger.

Where are you going, Siguiriya,
with a headless rhythm?
What moon will gather up
your sorrow of lime and oleander?

Earth of light,
sky of earth.

Afterwards

The children gaze
at a distant spot.

The lamps are put out.
Some blind girls
ask questions of the moon
and spirals of weeping
rise through the air.

The mountains gaze
at a distant spot.

And Then

The labyrinths
that time creates
vanish.

(Only the desert
remains.)

El corazón,
fuente del deseo,
se desvanece.

(Sólo queda
10 el desierto.)

La ilusión de la aurora
y los besos,
se desvanecen.

Sólo queda
el desierto.
Un ondulado
desierto.

De *Poema de la Soleá*

A Jorge Zalamea

Tierra seca,
tierra quieta
de noches
inmensas.

(Viento en el olivar,
viento en la sierra.)

Tierra
vieja
del candil
10 y la pena.
Tierra
de las hondas cisternas.
Tierra
de la muerte sin ojos
y las flechas.

(Viento por los caminos.
Brisa en las alamedas.)

Puñal

El puñal
entra en el corazón,

The heart
fountain of desire
vanishes.

(Only the desert
10   remains.)

The illusion of dawn
and kisses
vanish.

Only the desert
remains.
Undulating
desert.

From *Poem of the* Soleá

For Jorge Zalamea

Dry land,
quiet land
of immense
nights.

(Wind in the olive grove,
wind in the sierra.)

Old
land
of oil lamps
10   and sorrow.
Land
of deep cisterns.
Land
of death without eyes
and of arrows.

(Wind along the roadways.
Breeze in the poplars.)

Dagger

The dagger
goes into the heart

como la reja del arado
en el yermo.

No.
No me lo claves.
No.

El puñal,
como un rayo de sol,
10   incendia las terribles
hondonadas.

No.
No me lo claves.
No.

Cueva

De la cueva salen
largos sollozos.

(Lo cárdeno
sobre lo rojo.)

El gitano evoca
países remotos.

(Torres altas y hombres
misteriosos.)

En la voz entrecortada
10   van sus ojos.

(Lo negro
sobre lo rojo.)

Y la cueva encalada
tiembla en el oro.

(Lo blanco
sobre lo rojo.)

like the blade of a plow
into barren land.

     No.
Don't run it through me.
     No.

The dagger
like a ray of the sun
10 sets fire
to terrible
depths.

     No.
Don't run it through me.
     No.

Cave

From the cave come
long sobs.

(Purple
over red.)

The gypsy conjures up
distant lands.

(Tall towers and mysterious
men.)

His eyes follow
10 the faltering voice.

(Black
over red.)

The whitewashed cave
trembles in the gold.

(White
over red.)

De *Poema de la Saeta*

A Francisco Iglesias

Procesión

Por la calleja vienen
extraños unicornios.
¿De qué campo,
de qué bosque mitológico?
Más cerca,
ya parecen astrónomos.
Fantásticos Merlines
y el Ecce Homo,
Durandarte encantado,
10 Orlando furioso.

Saeta

Cristo moreno
pasa
de lirio de Judea
a clavel de España.

¡Miradlo por dónde viene!

De España.
Cielo limpio y oscuro,
tierra tostada,
y cauces donde corre
10 muy lenta el agua.
Cristo moreno,
con las guedejas quemadas,
los pómulos salientes
y las pupilas blancas.

¡Miradlo por dónde va!

Madrugada

Pero como el amor
los saeteros
están ciegos.

From *Poem of the* Saeta

For Francisco Iglesias

Procession

Along the side street come
strange unicorns.
From what field,
what mythological grove?
Close by
they resemble astronomers,
Fantastic Merlins
and the Ecce Homo.
Enchanted Durandarte.
10   Orlando furioso.

Saeta

Dark-skinned Christ
passes
from lily of Judea
to carnation of Spain.

Look here he comes!

From Spain.
Sky clear and dark,
browned earth,
and stream beds where the water
10   barely trickles.
Dark-skinned Christ,
with long locks burnt
high cheekbones
and white pupils.

Look there he goes!

Before Dawn

But like love
the archers
are blind.

Sobre la noche verde,
las saetas
dejan rastros de lirio
caliente.

La quilla de la luna
rompe nubes moradas
10   y las aljabas
se llenan de rocío.

¡Ay, pero como el amor
los saeteros
están ciegos!

De *Gráfico de la Petenera*

A Eugenio Montes

Campana
(Bordón)

En la torre
amarilla
dobla una campana.

Sobre el viento
amarillo
se abren las campanadas.

En la torre
amarilla
cesa la campana.

10   El viento con el polvo
hace proras de plata.

Las seis cuerdas

La guitarra
hace llorar a los sueños.
El sollozo de las almas
perdidas
se escapa por su boca
redonda.

Above the green night
arrows
leave traces of ardent
lily.

The keel of the moon
rips purple clouds
10 and the quivers
fill with dew.

Oh, but like love
the archers
are blind!

From *Graphic of the* Petenera

For Eugenio Montes

Bell
(Bass String)

In the yellow
tower
a bell tolls.

Over the yellow
wind
the bell-notes flower.

In the yellow
tower
the bell stops.

10 With dust the wind
shapes silver prows.

The Six Strings

The guitar
causes dreams to weep.
The sobs of lost
souls
escape through its round
mouth.

41   *from* POEM OF THE DEEP SONG

Y como la tarántula,
teje una gran estrella
para cazar suspiros,
10   que flotan en su negro
aljibe de madera.

De *Viñetas flamencas*

A Manuel Torres, "Niño de Jerez,"
que tiene tronco de Faraón

Juan Breva

Juan Breva tenía
cuerpo de gigante
y voz de niña.
Nada como su trino.
Era la misma
Pena cantando
detrás de una sonrisa.
Evoca los limonares
de Málaga la dormida,
10   y hay en su llanto dejos
de sal marina.
Como Homero, cantó
ciego. Su voz tenía
algo de mar sin luz
y naranja exprimida.

Café cantante

Lámparas de cristal
y espejos verdes.

Sobre el tablado oscuro,
la Parrala sostiene
una conversación
con la muerte.
La llama,
no viene,
y la vuelve a llamar.
10   Las gentes
aspiran los sollozos.
Y en los espejos verdes,

And like the tarantula
it weaves a large star
to trap the sighs
10   floating in its black
wooden cistern.

From *Flamenco Vignettes*

For Manuel Torres "Niño de Jerez,"
descended from a line of Pharaohs

Juan Breva

Juan Breva had
a giant's body
and the voice of a girl.
Nothing like his trill.
Pain itself
singing
behind a smile.
He conjures up the lemon groves
of slumbrous Málaga,
10   his lament carries
hints of sea salt.
Like Homer he sang
blind. His voice had
something of sea without light,
and orange squeezed dry.

Cabaret

Glass lamps
and green mirrors.

On the dark stage
Parrala carries on
a conversation
with death.
Calls her,
she doesn't come,
calls her again.
10   The people
swallow their sobs.
And in the green mirrors

largas colas de seda
se mueven.

Conjuro

La mano crispada
como una Medusa
ciega el ojo doliente
del candil.

As de bastos.
Tijeras en cruz.

Sobre el humo blanco
del incienso, tiene
algo de topo y
10   mariposa indecisa.

As de bastos.
Tijeras en cruz.

Aprieta un corazón
invisible, ¿la véis?
Un corazón
reflejado en el viento.

As de bastos.
Tijeras en cruz.

Memento

Cuando yo me muera,
enterradme con mi guitarra
bajo la arena.

Cuando yo me muera,
entre los naranjos
y la hierbabuena.

Cuando yo me muera,
enterradme, si queréis,
en una veleta.

10   ¡Cuando yo me muera!

long silken trains
begin to stir.

Spell

The rigid hand
like a medusa
blinds the sickly eye
of the candle.

Ace of spades.
Crossed scissors.

Above the white smoke
of the incense, it looks
something like a mole and
hesitant butterfly.

Ace of spades.
Crossed scissors.

It clenches an
invisible heart, see it?
A heart
reflected in the wind.

Ace of spades.
Crossed scissors.

Memento

Whenever I die
bury me with my guitar
beneath the sand.

Whenever I die
among orange trees
and mint.

Whenever I die,
bury me if you wish
in a weather vane.

Whenever I die!

De *Tres ciudades*

A Pilar Zubiaurre

Malagueña

La muerte
entra y sale
de la taberna.

Pasan caballos negros
y gente siniestra
por los hondos caminos
de la guitarra.

Y hay un olor a sal
y a sangre de hembra
10 en los nardos febriles
de la marina.

La muerte
entra y sale,
y sale y entra
de la taberna.

Barrio de Córdoba
Tópico nocturno

En la casa se defienden
de las estrellas.
La noche se derrumba.
Dentro hay una niña muerta
con una rosa encarnada
oculta en la cabellera.
Seis ruiseñores la lloran
en la reja.

Las gentes van suspirando
10 con las guitarras abiertas.

From *Three Cities*

For Pilar Zubiaurre

Malagueña

Death
goes in and out
of the tavern.

Black horses
and sinister people
pass along the sunken roads
of the guitar.

There's an odor of salt
and female blood
10 in the feverish spikenard
along the shore.

Death
goes in and out,
out and in
of the tavern goes
death.

Neighborhood of Córdoba
Nocturnal Theme

Inside the house they take shelter
from the stars.
Night collapses.
Within, a dead girl,
a crimson rose
hidden in her hair.
Six nightingales on the railing
weep for her.

The people keep sighing
10 with gaping guitars.

De *Seis caprichos*

A Regino Sainz de la Maza

Adivinanza de la guitarra

En la redonda
encrucijada,
seis doncellas
bailan.
Tres de carne
y tres de plata.
Los sueños de ayer las buscan,
pero las tiene abrazadas
un Polifemo de oro.
¡La guitarra!

Candil

¡Oh, qué grave medita
la llama del candil!

Como un faquir indio
mira su entraña de oro
y se eclipsa soñando
atmósferas sin viento.

Cigüeña incandescente
pica desde su nido
a las sombras macizas
y se asoma temblando
a los ojos redondos
del gitanillo muerto.

Crótalo

Crótalo.
Crótalo.
Crótalo.
Escarabajo sonoro.

En la araña
de la mano
rizas el aire

From *Six Capriccios*

For Regino Sainz de la Maza

Riddle of the Guitar

At the round
crossway
six maidens
dance.
Three of flesh
and three of silver.
Dreams of yesterday seek them
but a golden Polyphemus
holds them in his embrace.
10 Guitar!

Oil Lamp

Oh, how gravely the flame
of the oil lamp meditates!

Like an Indian fakir
it gazes at its golden entrails
then goes into eclipse dreaming
atmospheres with no wind.

Incandescent stork
from its nest pecks
at the massive shadows
10 and trembling approaches
the round eyes
of the dead gypsy boy.

Castanet

Castanet.
Castanet.
Castanet.
Sonorous scarab.

In the spider
of the hand
you crimp the warm

cálido
y te ahogas en tu trino
10   de palo.

Crótalo.
Crótalo.
Crótalo.
Escarabajo sonoro.

Chumbera

Laoconte salvaje.

¡Qué bien estás
bajo la media luna!

Múltiple pelotari.

¡Qué bien estás
amenazando el viento!

Dafne y Atis
saben de tu dolor.
Inexplicable.

Pita

Pulpo petrificado.

Pones cinchas cenicientas
al vientre de los montes
y muelas formidables
a los desfiladeros.

Pulpo petrificado.

air,
and drown in your wooden
10   trill.

Castanet.
Castanet.
Castanet.
Sonorous scarab.

Prickly Pear

Wild Laocoön.

How grand you look
beneath the half-moon!

Multiplied ball player.

How grand you look
threatening the wind!

Daphne and Attis
know of your pain.
Inexplicable.

Agave

Petrified octopus.

You put dusty cinch straps
around the belly of the mountains
and formidable molars
along the defiles.

Petrified octopus.

De

SUITES

From

SUITES

Translated by

Jerome Rothenberg

[*The Griffin, ca. 1923*]

La suite de los espejos

Símbolo

Cristo
tenía un espejo
en cada mano.
Multiplicaba
su propio espectro.
Proyectaba su corazón
en las miradas
negras.
¡Creo!

El gran espejo

Vivimos
bajo el gran espejo.
¡El hombre es azul!
¡Hosanna!

Reflejo

Doña Luna.
(¿Se ha roto el azogue?)
No.
¿Un muchacho ha encendido
su linterna?
Sólo una mariposa
basta para apagarte.
Calla . . . ¡pero es posible!
¡Aquella luciérnaga
es la luna!

Rayos

Todo es abanico.
Hermano, abre los brazos.
Dios es el punto.

Mirror Suite

Symbol

Christ,
a mirror
in each hand.
He multiplies
his shadow.
He projects his heart
through his black
visions.
I believe!

The Giant Mirror

We live beneath
a giant mirror.
Man is blue!
Hosanna!

Reflection

Lady Moon.
(Did someone shatter the quicksilver?)
No.
Has a child flicked on
the lantern?
Even a butterfly could
blow you out.
Be quiet! . . . (Can it really!)
That glowworm
is the moon!

Rays

Everything's a fan.
Brother, open up your arms.
God is the pivot.

Réplica

Un pájaro tan sólo
canta.
El aire multiplica.
Oímos por espejos.

Tierra

Andamos
sobre un espejo
sin azogue,
sobre un cristal
sin nubes.
Si los lirios nacieran
al revés,
si las rosas nacieran
al revés,
10 si todas las raíces
miraran las estrellas
y el muerto no cerrara
sus ojos,
seríamos como cisnes.

Capricho

Detrás de cada espejo
hay una estrella muerta
y un arco iris niño
que duerme.

Detrás de cada espejo
hay una calma eterna
y un nido de silencios
que no han volado.

El espejo es la momia
10 del manantial, se cierra
como concha de luz
por la noche.

El espejo
es la madre-rocío,
el libro que diseca
los crepúsculos, el eco hecho carne.

Replica

Only a single bird
is singing.
The air is cloning it.
We hear through mirrors.

Earth

We walk on
an unsilvered
mirror,
a crystal surface
without clouds.
If lilies would grow
backwards,
if roses would grow
backwards,
10 if all those roots
could see the stars
& the dead not close
their eyes,
we would become like swans.

Capriccio

Behind each mirror
is a dead star
& a baby rainbow
sleeping.

Behind each mirror
is a blank forever
& a nest of silences
too young to fly.

The mirror is the wellspring
10 become mummy, closes
like a shell of light
at sunset.

The mirror
is the mother dew,
the book of desiccated
twilights, echo become flesh.

Sinto

Campanillas de oro.
Pagoda dragón.
Tilín tilín
sobre los arrozales.

Fuente primitiva,
fuente de la verdad.

A lo lejos,
garzas color de rosa
y un volcán marchito.

Los ojos

En los ojos se abren
infinitos senderos.
Son dos encrucijadas
de la sombra.
La muerte llega siempre
de esos campos ocultos.
(Jardinera que troncha
las flores de las lágrimas.)
Las pupilas no tienen
10   horizontes.
Nos perdemos en ellas
como en la selva virgen.
Al castillo de irás
y no volverás
se va por el camino
que comienza en el iris.
¡Muchacho sin amor,
Dios te libre de la yedra roja!
¡Guárdate del viajero,
20   Elenita que bordas
corbatas!

Initium

Adán y Eva.
La serpiente
partió el espejo
en mil pedazos,

Shinto

Small golden bells.
Dragon pagoda.
Tinkle tinkle
over the ricefields.

Primal fountain.
Fountain of the real.

Far off,
pink-colored herons
& the spent volcano.

Eyes

In our eyes the roads
are endless.
Two are crossroads of
the shadow.
Death always emerging
from those secret fields.
A woman working a garden:
teardrops like flowers
she breaks.
10 Horizonless pupils.
Virgin forests
we're lost in.
Castle of no return
that you reach
from the road that starts in the iris.
Oh boy without love, may God
set you free from red ivy.
And you, Elenita,
who sit there
20 embroidering neckties,
keep clear of that traveler.

Initium

Adam & Eve.
The serpent cracked
the mirror
in a thousand pieces,

y la manzana
fue la piedra.

Berceuse al espejo dormido

   Duerme.
No temas la mirada
errante
   Duerme.

Ni la mariposa
ni la palabra
ni el rayo furtivo
de la cerradura
te herirán.
10   Duerme.

Como mi corazón,
así tú,
espejo mío.
Jardín donde el amor
me espera.

Duérmete sin cuidado,
pero despierta
cuando se muera el último
beso de mis labios.

Aire

El aire
preñado de arcos iris
rompe sus espejos
sobre la fronda.

Confusión

¿Mi corazón
es tu corazón?
¿Quién me refleja pensamientos?
¿Quién me presta
esta pasión
sin raíces?

& the apple
was his rock.

Berceuse for a Sleeping Mirror

Sleep.
Do not fear the roaming.
eye.
Sleep.

The butterfly,
the word,
the furtive light
in through the keyhole,
will not wound you.
Sleep.

As my heart is,
so you are,
my mirror.
Garden where my love
is waiting.

Sleep easy,
but awaken
when the last kiss dies against
my lips.

Air

The air
pregnant with rainbows
shatters its mirrors
over the grove.

Confusion

Is my heart
your heart?
Who is mirroring my thoughts?
Who lends me this un-
rooted passion?
Why are my clothes

¿Por qué cambia mi traje
de colores?
¡Todo es encrucijada!
10 ¿Por qué ves en el cieno
tanta estrella?
¿Hermano, eres tú
o soy yo?
¿Y estas manos tan frías
son de aquél?
Me veo por los ocasos,
y un hormiguero de gente
anda por mi corazón.

Remanso

El búho
deja su meditación,
limpia sus gafas
y suspira.
Una luciérnaga
rueda monte abajo
y una estrella
se corre.
El búho bate sus alas
10 y sigue meditando.

Noche
(Suite para piano y voz emocionada)

Rasgos

Aquel camino
sin gente.
Aquel camino.

Aquel grillo
sin hogar.
Aquel grillo.

Y esta esquila
que se duerme.
Esta esquila . . .

changing color?
Everything is a crossroads!
Why does this slime
10   look so starry?
Brother, are you you
or am I I?
And these cold hands,
are they his?
I see myself in sunsets
& a swarm of people
wanders through my heart.

The Pool

Horned owl
stops his meditations,
cleans his glasses,
sighs.
A firefly
spins downhill
& a star
slides by.
Old owl shakes his wings,
10   takes up his meditations.

Night
(Suite for Piano and Poet's Voice)

Sketches

That road
got no people.
That road.

That weevil
got no home.
That weevil.

And this sheepbell
gone to sleep.
This sheepbell.

Preludio

El buey
cierra sus ojos
lentamente . . .
(Calor de establo.)

Este es el preludio
de la noche.

Rincón del cielo

La estrella
vieja
cierra sus ojos turbios.

La estrella
nueva
quiere azular
la sombra.

(En los pinos del monte
hay luciérnagas.)

Total

La mano de la brisa
acaricia la cara del espacio
una vez
y otra vez.
Las estrellas entornan
sus párpados azules
una vez
y otra vez.

Un lucero

Hay un lucero quieto,
un lucero sin párpados.
—¿Dónde?
—Un lucero . . .
En el agua dormida
del estanque.

Prelude

The bullock
slowly
shuts his eyes.
Heat in the stable.

Prelude to
the night.

In a Corner of the Sky

The old
star
shuts her bleary eyes.

The new
star
wants to paint the night
blue.

(in the firtrees on the mountain:
fireflies.)

The Whole Works

The wind's hand
creases the forehead of space
again &
again.
The stars half-close
their blue eyelids
again &
again.

A Star

There is a tranquil star,
a star that has no eyelids.
—Where?
—A star . . .
In sleepy water.
In the pond.

Franja

El camino de Santiago
(Oh noche de mi amor,
cuando estaba la pájara pinta
pinta
pinta
en la flor del limón.)

Una

Aquella estrella romántica
(para las magnolias,
para las rosas.)
Aquella estrella romántica
se ha vuelto loca.

Balalín,
balalán.

(Canta, ranita,
en tu choza
de sombra.)

Madre

La osa mayor
da teta a sus estrellas
panza arriba.
Gruñe
y gruñe.
¡Estrellas niñas, huid,
estrellitas tiernas!

Recuerdo

Doña Luna no ha salido.
Está jugando a la rueda
y ella misma se hace burla.
Luna lunera.

Swath

O St. James Road.
O Milky Way.
(O night of love for me
when the yellow bird was painted
painted
painted
up in the lemontree.)

One

That romantic star
(one for magnolia,
one for the roses).
That romantic star
just went crazy.

Tralalee,
tralala.

(Sing, little frog,
in your shadowy
10   hut.)

Ursa Major

Bear mother
gives suck to the stars
astride her belly:
Grunt
grunt.
Run off, star babies,
tender little stars.

Memory

Our Lady Moon still hidden,
playing ring around a wheel.
She makes herself look silly.
Loony moon.

Hospicio

Y las estrellas pobres,
las que no tienen luz,

¡qué dolor,
qué dolor,
qué pena!

están abandonadas
sobre un azul borroso.

¡Qué dolor,
qué dolor,
10   qué pena!

Cometa

En Sirio
hay niños.

Venus

Ábrete, sésamo
del día.
Ciérrate, sésamo
de la noche.

Abajo

El espacio estrellado
se refleja en sonidos.
Lianas espectrales.
Arpa laberíntica.

La gran tristeza

No puedes contemplarte
en el mar.
Tus miradas se tronchan
como tallos de luz.
Noche de la tierra.

At the Poorhouse

And the poor stars
that have no light

—o sorrow,
sorrow,
o lamentation!—

end up stuck
in muddy blue.

O sorrow,
sorrow,
10   o lamentation!

Comet

There on Sirius
are babes.

Venus

Open sesame
by day.
Shut sesame
at night.

Below

Space & stars
reflected into sound.
Liana ghosts.
Harp labyrinths.

The Great Sadness

You can't look at yourself
in the ocean.
Your looks fall apart
like tendrils of light.
Night on earth.

Remansos

(Margarita, ¿quién soy yo?)

Ciprés
(Agua estancada.)

Chopo
(Agua cristalina.)

Mimbre
(Agua profunda.)

Corazón
(Agua de pupila.)

Variación

El remanso del aire
bajo la rama del eco.

El remanso del agua
bajo fronda de luceros.

El remanso de tu boca
bajo espesura de besos.

Remansillo

Me miré en tus ojos
pensando en tu alma.

Adelfa blanca.

Me miré en tus ojos
pensando en tu boca.

Adelfa roja.

Me miré en tus ojos
¡pero estabas muerta!

Adelfa negra.

70

Backwaters

(Margarita, who am I?)

Cypress
(Stagnant water.)

Poplar.
(Crystal water.)

Willow.
(Deep Water.)

Heart.
(Eyeball water.)

Variation

The backwater of air
under this echo's branches.

The backwater of water
under that frond of stars.

The backwater of your mouth
under our thickening kisses.

Little Backwater

I saw myself in your eyes
& thinking about your soul.

    O oleander white.

I saw myself in your eyes
& thinking about your mouth.

    O oleander red.

I saw myself in your eyes
but saw that you were dead.

    O oleander black.

Canción

Ya viene la noche.

Golpean rayos de luna
sobre el yunque de la tarde.

Ya viene la noche.

Un árbol viejo se abriga
con palabras de cantares.

Ya viene la noche.

Si tú vinieras a verme
por los senderos del aire,

10   *Ya viene la noche.*

me encontrarías llorando
bajo los álamos grandes.
   ¡Ay morena!
Bajo los álamos grandes.

Sigue

Cada canción
es un remanso
del amor.

Cada lucero
es un remanso
del tiempo.
Un nudo
del tiempo.

Y cada suspiro
10 un remanso
del grito.

Song

      Night here already.

Moon's rays been striking
evening like an anvil.

      Night here already.

An old tree keeping warm
wrapped in words of songs.

      Night here already.

If you should come to see me
walking on the air—

10   Night here already—

you'd find me crying here
under the poplar trees.

      Ah, morena, my high brown!

Under the poplar trees.

Keep It Going

Each song's
a backwater
of love.

Each star's
a backwater
of time.
Of time tied
in a knot.

And each sigh's
10 the backwater
of a scream.

Media luna

La luna va por el agua.
¿Cómo está el cielo tranquilo?
Va segando lentamente
el temblor viejo del río
mientras que una rana joven
la toma por espejito.

(Margarita, ¿quién soy yo?)

Cuatro baladas amarillas

A Claudio Guillén

I

En lo alto de aquel monte
hay un arbolito verde.

> *Pastor que vas,*
> *pastor que vienes.*

Olivares soñolientos
bajan al llano caliente.

> *Pastor que vas,*
> *pastor que vienes.*

Ni ovejas blancas ni perro,
10 ni cayado ni amor tienes.

> *Pastor que vas.*

Como una sombra de oro
en el trigal te disuelves.

> *Pastor que vienes.*

II

La tierra estaba
amarilla.

> *Orillo, orillo,*
> *pastorcillo.*

Half Moon

Moon goes through the water.
How peaceable the sky is!
Slowly going gathering
old tremors from the river
while a young frog takes her
for a tiny mirrror.

(Margarita, who am I?)

Four Ballads in Yellow

For Claudio Guillén

I

High up on the mountain
a little green tree

    & a shepherd who comes
    & a shepherd who goes.

Sleepy old olive trees
going down the warm valley

    & a shepherd who comes
    & a shepherd who goes.

Not white ewes nor a dog
nor a sheephook nor love

    for the shepherd who goes.

Like a shadow in gold
you dissolve in the wheat

    you shepherd who comes.

II

The earth was
yellow.

    Catch as catch can,
    little shepherd man.

Ni luna blanca
ni estrella lucían.

Orillo, orillo,
pastorcillo.

Vendimiadora morena
10 corta el llanto de la viña.

Orillo, orillo,
pastorcillo.

III

Dos bueyes rojos
en el campo de oro.

Los bueyes tienen ritmo
de campanas antiguas
y ojos de pájaro.
Son para las mañanas
de niebla, y sin embargo,
horadan la naranja
del aire en el verano.
10 Viejos desde que nacen,
no tienen amo.
Y recuerdan las alas
de sus costados.
Los bueyes
siempre van suspirando
por los campos de Ruth
en busca del vado,
del eterno vado,
borrachos de luceros
20 a rumiarse sus llantos.

Dos bueyes rojos
en el campo de oro.

IV

Sobre el cielo
de las margaritas ando.

Yo imagino esta tarde
que soy santo.
Me pusieron la luna

Not a white moon, no,
not a star aglow.

    Catch as catch can,
    little shepherd man.

Brown grapepicking woman
gets tears from the vine.

    Catch as catch can,
    little shepherd man.

III

    Two red bulls
    in one gold field.

Bulls got a rhythm
like oldtime bells
& eyes like a bird's.
Made for foggy
mornings, & even so
they bore through the air-
orange, in summer.
Old from their birth
they don't have no boss
& think back to the wings
down their sides.
Two red bulls
that go around sighing
through fields of Ruth
for a shoal to cross over,
that eternal shoal,
drunk on starshine,
are chewing their cuds,
        two red bulls
        in one gold field,
are chewing their sorrows.

IV

Over a sky
made of daisies
I walk.

I imagine today
that I'm holy.

en las manos.
Yo la puse otra vez
en los espacios,
y el Señor me premió
10 con la rosa y el halo.

Sobre el cielo
de las margaritas ando.

Y ahora voy
por este campo.
A librar a las niñas
de galanes malos
y dar monedas de oro
a todos los muchachos.

Sobre el cielo
20 *de las margaritas ando.*

El regreso

Yo vuelvo
por mis alas.

¡Dejadme volver!
¡Quiero morirme siendo
amanecer!

¡Quiero morirme siendo
ayer!

Yo vuelvo
por mis alas.

10 ¡Dejadme retornar!

Quiero morirme siendo
manantial.

Quiero morirme fuera
de la mar.

That they placed the moon
in my hands.
That I set her back
into space.
10　And the Lord awarded me
a rose & a halo.

Over a sky
made of daisies
I walk.

And now I move
down this field
rescuing maidens from
evil suitors,
giving gold coins
20　to all the young boys.

Over a sky
made of daisies
I walk.

The Return

　　I'm coming back
　　for my wings.

O let me come back!
I want to die where
it's dawn!

I want to die where
it's yesterday!

　　I'm coming back
　　for my wings.

10　O let me get back!

I want to die where
it's origin.

I want to die
out of sight
of the sea.

Corriente

El que camina
se enturbia.

El agua corriente
no ve las estrellas.

El que camina
se olvida.

Y el que se para
sueña.

Hacia . . .

Vuelve,
¡corazón!
vuelve.

Por las selvas del amor
no verás gentes.
Tendrás claros manantiales.
En lo verde
hallarás la rosa inmensa
del siempre.

10 Y dirás: ¡Amor! ¡amor!
sin que tu herida
se cierre.

Vuelve,
¡corazón mío!
vuelve.

Recodo

Quiero volver a la infancia
y de la infancia a la sombra.

¿Te vas, ruiseñor!
Vete.

Quiero volver a la sombra
y de la sombra a la flor.

In Motion

You walk,
you get muddy.

Water in motion
will not see the stars.

You walk,
you go blank.

You stop walking,
you dream.

Towards . . .

Return,
corazón!
return.

Through forests where love is
you won't see a soul.
You will come on sweet waters.
Out where it's green
you will spot the great rose
named forever.
10   And will call out: Love! love!
without your wound
closing

Return,
mi corazón!
return.

Oxbow

I want to go back to childhood
& from childhood to shadow.

You going too, nightingale?
Better get going!

I want to go back to the shadow
& from the shadow to the flower.

¿Te vas, aroma?
　　　Vete.

Quiero volver a la flor
10　y de la flor
a mi corazón.

　　　¿Te vas, amor?
　　　　　¡Adiós!

(¡A mi desierto corazón!)

Despedida

Me despediré
en la encrucijada
para entrar en el camino
de mi alma.

Despertando recuerdos
y horas malas
llegaré al huertecillo
de mi canción blanca
y me echaré a temblar como
10　la estrella de la mañana.

Ráfaga

Pasaba mi niña.
¡Qué bonita iba!
Con su vestidito
de muselina.
Y una mariposa
prendida.

¡Síguela, muchacho,
la vereda arriba!
Y si ves que llora
10　o medita,
píntale el corazón
con purpurina
y dile que no llore
si queda solita.

You going too, perfume?
Better get going!

I want to go back to the flower
10 & from the flower
to my heart.

You going too, love?
Adios.

My bare heart.

Saying Goodbye

I'll be saying goodbye
at the crossroads,
heading off down that road
through my soul.

I'll arouse reminiscences,
stir up mean hours.
I'll arrive at the garden spot
in my song (my white song),
& I'll start in to shiver & shake
10 like the morning star.

Wind Gust

My girl coming by,
how sweet she looks walking!
with her cute muslin
dress
& a newly caught
butterfly.

Trail her, muchacho,
down every byway,
& if you once catch her crying
10 or thinking it over,
paint this onto her heart
& spray it with glitter
& tell her not to cry
if she should stay single.

De *Seis canciones de anochecer*

Solitario
(Zujaira)

Sobre el pianísimo
del oro . . .
mi chopo
solo.

Sin un pájaro
armónico.

Sobre el pianísimo
del oro . . .

El río a sus pies
10 corre grave y hondo
bajo el pianísimo
del oro . . .

Y yo con la tarde
sobre mis hombros
como un corderito
muerto por el lobo
bajo el pianísimo
del oro.

De *Tres crepúsculos*

III

¡Adiós, sol!

Bien sé que eres la luna,
pero yo
no lo diré a nadie,
sol.
Te ocultas
detrás del telón
y disfrazas tu rostro
con polvos de arroz.
10 De día, la guitarra
del labrador;

From *Six Songs at Nightfall*

Solitaire
(Zujaira)

Over the pianissimo
of gold . . .
my lonely
poplar.

Without some harmonical
bird.

Over the pianissimo of gold . . .

The river at its feet
runs dark & deep
10 beneath the pianissimo
of gold . . .

And I with evening
on my shoulders
like a little lamb
the wolf has slain
beneath the pianissimo
of gold.

From *Three Crepuscular Poems*

III
(For Diane Rothenberg)

Adios, sun!

I know for sure that you're the moon,
but I
won't tell nobody,
sun.

You sneak
behind the curtain
& cover your face
with rice powder.

de noche, la mandolina
de Pierrot.
¡Qué más da!
Tu ilusión
es crear el jardín
multicolor.
¡Adiós, sol!
No olvides lo que te ama
20 el caracol,
la viejecilla
del balcón,
y yo . . .
que juego al trompo con mi . . .
corazón.

Madrigales

[1]

Como las ondas concéntricas
sobre el agua,
así en mi corazón
tus palabras.

Como un pájaro que choca
con el viento,
así sobre mis labios
tus besos.

Como fuentes abiertas
10 frente a la tarde,
así mis ojos negros
sobre tu carne.

II

Estoy preso
en tus círculos

10 By day, the farmhand's
guitar,
by night, Pierrot's
mandolin.

I should care!

Your illusion,
sun, is to make
the garden
turn Technicolor.

Adios, sun!

20 And don't forget who loves you:
the snail,
the little old lady
on her balcony,
& me . . .
spinning my heart like a . . .
top.

Madrigals

[1]

Like concentric waves
on the water,
your words
in my heart.

Like a bird that collides
with the wind,
your kiss
on my lips.

Like open fountains
10 fronting the night,
my dark eyes
on your skin.

II

I'm caught
in your concentric

concéntricos.
Como Saturno
llevo
los anillos
de mi sueño.
Y no acabo de hundirme
ni me elevo.

Castillo de fuegos artificiales
quemado con motivo del cumpleaños del poeta

Primera cohetería

Tú tú tú tú
Yo yo yo yo
¿Quién? . . .
¡Ni tú
ni yo!

Rueda Catalina

Doña Catalina
tenía un pelo de oro
entre su cabellera
de sombra.

(¿A quién espero,
Dios mío,
a quién espero?)

Doña Catalina
camina despacio
poniendo estrellitas
verdes en la noche.

(Ni aquí
ni allí,
sino aquí.)

Doña Catalina
se muere y le nace

circles.
Like Saturn
I lug around
rings
from my dreams.
I'm not totally sunk,
I'm not rising.
10 My love!

Barrage of Firework Poems
on the Occasion of the Poet's Birthday

First Launching

You you you you
me me me me
Who? . . .
not you!
not me!

Catherine Wheel

Doña Catalina
had a single gold hair
among her shadowy
tresses.

(For whom am I waiting,
dear God,
for whom am I waiting?)

Doña Catalina
walks slowly
10 scattering little green stars
in the night.

(Not here
& not there
but here.)

Doña Catalina:
a grenade of light

from SUITES

una granadeta de luz
en la frente.

¡Chsssssssssssss!

Cohetes

Seis lanzas de fuego
suben.
(La noche es una guitarra.)
Seis sierpes enfurecidas.
(Por el cielo vendrá San Jorge.)
Seis sopletes de oro y viento.
(¿Se agrandará la ampolla
de la noche?)

Jardín chino

En los bosquecillos
de grana y magnesio
saltan las princesitas
Chispas.

Hay una lluvia de naranjas
sobre el zig-zag de los cerezos
y entre comas vuelan azules
dragoncillos amaestrados.

Niña mía, este jardincillo
10 es para verlo en los espejitos
de tus uñas.
Para verlo en el biombo
de tus dientes.
Y ser como un ratoncito.

Girasol

Si yo amara a un cíclope
suspiraría
bajo esta mirada
sin párpados.
¡Oh girasol de fuego!
El gentío lo mira

dies & is born
on her forehead.

chsssssssssssss!

Rockets

Six fiery spears
zoom up.
(The night's a guitar.)
Six fuming serpents.
(St. George will dive through the sky.)
Six torches of gold & of wind.
(Will they puff up the bell jars
of night?)

Chinese Garden

In the little woodlets
with their purples & magnesiums
the princesitas jumping
are baby sparkadillos.

There's a rain of oranges
above the zigzag cherryos—
& between commas comes a flight
of prancing blue dragondolas.

My little girl this gardenette's
best looked at in the mirrorettes
that are thy fingernails.
And in those screens that are thy teeth.
As by a little mouselet.

Sunflower

If I did love a cyclops
I would swoon
beneath his stronger gaze
sans eyelids.
O fiery sunflower, ay!
The people stare at it

sin estremecimiento.
¡Ojo de la providencia
ante una muchedumbre
10   de Abeles!

¡Girasol girasol!
¡Ojo salvaje y puro
sin la ironía del guiño!

Girasol girasol.
¡Estigma ardiente sobre
los gentíos de feria!

Disco de rubíes

Gira y se estremece
como loco.
No sabe nada
¿y lo sabe todo?
¡Todas las flechas
a este corazón
redondo!

Todas las pupilas
a este corazón
10   redondo.
¡Lupa sangrienta entre
el misterio
y nosotros!

Capricho

   ¡Tris! . . .
¿Has cerrado
los ojos?
   ¡Triis! . . .
¿Más aún? Serás una
muchacha de brisa.
Yo soy un hombre.
   ¡Tras! . . .
Ya te vas, amor mío,
10   ¿y tus ojos?
   ¡Traaas! . . .
Si los cierras yo tengo dos plumas.

sans shuddering.
Eyeball of Providence
eyeing a crowdful of
10   Abels!

Sunflower sunflower!
Pure savage eyeball
sans winkage sans irony!

Sunflower sunflower!
Stigmata raging above
a fair full of peoples.

The Ruby Disc

gyrates & shakes
like crazy.
Knowing nothing—
knows it all?
All those arrows aimed
at this round
heart.
All those eyeballs aimed
at this round
10   heart.
A bloody lens between
the mystery
& us.

Capriccio

    Zip! . . .
Did you just close
your eyes?
    Ziiip! . . .
Even more? That's a
breezy young girl.
And I am an hombre.
    Zap!
Already you're gone, o my love,
10   & your eyes?
    Zaaap! . . .
If you close them, I have here two feathers,

93

¿Lo oyes? Dos plumas que miran
de mi pavo real.
   ¡Tris! . . .
¿Me has oído?
   ¡Traaas! . . .

Juego de lunas

La luna está redonda.
Alrededor, una noria
de espejos.
Alrededor, una rueda
de agua.
La luna se ha hecho láminas
como un pan de oro blanco.
La luna
se ha deshojado
en lunas.
Bandadas de fuentes
vuelan por el aire.
En cada fuente yace
una luna difunta.
La luna
se hace un bastón de luz
en el torrente claro.
La luna,
como una gran vidriera
rota, cae sobre el mar.
La luna
se va por un biombo
infinito.
¿Y la Luna? ¿Y la Luna?

(Arriba,
no queda más que un aro
de cristalillos.)

you hear? two feathers staring out
from my peacock.
    Zip!
Did you hear me?
    Zaaap! . . .

A Game of Moons

Moon is round.
Roundabout it is a treadmill
built with mirrors.
Roundabout it is a wheel
like a waterwheel.
Moon's become a gilt leaf
like a loaf of white gold.
Moon sheds its petals
like moons.
10 Swarms of fountains
float through the sky.
In each fountain 's a moon
lying dead.
Moon
becomes a cane made of light
in bright torrents.
Moon
like a large stainedglass window
that breaks on the ocean.
20 Moon
through an infinite
screen.
And the Moon? And the Moon?

(Up above
nothing left but a ring
of small crystals.)

En el jardín de las toronjas de luna

Prólogo

Asy como la sombra nuestra vida se va,
que nunca más torna nyn de nos tornará
—Pero López de Ayala (*Consejos morales*)

Me he despedido de los amigos que más quiero par emprender un corto pero dramático viaje. Sobre un espejo de plata encuentro mucho antes de que amanezca el maletín con la ropa que debo usar en la extraña tierra a que me dirijo.

El perfume tenso y frío de la madrugada bate misteriosamente el inmenso acantilado de la noche.

En la página tersa del cielo temblaba la inicial de una nube, y debajo de mi balcón un ruiseñor y una rana levantan en el aire un aspa soñolienta de sonido.

Yo, tranquilo pero melancólico, hago los últimos preparativos, embargado por sutilísimas emociones de alas y círculos concéntricos. Sobre la blanca pared del cuarto, yerta y rígida como una serpiente de museo, cuelga la espada gloriosa que llevó mi abuelo en la guerra contra el rey don Carlos de Borbón.

Piadosamente descuelgo esa espada, vestida de herrumbre amarillenta como un álamo blanco, y me la ciño recordando que tengo que sostener una gran lucha invisible antes de entrar en el jardín. Lucha extática y violentísima con mi enemigo secular el gigantesco dragón del Sentido Común.

Una emoción aguda y elegíaca por las cosas que no han sido, buenas y malas, grandes y pequeñas, invade los paisajes de mis ojos casi ocultos por unas gafas de luz violeta. Una emoción amarga que me hace caminar hacia este jardín que se estremece en las altísimas llanuras del aire.

Los ojos de todas las criaturas golpean como puntos fosfóricos sobre la pared del porvenir . . . lo de atrás se queda lleno de maleza amarilla, huertos sin frutos y ríos sin agua. Jamás ningún hombre cayó de espaldas sobre la muerte. Pero yo, por un momento, contemplando ese paisaje abandonado e infinito, he visto planos de vida inédita, mútiples y superpuestos como los cangilones de una noria sin fin.

Antes de marchar siento un dolor agudo en el corazón. Mi familia duerme y toda la casa está en un reposo absoluto. El alba, revelando torres y contando una a una las hojas de los árboles, me pone un crujiente vestido de encaje lumínico.

Algo se me olvida . . . no me cabe la menor duda . . . ¡tanto tiempo preparándome! y . . . Señor, ¿qué se me olvida? ¡Ah! Un pedazo de madera . . . uno bueno de cerezo sonrosado y compacto.

Creo que hay que ir bien presentado . . . De una jarra con flores puesta

In the Garden of the Lunar Grapefruits

Prologue

So like the shadow our life doth slip away
that never doth return nor us restore.
—Pero López de Ayala (*Consejos morales*)

I have taken leave of the friends I love the most & have set out on a short dramatic journey. On a silver mirror I find, long before dawn, the satchel with the clothing I'll need for the exotic country to which I'm heading.

The tight, cold scent of sunrise beats weirdly on the huge escarpment we call night.

On the sky's stretched page a cloud's initial letter trembles, & below my balcony a nightingale & frog raise up a sleepy cross of sound.

I—tranquil, melancholy man—make my final preparations, impeded by those subtlest feelings aroused in me by wings & by concentric circles. On the white wall in my room, stiff & rigid like a snake in a museum, hangs the noble sword my grandfather carried in the war against Don Carlos the Pretender.

With reverence I take the sword down, coated with yellow rust like a white poplar, & I gird it on me while remembering that I'll have to go through an awful invisible fight before I enter the garden. An ecstatic & ferocious fight against my secular enemy, the giant dragon Common Sense.

A sharp & elegiac feeling for things that haven't been—good & evil, large & small—invades those landscapes in back of my eyes that my ultraviolet glasses have all but occulted. A bitter feeling that makes me travel toward this garden that shimmers on its skyhigh prairie.

The eyes of all creatures pound like phosphorescent points against the wall of the future . . . what was past stays filled with yellowing under-brush, orchards without any fruit, waterless rivers. No man ever fell backwards into death. But I, absorbed for now by this abandoned & infinite landscape, catch a glimpse of life's unpublished blueprints—mul-tiplied, superposed, like buckets in an endless waterwheel.

Before taking off just now I felt a sharp pain in my heart. My family is sleeping & the whole house is in a state of absolute repose. The dawn reveals towers & one by one counts up the tree leaves. It slips a costume on me: crackling, made of spangled lace.

Must be something I've forgotten . . . can't be any doubt about it, so much time spent getting ready & . . . lord, what is it that escapes me? Ah, a piece of wood . . . a piece of good old cherry wood . . . rose-colored, tight-grained.

I believe in being well-groomed when I travel. . . . From a jar of

sobre mi mesilla me prendo en el ojal siniestro una gran rosa pálida que
tiene un rostro enfurecido pero hierático.

Ya es la hora.

(En las bandejas irregulares de las campanadas, vienen los kikirikís de los
gallos.)

Pórtico

> NIÑO: *Yo voy por las plumas*
> *del pájaro Grifón.*
> ENANO: *Hijo mío, me es imposible*
> *ayudarte en esta empresa.*
> —*Cuento popular*

    Tan-tan

El aire se había muerto.
Estaba inmóvil y arrugado.

Los pinos yacían en tierra.
Sus sombras de pie, ¡temblando!

    Yo—Tú—Él
(en un solo plano)

    Tan-tan

[. . .]

Perspectiva

Dentro de mis ojos
se abre el canto hermético
de las simientes que
no florecieron.

Todas sueñan un fin
irreal y distinto.
(El trigo sueña enormes
flores amarillentas.)

Todas sueñan extrañas
aventuras de sombra.

flowers on my nightstand, I pick out a huge pale rose & pin it to my left lapel. It has a fierce but hieratic face.

And so the time has come.

(With the scatterbrained sound of the bells' tongues come the cocka-doodledoos of the roosters.)

Portico

CHILD: *I am going in search of*
the gryphon-bird's wings.
DWARF: *My child, there is no way*
I can help you in this matter.
—*Old folk tale*

Clang clang

The breeze, having been killed,
lay motionless & shriveled.

The pinetrees, living, lay on the earth.
Their shadows uprisen, trembling!

I—You—He
(on a single plane)

Clang clang

[. . .]

Perspective

From behind my eyes
hermetic song breaks open—
song of the seedling that
did not ever flower.

Each one dreams about an
unreal, quirky end.
(The wheat dreams it's got
enormous yellow flowers.)

All of them dreaming strange
adventures in the shade.

Frutos inaccesibles
y vientos amaestrados.

Ninguna se conoce.
Ciegas y descarriadas.
Les duelen sus perfumes
enclaustrados por siempre.

Cada semilla piensa
un árbol genealógico
que cubre todo el cielo
20 de tallos y racimos.

Por el aire se extienden
vegetaciones increíbles.
Ramas negras y grandes,
rosas color ceniza.

La luna casi ahogada
de flores y ramajes
se defiende con sus rayos
como un pulpo de plata.

Dentro de mis ojos
30 se abre el canto hermético
de las simientes que
no florecieron.

El jardín

Jamás nació, ¡jamás!
Pero pudo brotar.

Cada segundo se
profundiza y renueva.

Cada segundo abre
nuevas sendas distintas.

¡Por aquí! ¡Por allí!
Va mi cuerpo multiplicado.

Atravesando pueblos
10 o dormido en el mar.

Fruits hanging out of reach
& domesticated winds.

None of them know each other,
blind & gone astray,
their perfumes paining them
but cloistered now forever.

Each seed thinks up
a genealogical tree—
covers the whole sky
20   with its stalks & roots.

The air's smeared over with
improbable vegetations.
Black & heavy branches.
Cinder-colored roses.

The moon nearly smothered
with flowers & with branches
fights them off with moonbeams
like an octopus in silver.

From behind my eyes
30   hermetic song breaks open—
song of the seedlings that
did not ever flower.

The Garden

was never born, never,
but could burst into life.

Every moment it's
deepened, restored.

Every moment it opens new
unheard-of pathways.

Over here! over there!
See my multiple bodies

passing through pueblos
10   or asleep in the ocean?

¡Todo está abierto! Existen
llaves para las claves.
Pero el sol y la luna
nos pierden y despistan.
Y bajo nuestros pies
se enmarañan los caminos.

Aquí contemplo todo
lo que pude haber sido.
Dios o mendigo,
20   agua o vieja margarita.

Mis múltiples senderos
teñidos levemente
hacen una gran rosa
alrededor de mi cuerpo.

Como un mapa imposible,
el jardín de lo posible.
Cada segundo se
profundiza y renueva.

Jamás nació, ¡jamás!
30   ¡Pero pudo brotar!

Glorieta

Sobre el surtidor inmóvil
duerme un gran pájaro muerto.

Los dos amantes se besan
entre fríos cristales de sueño.

«La sortija, ¡dame la sortija!»
«No sé dónde están mis dedos».
«¿No me abrazas?» «Me dejé los brazos
cruzados y fríos en el lecho».

Entre las hojas se arrastraba
10   un rayo de luna viejo

Everything open! Locks
to fit every key.
But the sun & moon
lose & delude us
& under our feet
the highways are tangled.

Here I'll mull over all
I once could have been.
God or beggar,
20   water or old marguerite.

My multiple paths
barely stained
now form this enormous rose
encircling my body.

Like an impossible map
the garden of the possible
every moment is
deepened, restored.

Was never born, never,
but could burst into life.

Pergola

A static jet of water,
over which
a large dead bird's
asleep.

Two lovers kissing
in among
Dream's icy
crystals.

"The ring, hand me the ring."
10   "I can't see where my fingers are."

"Why don't you hold me?"

        "No, my arms
are bent & freezing
on the bed."

Avenida

Las blancas teorías
con los ojos vendados
danzaban por el bosque.

Lentas como cisnes
y amargas como adelfas.

Pasaron sin ser vistas
por los ojos del hombre,
como de noche pasan
inéditos los ríos,
10   como por el silencio
un rumor nuevo y único.

Alguna entre su túnica
lleva una gris mirada
pero de moribundo.
                Otras
agitan largos ramos
de palabras confusas.
No viven y están vivas.
Van por el bosque extático.
20   ¡Enjambre de sonámbulas!
(Lentas como cisnes
y amargas como adelfas.)

Las doncellas dejan un olor
mental ausente de miradas.
El aire se queda indiferente,
camelia blanca de cien hojas.

Canción del jardinero inmóvil

Lo que no sospechaste
vive y tiembla en el aire.

Al tesoro del día
apenas si tocáis.

Dragging along, between
the leaves,
a trace of the old moon.

Avenue

Pallid white theories
with blindfolded eyes
would dance through the forest.

Sluggish like swans
& bitter like oleander.

They passed by, unseen
by a man's eyes,
as at nightfall the rivers
pass by, unreported.
10 As in the silence, a new-
fangled murmuring.

One of them inside her gown
has a gray heavy look
as of somebody dying.
                  Others
shake outsized branches of
disjuncted words.
They don't live, are alive,
pass through the ecstatic forest.
20 A swarm of sleepwalking women!
(Sluggish like swans
& bitter like oleander.)

Women leaving an odor behind them,
mental, stripped of appearances,
the air as indifferent as ever,
like a white camellia, a hundred blossoms.

Song of the Motionless Gardener

What you wouldn't have suspected
lives & trembles in the air.

Those treasures of the day
you keep just out of reach.

Van y vienen cargados
sin que los mire nadie.

Vienen rotos pero vírgenes
y hechos semilla salen.

Os hablan las cosas y
10   vosotros no escucháis.

El mundo es un surtidor
fresco, distinto y constante.

Al tesoro del día
apenas si tocáis.

Os veda el puro silencio,
el torrente de la sangre.

Pero dos ojos tenéis
para remontar los cauces.

Al tesoro del día
20   apenas si tocáis.

Lo que no sospechaste
vive y tiembla en el aire.

El jardin se enlazaba
por sus perfumes estancados.

Cada hoja soñaba
un sueño diferente.

Los puentes colgantes

¡Oh qué gran muchedumbre,
invisible y renovada,
la que viene a este jardín
a descansar para siempre!

Cada paso en la tierra
nos lleva a un mundo nuevo.
Cada pie lo apoyamos
sobre un puente colgante.

These come & go in truckloads
but no one stops to see them.

Banged up they come but virgin,
& gone back to seed they leave.

Things speak to you but no one
10 bothers to stop & listen.

The world's waterspout of
objects, various & steady.

Those treasures of the day
you keep just out of reach.

The hot rush of your blood
drowning the virgin silence.

But the two good eyes you have
would draw you to the source.

Those treasures of the day
20 you keep just out of reach.

What you wouldn't have suspected
lives & trembles in the air.

The garden joined together
by its putrefying perfumes.

Every leaf inside it dreaming
a different kind of dream.

Floating Bridges

Oh what a crush of people
invisible   reborn
make their way into this garden
for their eternal rest!

Every step we take on earth
brings us to a new world.
Every foot supported
on a floating bridge.

Comprendo que no existe
10 el camino derecho.
Sólo un gran laberinto
de encrucijadas múltiples.

Constantemente crean
nuestros pies al andar
inmensos abanicos
de senderos en germen.

¡Oh jardín de las blancas
teorías! ¡Oh jardín
de lo que no soy pero
20 pude y debí haber sido!

El sátiro blanco

Sobre narcisos inmortales
dormía el sátiro blanco.

Enormes cuernos de cristal
virginizaban su ancha frente.

El sol como un dragón vencido
lamía sus largas manos de doncella.

Flotando sobre el río del amor
todas las ninfas muertas desfilaban.

El corazón del sátiro en el viento
10 se oreaba de viejas tempestades.

La siringa en el suelo era una fuente
con siete azules caños cristalinos.

Estampas del jardín

[1]

Las antiguas doncellas
que no fueron amadas
vienen con sus galanes
entre las quietas ramas.

And I know that there is no
10 straight road in this world—
only a giant labyrinth
of intersecting crossroads.

And steadily our feet
keep walking & creating
—like enormous fans—
these roads in embryo.

Oh garden of white
theories! garden
of all I am not, all
20 I could & should have been!

White Satyr

Atop deathless narcissuses
the white satyr slept.

Huge horns made of crystal
virginized his deep brows.

The sun, a tamed dragon,
licked his ladylike hands.

On the river of love
dead nymphs drifted by.

The satyr's heart in the wind
10 dried out from old storms.

The syringe on the ground
was a fountain,
it had seven blue tubes
cut in glass.

Engravings of the Garden

[1]

Those antique virgins
still unloved,
walk with their loverboys
through silent leaves.

Los galanes sin ojos
y ellas sin palabras
se adornan con sonrisas
como plumas rizadas.

Desfilan bajo grises
10 tulipanes de escarcha
en un blanco delirio
de luces enclaustradas.

La ciega muchedumbre
de los perfumes vaga
con los pies apoyados
sobre flores intactas.

¡Oh luz honda y oblicua
de las yertas naranjas!
Los galanes tropiezan
20 con sus rotas espadas.

II

La viuda de la luna
¿quién la olvidará?
Soñaba que la tierra
fuese de cristal.

Enfurecida y pálida,
quería dormir al mar,
peinando sus melenas
con gritos de coral.

Sus cabellos de vidrio
10 ¿quién los olvidará?
En su pecho los cien
labios de un manantial.

Alabardas de largos
surtidores la van
guardando por las ondas
quietas del arenal.

Pero la luna luna
¿cuándo volverá?
La cortina del viento
20 tiembla sin cesar.

The boys, how eyeless
& how wordless they,
who cover themselves with smiles
like curlicues of feathers.

Strutting beneath the gray
& frosty tulips—
a white delirium
of cloistered lights.

Blind crowd—the perfumes
drifting past—
their feet propped up on
uncut flowers.

Oh deep & crooked light
from oranges gone numb!
And loverboys who stumble
over their broken swords.

II

Widow of the moon—
who could forget her?
Dreaming that the earth
be crystal,

she, furious & pale,
would rock the sea to sleep,
comb out her tresses
with coral, like a cry.

Hairs spun of glass—
who could forget them?
At her breast a hundred
lips, a single fountain.

Halberds from giant
jets spurt up,
keep guard of her by silent
waves, by dunes.

But moon, the moon,
when will the moon come back?
A curtain made of wind
that trembles on and on.

La viuda de la luna
¿quién la olvidará?
Soñaba que la tierra
fuese de cristal.

Como el buen conde Arnaldo
¿quién te olvidará?
También soñaba toda
la tierra de cristal.

●

[. . . . .]

Yo
¿Qué quieres de mí
que no me dejas, Sueño?

Sueño
Doce cisnes de oro
y doce lunas negras.

Yo
Quiero días y noches
claros y sin secretos.

Sueño
[. . . . .]

Arco de lunas

Un arco de lunas negras
sobre el mar sin movimiento.

Mis hijos que no han nacido
me persiguen.

«¡Padre, no corras, espera!
El más chico viene muerto».
Se cuelgan de mis pupilas.
Canta el gallo.

El mar hecho piedra ríe
10 su última risa de olas.

Widow of the moon—
who could forget her?
Dreaming that the earth
be crystal.

Like thee, good count Arnaldo,
who would forget thee too?
Thee, dreaming a whole earth
in crystal.

•

[. . . . .]

I
What do you want from me, Dream,
that you won't let me be?

Dream
A dozen gold swans
& a dozen black moons.

I
I want clear days & nights
& no secrets.

Dream
[. . . . .]

Moonbow

A bow of black moons
over the motionless sea.

My unborn children
10 track me down.

"Father, don't run from us, wait,
the youngest of us is dying."

They hang themselves from my eyes.
The cock starts to crow.

The sea, turned to stone, is laughing
a last laugh made of waves.

«¡Padre, no corras!»
                          Mis gritos
se hacen nardos.

●

Altas torres.
Largos ríos.

Hada
Toma el anillo de bodas
de tus abuelos.
Cien manos bajo la tierra
lo echarán de menos.

Yo
Voy a sentir en mis manos
una inmensa flor de dedos,
y el símbolo del anillo
¡no lo quiero!

Altas torres.
Largos ríos.

Cancioncilla del niño que no nació

¡Me habéis dejado sobre una flor
de oscuros sollozos de agua!

El llanto que aprendí
se pondrá viejecito
arrastrando su cola
de suspiros y lágrimas.

Sin brazos, ¿cómo empujo
la puerta de la luz?
Sirvieron a otro niño
de remos en su barca.

Yo dormía tranquilo.
¿Quién taladró mi sueño?
Mi madre tiene ya
la cabellera blanca.

"Father, don't run from us!" . . .

                                 And my screams

turning to spikenards.

•

Tall towers.
Wide waters.

Fairy
Take this wedding ring
that your grandfathers wore.
A hundred hands under the earth
will be grieving its absence.

I
I'm going to feel in my hands
a huge flower of fingers
& the symbol of that ring.
10   Oh ring I do not want!

Tall towers.
Wide waters.

Little Song of the Unborn Child

On a flower of dark sobs
& waters you left me.

The lament that I learned
will be a shriveled old man
dragging sighs & tears
behind it like a tail.

If I have no arms,
how will I force daylight's door?
Those oars served another
10   child on his boat.

I was sleeping in peace.
Who ripped into my dream?
My mother has long had
a head of white hair.

115

¡Me habéis dejado sobre una flor
de oscuros sollozos de agua!

Canción del muchacho de siete corazones

Siete corazones
tengo.
Pero el mío no lo encuentro.

En el alto monte, madre,
tropezábamos yo y el viento.
Siete niñas de largas manos
me llevaron en sus espejos.

He cantado por el mundo
con mi boca de siete pétalos.
10   Mis galeras de amaranto
iban sin jarcias y sin remos.

He vivido los paisajes
de otras gentes. Mis secretos
alrededor de la garganta
¡sin darme cuenta! iban abiertos.

En el alto monte, madre,
(mi corazón sobre los ecos
dentro del álbum de una estrella)
tropezábamos yo y el viento.

20   Siete corazones
tengo.
Pero el mío no lo encuentro.

Olor blanco

¡Oh qué frío perfume
de jacintos!
Por los cipreses blancos
viene una doncella.
Trae sus senos cortados
[en] un plato de oro.

(Dos caminos.
Su larguísima cola
y la Vía Láctea.)

On a flower of dark sobs
& waters you left me.

Song of the Seven-Hearted Boy

Seven hearts
are the hearts that I have.
But mine is not there among them.

In the high mountains, mother,
where I sometimes ran into the wind,
seven girls with long hands
carried me around in their mirrors.

I have sung my way through this world
with my mouth with its seven petals.
10   My crimson-colored galleys
have cast off without rigging or oars.

I have lived my life in landsacpes
that other men have owned.
And the secrets I wore at my throat,
unbeknownst to me, had come open.

In the high mountains, mother,
where my heart rises over its echoes
in the memory book of a star,
20   I sometimes ran into the wind.

Seven hearts
are the hearts that I have.
But mine is not there among them.

White Smell

Oh what cold perfumes
what hyacinths!
What maiden who comes
through white cypresses.
Carries her two severed breasts
on a platter of gold.

(Two highways.
Her very long train
& the milky way.)

Madre
de los niños muertos
tiembla con el delirio
de los gusanos de luz.

¡Oh qué frío perfume
de jacintos!

Encuentro

Flor de sol.
Flor de río.

Yo
¿Eras tú? Tienes el pecho
iluminado y no te he visto.

Ella
¡Cuántas veces te han rozado
las cintas de mi vestido!

Yo
Sin abrir, oigo en tu garganta
las blancas voces de mis hijos.

Ella
Tus hijos flotan en mis ojos
como diamantes amarillos.

Yo
¿Eras tú? ¿Por dónde arrastrabas
esas trenzas sin fin, amor mío?

Ella
En la luna. ¿Te ríes? Entonces,
alrededor de la flor del narciso.

Yo
En mi pecho se agita sonámbula
una sierpe de besos antiguos.

Ella
Los instantes abiertos clavaban
sus raíces sobre mis suspiros.

Mother of stillborns
who shudders
with the frenzy of light-worms.

Oh what cold perfumes
what hyacinths!

Encounter

   Sun flower.
   River flower.

I
Was it you? Your breast so blazing
with light I lost sight of you.

She
And my dress with its ribbons—
how many times did it brush you?

I
In your throat I can hear, unopened,
my children's white voices.

She
Your children afloat in my eyes
are yellow like diamonds.

I
Was it you? Where were you dragging
your unending tresses, my love?

She
On the moon—are you laughing?
then circling Narcissus' flower.

I
In my breast a snake that won't sleep
but quakes with old kisses.

She
The moments fell open & fastened
their roots on my sighs.

from SUITES

Yo
Enlazados por la misma brisa
20 frente a frente ¡no nos conocimos!

Ella
El ramaje se espesa, vete pronto.
¡Ninguno de los dos hemos nacido!

Flor de sol.
Flor de río.

Duna

Sobre la extensa duna
de la luz antiquísima
me encuentro despistado
sin cielo ni camino.

El Norte moribundo
apagó sus estrellas.
Los cielos naufragados
se ondulaban sin prisa.

Por el mar de la luz
10 ¿dónde voy? ¿A quién busco?
Aquí gime el reflejo
de las lunas veladas.

¡Ay, mi fresco pedazo
de madera compacta,
vuélveme a mi balcón
y a mis pájaros vivos!

El jardín seguirá
moviendo sus arriates
sobre la ruda espalda
20 del silencio encallado.

¡Amanecer y repique!
(Fuera del jardín)

El sol con sus cien cuernos
levanta el cielo bajo.

I
Joined by one breeze
face to face, we were strangers!

She
The branches are burgeoning,
                                    go from me!
Neither of us has been born.

   Sun flower.
   River flower

Dune

Atop that vast dune
—most ancient light—
I find myself lost
with no sky, no road.

The North near to death
had switched off its stars.
The skies were shipwrecked,
slowly rising & falling.

Through a sea made of light
I go where? I seek whom?
A reflection that cries here
—of moons hidden by veils.

May the cool piece of tight-grained
wood in my hand
take me back to my balcony—
my still living birds.

Then the garden will follow,
will be moving its borders
on the coarse-grained shoulders
of a silence run aground.

Wake Up/Ring Out
(Outside the garden)

Sun with his hundred horns
lifts the downed sky.

121

El mismo gesto repiten
los toros en la llanura.

La pedrea estremecida
de los viejos campanarios

despierta y pone en camino
al gran rebaño del viento.

En el río ahora comienzan
10   las batallas de los peces.

Alma mía, niño y niña,
¡¡silencio!!

Same motion repeated by
the bulls on the prairie.

Spectacular rain of stones
around the old bell towers

arouses the wind, drives
its vast herd down the road.

In the river the wars
of the fish are beginning.

My soul, boy & girl,
be silent, *silent!*

De

CANCIONES

1921-1924

A Pedro Salinas, Jorge Guillén

y Melchorito Fernández Almagro

[*Leyenda japonesa, 1926*]

From

SONGS

1921–1924

To Pedro Salinas, Jorge Guillén,

and Melchor Fernández Almagro

Translated by Alan S. Trueblood

[*Japanese Legend, 1926*]

Canción de las siete doncellas
(Teoría del arco iris)

Cantan
las siete doncellas.

(Sobre el cielo un arco
de ejemplos de ocaso.)

Alma con siete voces
las siete doncellas.

(En el aire blanco,
siete largos pájaros.)

Mueren las siete
10   doncellas.

(¿Por qué no han sido nueve?
¿Por qué no han sido veinte?)

El río las trae.
Nadie puede verlas.

Nocturno esquemático

Hinojo, serpiente y junco.
Aroma, rastro y penumbra.
Aire, tierra y soledad.

(La escala llega a la luna.)

La canción del colegial

Sábado.
Puerta de jardín.

Domingo.
Día gris.
Gris.

Theories

Song of the Seven Maidens
(Theory of the Rainbow)

Singing,
the seven maidens.

(Across the sky in a bow,
a choice of sunsets.)

One soul with seven voices,
the seven maidens.

(In the white air
seven long birds.)

Dying, the seven
10 maidens.

(Why weren't there nine?
Why weren't there twenty?)

The river brings them.
No one can see them.

Nocturne in Outline

Fennel, serpent, and rushes.
Aroma, trail, and half-shadow.
Air, earth, and apartness.

(The ladder stretches to the moon.)

Schoolboy's Song

Saturday.
Garden gate.

Sunday.
Gray day.
Gray.

Sábado.
Arcos azules.
Brisa.

Domingo.
Mar con orillas.
Metas.

Sábado.
Semilla,
estremecida.

Domingo.
(Nuestro amor se pone,
amarillo.)

•

El canto quiere ser luz.
En lo oscuro el canto tiene,
hilos de fósforo y luna.
La luz no sabe qué quiere.
En sus límites de ópalo,
se encuentra ella misma,
y vuelve.

Tiovivo

A José Bergamín

Los días de fiesta
van sobre ruedas.
El tiovivo los trae
y los lleva.

Corpus azul.
Blanca Nochebuena.

Los días abandonan
su piel, como las culebras,
con la sola excepción
de los días de fiesta.

Estos son los mismos
de nuestras madres viejas.

Saturday.
Blue archway.
Breeze.

Sunday.
10 Sea and seashore.
Goals.

Saturday.
Seed
quivering.

Sunday.
(Our love sets,
yellow.)

•

Song would like to be light.
Song in the dark shows
filaments of phosphorus and moon.
Light doesn't know what it wants.
At its opaline edge
it meets up with itself
and returns.

Merry-go-round

To José Bergamín

Holidays
travel on wheels.
The merry-go-round brings them
and takes them away.

Blue Corpus Christi.
White Christmas Eve.

Days shed their skins
just like snakes,
with the single exception
10 of holidays.
These haven't changed
since our old mothers' time.

129

Sus tardes son largas colas
de moaré y lentejuelas.

Corpus azul.
Blanca Nochebuena.

El tiovivo gira
colgado de una estrella.
Tulipán de las cinco
20 partes de la tierra.

Sobre caballitos
disfrazados de panteras
los niños se comen la luna
como si fuera una cereza.

¡Rabia, rabia, Marco Polo!
Sobre una fantástica rueda,
los niños ven lontananzas
desconocidas de la tierra.

Corpus azul.
30 Blanca Nochebuena.

Friso

A Gustavo Durán

TIERRA	CIELO
Las niñas de la brisa	Los mancebos del aire
van con sus largas colas.	saltan sobre la luna.

Cazador

¡Alto pinar!
Cuatro palomas por el aire van.

Cuatro palomas
vuelan y tornan.
Llevan heridas
sus cuatro sombras.

¡Bajo pinar!
Cuatro palomas en la tierra están.

Their afternoons are long trains
of moiré and sequins.

   Blue Corpus Christi.
White Christmas Eve.

   The merry-go-round turns,
suspended from a star.
Tulip of the five
20   corners of the earth.

   On wooden horses
disguised as panthers
children gobble the moon
as they would a cherry.

   Now hear *this*, Marco Polo:
From their fabulous wheel
children see far-off places
nowhere in this world.

   Blue Corpus Christi.
30   White Christmas Eve.

Frieze

To Gustavo Durán

EARTH
   The girls of the breeze
pass in their trailing gowns.

SKY
   The youths of the air
jump over the moon.

Hunter

   Tall pine grove!
Four doves ply the air.

   Four doves
fly off and return.
There are wounds
in their four shadows.

   Low pine grove!
Four doves are on the ground.

131   *from* SONGS, 1921–1924

Fábula

Unicornios y cíclopes.

Cuernos de oro
y ojos verdes.

Sobre el acantilado,
en tropel gigantesco
ilustran el azogue
sin cristal, del mar.

Unicornios y cíclopes.

Una pupila
10   y una potencia.

¿Quién duda la eficacia
terrible de esos cuernos?

¡Oculta tus blancos,
Naturaleza!

•

Agosto,
contraponientes
de melocotón y azúcar,
y el sol dentro de la tarde,
como el hueso en una fruta.

La panocha guarda intacta,
su risa amarilla y dura.

Agosto.
Los niños comen
10   pan moreno y rica luna.

Arlequín

Teta roja del sol.
Teta azul de la luna.

Torso mitad coral
mitad plata y penumbra.

Fable

    Unicorns and cyclops.

    Gold horns
and green eyes.

    On the headland
in a gigantic throng
they luster the glassless
quicksilver of the sea.

    Unicorns and cyclops.

    One eye
10 and one potency.

    Who can question the awful
efficacy of those horns?

    Conceal your bull's eyes,
Nature!

•

August.
Facing the sunset
peaches and sugar,
and the sun inside the evening
like the stone in a fruit.

The ear of corn holds intact
its hard yellow laughter.

August.
Children eat
10 dark bread and tasty moon.

Harlequin

    Red teat of the sun.
Blue teat of the moon.

    Torso half coral,
half silver and penumbra.

De *Canciones para niños*

A la maravillosa niña Colomba Morla Vicuña,
dormida piadosamente el día 12 de agosto de 1928

Canción china en Europa

A mi ahijada Isabel Clara

La señorita
del abanico,
va por el puente
del fresco río.

Los caballeros
con sus levitas,
miran el puente
sin barandillas.

La señorita
10   del abanico
y los volantes,
busca marido.

Los caballeros
están casados,
con altas rubias
de idioma blanco.

Los grillos cantan
por el Oeste.

(La señorita,
20   va por lo verde.)

Los grillos cantan
bajo las flores.

(Los caballeros,
van por el Norte.)

From *Songs for Children*

To the wonderful little girl Colomba Morla Vicuña,
who rested in the Lord August 12, 1928

Song of China in Europe

To my godchild Isabel Clara

The young lady
with the fan
is taking the bridge
across the river.

The gentlemen
in frock coats
are looking at the bridge
with no railings.

The young lady
10   with the fan
and the flounces
seeks a husband.

The gentlemen
are married
to tall blondes
of white speech.

Westward
crickets chirp.

(The young lady
20   walks the green.)

Crickets chirp
under flowers.

(Northward
the gentlemen go.)

Cancioncilla sevillana

A Solita Salinas

Amanecía
en el naranjel.
Abejitas de oro
buscaban la miel.

¿Dónde estará
la miel?

Está en la flor azul,
Isabel.
En la flor,
del romero aquel.

(Sillita de oro
para el moro.
Silla de oropel
para su mujer.)

Amanecía,
en el naranjel.

Caracola

A Natalita Jiménez

Me han traído una caracola.

Dentro le canta
un mar de mapa.
Mi corazón
se llena de agua
con pececillos
de sombra y plata.

Me han traído una caracola.

Sevillian Ditty

To Solita Salinas

Daybreak
in the orange grove.
Little gold bees
were out after honey.

And where can
the honey be?

It's in the blue blossom,
Isabel.
In the bloom
of that rosemary plant.

(A little gold seat
for the Moor.
A seat that glitters
for his wife.)

Daybreak
in the orange grove.

Seashell

To Natalita Jiménez

Someone brought me a seashell.

Singing inside
is a sea from a map.
My heart
fills up with water
and little tiny fish,
silvery, shadowy.

Someone brought me a seashell.

137

El lagarto está llorando.
La lagarta está llorando.

El lagarto y la lagarta
con delantaritos blancos.

Han perdido sin querer
su anillo de desposados.

¡Ay, su anillito de plomo,
ay, su anillito plomado!

Un cielo grande y sin gente
10 monta en su globo a los pájaros.

El sol, capitán redondo,
lleva un chaleco de raso.

¡Miradlos qué viejos son!
¡Qué viejos son los lagartos!

¡Ay cómo lloran y lloran,
¡ay!, ¡ay!, cómo están llorando!

Paisaje

La tarde equivocada
se vistió de frío.

Detrás de los cristales
turbios, todos los niños,
ven convertirse en pájaros
un árbol amarillo.

La tarde está tendida
a lo largo del río.
Y un rubor de manzana
10 tiembla en los tejadillos.

*To Mlle. Teresita Guillén
playing her six-note piano*

Mr. Lizard is crying.
Mrs. Lizard is crying.

Mr. and Mrs. Lizard
in little white aprons.

They've gone and lost
their wedding ring.

Oh, their little lead ring!
Their little leaden ring, oh!

A big peopleless sky
10 lifts the birds in its balloon.

The sun, a roly-poly captain,
wears a satin vest.

How old they are, just look!
How old the lizards are!

Oh, how they do weep,
and, oh, how they are weeping!

Landscape

To Rita, Concha, Pepe, and Carmencica

By mistake the evening
had dressed in cold.

Through the mist on the panes
all the children
watch a yellow tree
change into birds.

Evening is stretched out
all down the river.
And the flush of an apple
10 shivers over tile roofs.

Canción tonta

Mamá.
Yo quiero ser de plata.

Hijo,
tendrás mucho frío.

Mamá.
Yo quiero ser de agua.

Hijo,
tendrás mucho frío.

Mamá.
10   Bórdame en tu almohada.

¡Eso sí!
¡Ahora mismo!

De *Andaluzas*

A Miguel Pizarro (en la irregularidad simétrica del Japón)

Adelina de paseo

La mar no tiene naranjas,
ni Sevilla tiene amor.
Morena, qué luz de fuego.
Préstame tu quitasol.

Me pondrá la cara verde
—zumo de lima y limón—.
Tus palabras—pececillos—
nadarán alrededor.

La mar no tiene naranjas.
10   Ay amor.
¡Ni Sevilla tiene amor!

Canción de jinete

Córdoba.
Lejana y sola.

Silly Song

Mommy.
I want to be all silver.

Son,
you'll be awfully cold.

Mommy.
I want to be all water.

Son,
you'll be awfully cold.

Mommy.
10 Sew me onto your cushion.

That I will!
This very moment!

From *Andalusian Songs*

To Miguel Pizarro (in the symmetrical irregularity of Japan)

Adelina Out Walking

The sea has no oranges
nor Seville any love.
Dark girl, such fiery light!
Lend me your parasol.

It will turn my face green
—juice of lemon and lime.
Your words—little fish—
will swim roundabout.

The sea has no oranges.
10 Oh the pity, love.
Nor Seville any love!

Rider's Song

Córdoba.
Distant and lonely.

Jaca negra, luna grande,
y aceitunas en mi alforja.
Aunque sepa los caminos
yo nunca llegaré a Córdoba.

Por el llano, por el viento,
jaca negra, luna roja.
La muerte me está mirando
desde las torres de Córdoba.

¡Ay qué camino tan largo!
¡Ay mi jaca valerosa!
¡Ay que la muerte me espera,
antes de llegar a Córdoba!

Córdoba.
Lejana y sola.

•

Galán,
galancillo.
En tu casa queman tomillo.

Ni que vayas, ni que vengas,
con llave cierro la puerta.

Con llave de plata fina.
Atada con una cinta.

En la cinta hay un letrero:
Mi corazón está lejos.

No des vueltas en mi calle.
¡Déjasela toda al aire!

Galán,
galancillo.
En tu casa queman tomillo.

Black pony, large moon,
in my saddlebag olives.
Well as I know the roads,
I shall never reach Córdoba.

Over the plain, through the wind,
black pony, red moon.
Death keeps a watch on me
from Córdoba's towers.

Oh, such a long way to go!
And, oh, my spirited pony!
Ah, but death awaits me
before I ever reach Córdoba.

Córdoba.
Distant and lonely.

•

Suitor,
suitor of mine.
At your house they're burning thyme.

Come or go as you please,
I'll stay under lock and key.

A key made of fine silver.
On a ribbon for good measure.

On the ribbon words are written:
My heart is not smitten.

Don't roam my street day and night.
Only the wind has that right.

Suitor,
suitor of mine.
At your house they're burning thyme.

Tres retratos con sombra

Verlaine

La canción,
que nunca diré,
se ha dormido en mis labios.
La canción,
que nunca diré.

Sobre las madreselvas
había una luciérnaga,
y la luna picaba
con un rayo en el agua.

Entonces yo soñé,
la canción,
que nunca diré.

Canción llena de labios
y de cauces lejanos.

Canción llena de horas
perdidas en la sombra.

Canción de estrella viva
sobre un perpetuo día.

Baco

Verde rumor intacto.
La higuera me tiende sus brazos.

Como una pantera, su sombra,
acecha mi lírica sombra.

La luna cuenta los perros.
Se equivoca y empieza de nuevo.

Ayer, mañana, negro y verde,
rondas mi cerco de laureles.

¿Quién te querría como yo,
si me cambiaras el corazón?

Three Portraits with Shading

Verlaine

The song
I'll never speak,
on the tip of my tongue fell asleep.
The song
I'll never speak.

On the honeysuckle
a firefly blinked
and the moon was pricking
the water with a beam.

10   It was then I dreamed
the song
I'll never speak.

Song filled with lips,
flowing from far away.

Song filled with hours
whiled away in the shade.

Song of stars alive
in perpetual daytime skies.

Bacchus

Green sound intact.
The fig tree's arms open to me.

Its shadow, like a panther,
stalks my lyrical shadow.

The moon is counting dogs.
She slips and starts over.

Yesterday, tomorrow, black and green,
you haunt my laurel wreath.

No one would love you like me
10   if you'd only change my heart!

. . . Y la higuera me grita y avanza
terrible y multiplicada.

Juan Ramón Jiménez

En el blanco infinito,
nieve, nardo y salina,
perdió su fantasía.

El color blanco, anda,
sobre una muda alfombra
de plumas de paloma.

Sin ojos ni ademán
inmóvil sufre un sueño.
Pero tiembla por dentro.

10   En el blanco infinito,
¡qué pura y larga herida
dejó su fantasía!

En el blanco infinito.
Nieve. Nardo. Salina.

Venus
Así te vi.

La joven muerta
en la concha de la cama,
desnuda de flor y brisa
surgía en la luz perenne.

Quedaba el mundo,
lirio de algodón y sombra,
asomado a los cristales
viendo el tránsito infinito.

La joven muerta,
10   surcaba el amor por dentro.
Entre la espuma de las sábanas
se perdía su cabellera.

. . . And the fig tree shouts and comes at me
in frightful proliferation.

Juan Ramón Jiménez

In the infinity of white,
snow, spikenard, and salt flat,
his fantasy went astray.

The color white moves
over a soundless carpet
of pigeon feathers.

Eyeless, no gesture, stock-still,
he is haunted by a dream.
But inwardly he quivers.

10   In the infinity of white
what a clean, long gash
his fantasy left!

In the infinity of white.
Snow. Spikenard. Salt flat.

Venus
I saw you thus.

The dead maiden
in the shell of the bed,
stripped of blossom and breeze,
ascended in unending light.

The world was left behind,
a lily of cotton and shadow,
watching through the panes
the infinite passage.

The dead maiden
10   plied love from within.
In the foam of the sheets
her long hair disappeared.

Debussy

Mi sombra va silenciosa
por el agua de la acequia.

Por mi sombra están las ranas
privadas de las estrellas.

La sombra manda a mi cuerpo
reflejos de cosas quietas.

Mi sombra va como inmenso
cínife color violeta.

Cien grillos quieren dorar
10 la luz de la cañavera.

Una luz nace en mi pecho,
reflejado, de la acequia.

Juegos

*Dedicado a la cabeza de Luis Buñuel,
En gros plan*

Árbol de canción

Para Ana María Dalí

Caña de voz y gesto,
una vez y otra vez
tiembla sin esperanza
en el aire de ayer.

La niña suspirando
lo quería coger;
pero llegaba siempre
un minuto después.

¡Ay sol! ¡Ay luna, luna!
10 Un minuto después.
Sesenta flores grises
enredaban sus pies.

Mira cómo se mece
una vez y otra vez,

Debussy

My shadow glides in silence
over the watercourse.

On account of my shadow
the frogs are deprived of stars.

The shadow sends my body
reflections of quiet things.

My shadow moves like a huge
violet-colored mosquito.

10   A hundred crickets are trying
to gild the glow of the reeds.

A glow arises in my breast,
the one mirrored in the water.

Games

Dedicated to the head of Luis Buñuel
En gros plan

Tree of Song

For Ana María Dalí

A reed in voice and gesture
again and again
quivers forlorn
in yesterday's breeze.

The girl, with a sigh,
was trying to catch it
but she always arrived
a minute too late.

O sun! Moon, O moon!
10   A minute too late.
Sixty gray flowers
trammeled her feet.

She sees it swaying
again and again,

virgen de flor y rama,
en el aire de ayer.

•

Naranja y limón.

¡Ay la niña
del mal amor!

Limón y naranja.

¡Ay de la niña,
de la niña blanca!

Limón.

(Cómo brillaba
el sol.)

10   Naranja.

(En las chinas
del agua.)

La calle de los mudos

Detrás de las inmóviles vidrieras
las muchachas juegan con sus risas.

(En los pianos vacíos,
arañas titiriteras.)

Las muchachas hablan con sus novios
agitando sus trenzas apretadas.

(Mundo del abanico,
el pañuelo y la mano.)

Los galanes replican haciendo,
10 alas y flores con sus capas negras.

innocent of flower and branch,
in yesterday's breeze.

●

Orange and lemon.

Oh, the girl
unhappy in love!

Lemon and orange.

Alas for the girl,
the pale girl!

Lemon.

(How the sun was glinting.)

Orange.

(Off the pebbles
in the water.)

The Street of the Mute

Behind the unmoving glass doors
the girls play with their laughter.

      (On the empty pianos,
      puppeteer spiders.)

To talk with their suitors, the girls
shake their tight-knit braids.

      (World of the fan,
      the hand, and the handkerchief.)

In reply the suitors' black capes
10 describe flourishes and wings.

Canciones de luna

A José F. Montesinos

La luna asoma

Cuando sale la luna
se pierden las campanas
y aparecen las sendas
impenetrables.

Cuando sale la luna,
el mar cubre la tierra
y el corazón se siente
isla en el infinito.

Nadie come naranjas
10 bajo la luna llena.
Es preciso comer,
fruta verde y helada.

Cuando sale la luna
de cien rostros iguales,
la moneda de plata
solloza en el bolsillo.

Dos lunas de tarde

1

(*A Laurita, amiga de mi hermana*)

La luna está muerta, muerta;
pero resucita en la primavera.

Cuando en la frente de los chopos
se rice el viento del sur.

Cuando den nuestros corazones
su cosecha de suspiros.

Cuando se pongan los tejados
sus sombreritos de yerba.

La luna está muerta, muerta;
10 pero resucita en la primavera.

Moon Songs

To José F. Montesinos

The Moon Appears

At the rise of the moon
bells fade out
and impassable paths
appear.

At the rise of the moon
the sea overspreads the land
and the heart feels like an island
in the infinite.

No one eats oranges
10   in the full moon's light.
Fruit must be eaten
green and ice-cold.

At the rise of the moon
with its hundred faces alike,
silver coins
sob away in pockets.

Two Evening Moons

1

(To Laurita, my sister's friend)

The moon is dead, is dead
but in spring will come back to life.

When across the poplars' faces
the south wind is rippling.

When our hearts have yielded
their harvest of sighs.

When tiled roofs are wearing
their little grass hats.

The moon is dead, is dead
10   but in spring will come back to life.

153

2

(A Isabelita, mi hermana)

La tarde canta
una «berceuse» a las naranjas.

Mi hermanita canta:
La tierra es una naranja.

La luna llorando dice:
Yo quiero ser una naranja.

No puede ser, hija mía,
aunque te pongas rosada.
Ni siquiera limoncito.
10 ¡Qué lástima!

Segundo aniversario

La luna clava en el mar
un largo cuerno de luz.

Unicornio gris y verde,
estremecido pero extático.

El cielo flota sobre el aire
como una inmensa flor de loto.

(¡Oh, tú sola paseando
la última estancia de la noche!)

Flor

A Colin Hackforth

El magnífico sauce
de la lluvia, caía.

¡Oh la luna redonda
sobre las ramas blancas!

2

(To Isabelita, my sister)

The evening is singing
a *berceuse* to the oranges.

My little sister is singing:
The earth is an orange.

In tears, the moon says:
I want to be an orange.

No way, my child,
even if you turned rosy.
Not even a nice lemon.
10 Oh, what a pity!

Second Anniversary

The moon fastens on the sea
a long horn of light.

Unicorn gray and green,
trembling yet ecstatic.

The sky floats on the air
like a giant lotus flower.

(O you, girl, pacing alone
the final chamber of night!)

Flower

To Colin Hackforth

The magnificent willow
of the rain was falling.

Oh, round moon
on white branches!

Eros con bastón (1925)

(A Pepín Bello)

Susto en el comedor

Eras rosa.
Te pusiste alimonada

¿Qué intención viste en mi mano
que casi te amenazaba?

Quise las manzanas verdes.
No las manzanas rosadas . . .

alimonada . . .

(Grulla dormida la tarde,
puso en tierra la otra pata.)

Lucía Martínez

Lucía Martínez.
Umbría de seda roja.

Tus muslos como la tarde
van de la luz a la sombra.
Los azabaches recónditos
oscurecen tus magnolias.

Aquí estoy, Lucía Martínez.
Vengo a consumir tu boca
y arrastrarte del cabello
en madrugada de conchas.

Porque quiero, y porque puedo.
Umbría de seda roja.

La soltera en misa

Bajo el Moisés del incienso,
adormecida.

Ojos de toro te miraban.
Tu rosario llovía.

Eros with a Cane (1925)

To Pepín Bello

Fright in the Dining Room

You were rose color.
You turned lemon.

What design did you see in my hand
that seemed to be threatening you?

The apples I wanted were the green
Not the rosy apples . . .

lemon . . .

(The afternoon, a crane asleep,
put its other foot down.)

Lucía Martínez

Lucía Martínez.
Shadowy in red silk.

Like the evening, your thighs
move from light into shadow.
Hidden veins of jet
darken your magnolias.

Here I am, Lucía Martínez.
I've come to devour your mouth
and drag you off by the hair
into the seashells of daybreak.

Because I want to and I can.
Shadowy in red silk.

The Unmarried Woman at Mass

Under the Moses of the incense
you have dozed off.

Eyes of bulls looked you over.
Your rosary was raining.

Con ese traje de profunda seda,
no te muevas, Virginia.

Da los negros melones de tus pechos
al rumor de la misa.

Trasmundo

A Manuel Ángeles Ortiz

Malestar y noche

Abejaruco.
En tus árboles oscuros.
Noche de cielo balbuciente
y aire tartamudo.

Tres borrachos eternizan
sus gestos de vino y luto.
Los astros de plomo giran
sobre un pie.
                    Abejaruco.
En tus árboles oscuros.

10   Dolor de sien oprimida
con guirnalda de minutos.
¿Y tu silencio? Los tres
borrachos cantan desnudos.
Pespunte de seda virgen
tu canción.
                    Abejaruco.
Uco uco uco uco.
                    Abejaruco.

Desposorio

Tirad ese anillo
al agua.

(La sombra apoya sus dedos
sobre mi espalda.)

Tirad ese anillo. Tengo
más de cien años. ¡Silencio!

In that dress of yours, deep in silk,
don't stir, Virginia.

Yield the black melons of your breasts
to the drone of the mass.

Back of the World

To Manuel Ángeles Ortiz

Disquiet and Night

Bee-eating bird.
In the dark of your trees.
Night of skies slurred
and tongue-tied air.

Three drunks perpetuate
motions of wine and grief, blurred.
The leaden stars pirouette
on one foot.
                    Bee-eating bird.
In the dark of your trees.

10   Aching of temples confined
in a garland of minutes deferred.
What of your silence? The three
naked drunks are singing.
A backstitch in virgin silk:
your song.
                    Bee-eating bird.
Heard, slurred, blurred, deferred.
                    Bee-eating bird.

Marriage Vow

Throw that ring
in the water.

(Fingers of shadow are pressing
against my back.)

Throw away that ring. I am
over a hundred years old. Be still!

159

¡No preguntadme nada!

Tirad ese anillo
al agua.

Despedida

Si muero,
dejad el balcón abierto.

El niño come naranjas.
(Desde mi balcón lo veo.)

El segador siega el trigo.
(Desde mi balcón lo siento.)

¡Si muero,
dejad el balcón abierto!

Suicidio

*(Quizá fue por no saberte
la geometría)*

El jovencito se olvidaba.
Eran las diez de la mañana.

Su corazón se iba llenando
de alas rotas y flores de trapo.

Notó que ya no le quedaba,
en la boca más que una palabra.

·Y al quitarse los guantes, caía,
de sus manos, suave ceniza.

Por el balcón se veía una torre.
El se sintió balcón y torre.

Vio, sin duda, cómo le miraba
el reloj detenido en su caja.

Vio su sombra tendida y quieta,
en el blanco diván de seda.

Ask me no questions.

Throw that ring
in the water.

Leave-taking

If I die,
leave the balcony open.

The boy is eating oranges.
(From my balcony I can see him.)

The reaper is reaping the wheat.
(From my balcony I can hear him.)

If I die,
leave the balcony open!

Suicide

*(Maybe it was because you hadn't
mastered your geometry)*

The lad was going blank.
It was ten in the morning.

His heart was growing full
of broken wings and rag flowers.

He noticed there remained
just one word on his lips.

And when he took off his gloves
a soft ash fell from his hands.

A tower showed through the balcony door.
He felt he was balcony and tower.

No doubt he saw how the clock,
stopped in its case, surveyed him.

He saw his shadow quiet and prone
on the white silk divan.

Y el jovan rígido, geométrico,
con un hacha rompió el espejo.

Al romperlo, un gran chorro de sombra,
inundó la quimérica alcoba.

Amor
(con alas y flechas)

Cancioncilla del primer deseo

En la mañana verde,
quería ser corazón.
Corazón.

Y en la tarde madura
quería ser ruiseñor.
Ruiseñor.

(Alma,
ponte color naranja.
Alma,
10   ponte color de amor.)

En la mañana viva,
yo quería ser yo.
Corazón.

Y en la tarde caída
quería ser mi voz.
Ruiseñor.

¡Alma,
ponte color naranja.
Alma,
20   ponte color de amor!

Preludio

Las alamedas se van,
pero dejan su reflejo.

Las alamedas se van,
pero nos dejan el viento.

And the stiff, geometrical youth
smashed the mirror with a hatchet.

When it broke, a great burst of shadow
flooded the illusory room.

Love
(with wings and arrows)

Ditty of First Desire

In the green morning
I wanted to be a heart.
A heart.

And in the ripe evening
I wanted to be a nightingale.
A nightingale.

(Soul,
turn orange-colored.
Soul,
10   turn the color of love.)

In the vivid morning
I wanted to be myself.
A heart.

And at the evening's end
I wanted to be my voice.
A nightingale.

Soul,
turn orange-colored.
Soul,
20   turn the color of love.

Prelude

The poplar lanes move on
but leave their reflection.

The poplar lanes move on
but leave us the wind.

El viento está amortajado
a lo largo bajo el cielo.

Pero ha dejado flotando
sobre los ríos, sus ecos.

El mundo de las luciérnagas
10   ha invadido mis recuerdos.

Y un corazón diminuto
me va brotando en los dedos.

Soneto

Largo espectro de plata conmovida
el viento de la noche suspirando,
abrió con mano gris mi vieja herida
y se alejó: yo estaba deseando.

Llaga de amor que me dará la vida
perpetua sangre y pura luz brotando.
Grieta en que Filomela enmudecida
tendrá bosque, dolor y nido blando.

¡Ay qué dulce rumor en mi cabeza!
10   Me tenderé junto a la flor sencilla
donde flota sin alma tu belleza.

Y el agua errante se pondrá amarilla,
mientras corre mi sangre en la maleza
mojada y olorosa de la orilla.

Canciones para terminar

A Rafael Alberti

De otro modo

La hoguera pone al campo de la tarde,
unas astas de ciervo enfurecido.
Todo el valle se tiende. Por sus lomos,
caracolea el vientecillo.

El aire cristaliza bajo el humo.
—Ojo de gato triste y amarillo—.

The wind lies shrouded
full length beneath the sky.

But floating on the rivers
it has left its echoes.

The world of fireflies
10 has invaded my memories.

And a tiny little heart
is sprouting at my fingertips.

Sonnet

A specter trailing restless silver,
the night wind with its sighing,
reopened my old wound in its gray hands,
moved on, and left me there desiring.

Wound of love, source to sustain my life
with blood always new and light unblemished.
Cleft in which the tongueless Philomel
will find her nest, her grove, her grief replenished.

Ah, so sweet a sound inside my head!
10 I shall lie down beside the simple flower
on which your soulless beauty soars.

Then the meandering water will turn yellow
as my blood keeps flowing through the marshy,
moist and fragrant growth along the shores.

Songs to End With

To Rafael Alberti

In Another Manner

The bonfire gives the evening land
the antlers of a raging stag.
The valley stretches away. A little breeze
zigzags among the furrows.

Air crystallizes in the smoke
—a cat's eye sad and yellow.

Yo en mis ojos, paseo por las ramas.
Las ramas se pasean por el río.

Llegan mis cosas esenciales.
10 Son estribillos de estribillos.
Entre los juncos y la baja-tarde,
¡qué raro que me llame Federico!

Canción del naranjo seco

A Carmen Morales

Leñador.
Córtame la sombra.
Líbrame del suplicio
de verme sin toronjas.

¿Por qué nací entre espejos?
El día me da vueltas.
Y la noche me copia
en todas sus estrellas.

Quiero vivir sin verme.
10 Y hormigas y vilanos,
soñaré que son
mis hojas y mis pájaros.

Leñador.
Córtame la sombra.
Líbrame del suplicio
de verme sin toronjas.

Canción del día que se va

¡Qué trabajo me cuesta
dejarte marchar, día!
Te vas lleno de mí,
vuelves sin conocerme.
¡Qué trabajo me cuesta
dejar sobre tu pecho
posibles realidades
de imposibles minutos!

En la tarde, un Perseo
10 te lima las cadenas,

My eyes and I glide along the branches.
The branches do their gliding on the river.

Things essential to me come to hand.
10 Refrains of other refrains.
Between the rushes and the dropping day,
how strange my having Federico for a name!

Song of the Dead Orange Tree

To Carmen Morales

Woodcutter.
Cut down my shadow.
Deliver me from the torment
of bearing no fruit.

Why was I born among mirrors?
Day turns round and round me.
And night copies me
in all her stars.

Let me live unmirrored.
10 And then let me dream
that ants and thistledown
are my leaves and my birds.

Woodcutter.
Cut down my shadow.
Deliver me from the torment
of bearing no fruit.

Song of Departing Day

Day, what a hard time I have
letting you leave.
You go off filled with me.
You return and don't know me.
What a hard time I have
leaving in your bosom
possible concretions
of impossible minutes.

In the evening a Perseus
10 files away your chains,

y huyes sobre los montes
hiriéndote los pies.
No pueden seducirte
mi carne ni mi llanto,
ni los ríos en donde
duermes tu siesta de oro.

Desde Oriente a Occidente
llevo tu luz redonda.
Tu gran luz que sostiene
20   mi alma, en tensión aguda.
Desde Oriente a Occidente,
¡qué trabajo me cuesta
llevarte con tus pájaros
y tus brazos de viento!

and you flee over hills
where you cut your feet.
Powerless to lure you
are my flesh and my tears
and the rivers on which
you sleep your golden siesta.

From East to West
I bear your round light.
Your vast light that keeps
20　my soul highly tensed.
From East to West
what a hard time I have
bearing you with your birds
and your windy arms.

De

PRIMER ROMANCERO GITANO

1924–1927

From

THE

GYPSY

BALLADS

1924–1927

Translated by

Will Kirkland

[*Soledad Montoya, 1930*]

2

Preciosa y el aire

A Dámaso Alonso

Su luna de pergamino
Preciosa tocando viene,
por un anfibio sendero
de cristales y laureles.
El silencio sin estrellas,
huyendo del sonsonete,
cae donde el mar bate y canta
su noche llena de peces.
En los picos de la sierra
los carabineros duermen
guardando las blancas torres
donde viven los ingleses.
Y los gitanos del agua
levantan, por distraerse,
glorietas de caracolas
y ramas de pino verde.

★

Su luna de pergamino
Preciosa tocando viene.
Al verla se ha levantado
el viento, que nunca duerme.
San Cristobalón desnudo,
lleno de lenguas celestes,
mira a la niña tocando
una dulce gaita ausente.

—Niña, deja que levante
tu vestido para verte.
Abre en mis dedos antiguos
la rosa azul de tu vientre.

Preciosa tira el pandero
y corre sin detenerse.
El viento-hombrón la persigue
con una espada caliente.

Frunce su rumor el mar.
Los olivos palidecen.
Cantan las flautas de umbría
y el liso gong de la nieve.

2

Preciosa and the Wind

To Dámaso Alonso

Playing her parchment moon,
Preciosa comes along
an amphibious trail
of crystal and laurel.
Fleeing from the sound,
the starless silence falls
where the sea pounds and sings
its night full of fish.
On the mountain peaks,
10   guarding the white towers
where the English live,
the carabineers sleep.
And the water gypsies,
to pass away the hours,
make bowers out of sea snails
and wands of evergreen.

           ★

Playing her parchment moon,
Preciosa comes along.
Seeing her, the wind,
20   who never sleeps, begins to rise.
St. Christopher, naked giant,
full of sky-blue tongues,
watches as the gypsy pipes
a sweet, distracted tune.

"Missy, let me lift
your dress and see you.
Open in my ancient fingers
the blue rose of your womb."

Preciosa hurls her tambourine
30   and runs wildly away.
The wind-man chases her
with a burning sword.

The ocean ruffles up its roar.
The olive trees turn pale.
The flutes of cane-deep shadows sing,
and the smooth gong of the snow.

¡Preciosa, corre, Preciosa,
que te coge el viento verde!
¡Preciosa, corre, Preciosa!
40 ¡Míralo por dónde viene!
Sátiro de estrellas bajas
con sus lenguas relucientes.

★

Preciosa, llena de miedo,
entra en la casa que tiene
más arriba de los pinos,
el cónsul de los ingleses.

Asustados por los gritos
tres carabineros vienen,
sus negras capas ceñidas
50 y los gorros en las sienes.

El inglés da a la gitana
un vaso de tibia leche,
y una copa de ginebra
que Preciosa no se bebe.

Y mientras cuenta, llorando,
su aventura a aquella gente,
en las tejas de pizarra
el viento, furioso, muerde.

3

Reyerta

A Rafael Méndez

En la mitad del barranco
las navajas de Albacete,
bellas de sangre contraria,
relucen como los peces.
Una dura luz de naipe
recorta en el agrio verde
caballos enfurecidos
y perfiles de jinetes.
En la copa de un olivo
10 lloran dos viejas mujeres.
El toro de la reyerta

174

Preciosa, run, Preciosa,
or the old green wind will catch you!
Preciosa, run, Preciosa!
40 Watch out, here he comes!
Satyr of low stars
with his shimmering tongues.

★

Preciosa, full of fear,
runs into the house
where the English consul lives
up beyond the pines.

Frightened by her screams
three carabineers come,
their black capes belted in,
50 their caps to the cheekbone.

The consul gives the gypsy
a cup of warm milk,
and a bracer of gin
that Preciosa does not drink.

And while she cries
and tells them her ordeal,
the wind, on slate-gray tiles,
gnaws above them, furiously.

3

The Dispute

To Rafael Méndez

Halfway down the steep ravine
blades from Albacete,
lovely with the other's blood,
are glistening like fish.
Against the bitter green,
a card-hard light
traces raging horses
and riders' silhouettes.
Sitting in an olive tree,
10 two old women weep.
The bull of the dispute

se sube por las paredes.
Ángeles negros traían
pañuelos y agua de nieve.
Ángeles con grandes alas
de navajas de Albacete.
Juan Antonio el de Montilla
rueda muerto la pendiente,
su cuerpo lleno de lirios
20   y una granada en las sienes.
Ahora monta cruz de fuego
carretera de la muerte.

★

El juez, con guardia civil,
por los olivares viene.
Sangre resbalada gime
muda canción de serpiente.
Señores guardias civiles:
aquí pasó lo de siempre.
Han muerto cuatro romanos
30   y cinco cartagineses.

★

La tarde loca de higueras
y de rumores calientes,
cae desmayada en los muslos
heridos de los jinetes.
Y ángeles negros volaban
por el aire de poniente.
Ángeles de largas trenzas
y corazones de aceite.

4

Romance sonámbulo

A Gloria Giner y a Fernando de los Ríos

Verde que te quiero verde.
Verde viento. Verdes ramas.
El barco sobre la mar
y el caballo en la montaña.
Con la sombra en la cintura,
ella sueña en su baranda,
verde carne, pelo verde,

is driven up the walls.
Black angels were bringing
handkerchiefs and melted snow.
Angels with enormous wings
of blades from Albacete.
Juan Antonio from Montilla
tumbles down the incline, dead,
irises across his body,
20 a pomegranate in his head.
Now he rides a flaming cross
along the road of death.

★

The judge comes through the olive grove
with the Civil Guard.
The seeped-out blood is moaning
mute song of the serpent.
"Civil Guardsmen, Sirs,
it was just the usual thing:
four Romans dead
30 and five Carthaginians."

★

The afternoon, gone mad
with figs and heated sounds,
swoons and falls upon
the riders' wounded thighs.
Black angels were flying
on the western breeze.
Angels with long braids
and hearts of soothing oil.

4

Sleepwalking Ballad

To Gloria Giner and Fernando de los Ríos

Green oh how I love you green.
Green wind. Green boughs.
Ship on the sea,
horse on the mountain.
With waist of shadow,
she dreams at her rail,
green flesh, hair green,

con ojos de fría plata.
Verde que te quiero verde.
10   Bajo la luna gitana,
las cosas la están mirando
y ella no puede mirarlas.

★

Verde que te quiero verde.
Grandes estrellas de escarcha
vienen con el pez de sombra
que abre el camino del alba.
La higuera frota su viento
con la lija de sus ramas,
y el monte, gato garduño,
20   eriza sus pitas agrias.
Pero ¿quién vendrá? ¿Y por dónde? . . .
Ella sigue en su baranda,
verde carne, pelo verde,
soñando en la mar amarga.

★

—Compadre, quiero cambiar
mi caballo por su casa,
mi montura por su espejo.
mi cuchillo por su manta.
Compadre, vengo sangrando,
30   desde los puertos de Cabra.
—Si yo pudiera, mocito,
este trato se cerraba.
Pero yo ya no soy yo,
ni mi casa es ya mi casa.
—Compadre, quiero morir
decentemente en mi cama.
De acero, si puede ser,
con las sábanas de holanda.
¿No ves la herida que tengo
40   desde el pecho a la garganta?
—Trescientas rosas morenas
lleva tu pechera blanca.
Tu sangre rezuma y huele
alrededor de tu faja.
Pero yo ya no soy yo,
ni mi casa es ya mi casa.
—Dejadme subir al menos
hasta las altas barandas,
¡dejadme subir!, dejadme

and her eyes, cold silver.
Green oh how I love you green.
10 Beneath the gypsy moon
things are looking at her,
and she can't look at them.

★

Green oh how I love you green.
Giant stars of frost
come with the shadow-fish
that leads the way for dawn.
The fig tree chafes its wind
with its sandpapered branches,
and the mountain, untamed cat,
20 bristles sour maguey spears.
But who will come? From where?
Still she leans on her rail,
green flesh, hair green,
dreaming of the bitter sea.

★

"Compadre, I want to trade
my stallion for your house,
my saddle for your mirror,
my knife for your blanket.
Compadre, I have come here bleeding,
30 from the Cabra Pass."
"If I could, I would, lad.
Your offer would be taken.
But I am me no more,
nor is my house my own."
"Compadre, I want to die here,
decently, in my own bed;
of steel, if that can be,
with sheets of fine linen.
Don't you see this wound
40 that runs from throat to chest?"
"Three hundred brown roses
cover your white shirt.
Blood reeks and oozes
all around your sash.
But I am me no more,
nor is my house my own."
"Let me go at least
to the high rails of the house.
Oh let me go! Let me go

50 hasta las verdes barandas.
Barandales de la luna
por donde retumba el agua.

★

Ya suben los dos compadres
hacia las altas barandas.
Dejando un rastro de sangre.
Dejando un rastro de lágrimas.
Temblaban en los tejados
farolillos de hojalata.
Mil panderos de cristal
60 herían la madrugada.

★

Verde que te quiero verde,
verde viento, verdes ramas.
Los dos compadres subieron.
El largo viento, dejaba
en la boca un raro gusto
de hiel, de menta y de albahaca.
—¡Compadre! ¿Dónde está, dime,
dónde está tu niña amarga?
—¡Cuántas veces te esperó!
70 ¡Cuántas veces te esperara,
cara fresca, negro pelo,
en esta verde baranda!

★

Sobre el rostro del aljibe
se mecía la gitana.
Verde carne, pelo verde,
con ojos de fría plata.
Un carámbano de luna
la sostiene sobre el agua.
La noche se puso íntima
80 como una pequeña plaza.
Guardias civiles borrachos
en la puerta golpeaban.
Verde que te quiero verde.
Verde viento. Verdes ramas.
El barco sobre la mar.
Y el caballo en la montaña.

50 up to those rails of green!
Great railings of the moon,
where the water roars."

★

Up the two compadres climb,
to the high rails of the house,
leaving a trail of blood.
Leaving a trail of tears.
Tiny tin-leaf lanterns
were trembling on the tiles.
A thousand crystal tambourines
60 were wounding dawn's dark sky.

★

Green oh how I love you green,
green wind, green boughs.
Up the two compadres climbed.
The long wind left
a strange taste in the mouth
of basil, gall, and mint.
"Compadre! Tell me, where is she?
Where is your bitter girl?"
"How often she awaited you!
70 How often did she wait,
bright face, black hair,
upon this rail of green!"

★

Over the face of the rain-well
rocked the gypsy girl.
Green flesh, hair green,
and her eyes, cold silver.
An icicle of moonlight
holds her on the water.
The night drew in near
80 like a village square.
Drunken Civil Guardsmen
were beating on the door.
Green oh how I love you green.
Green wind, green boughs.
Ship on the sea.
Horse on the mountain.

7

Romance de la pena negra

A José Navarro Pardo

Las piquetas de los gallos
cavan buscando la aurora,
cuando por el monte oscuro
baja Soledad Montoya.
Cobre amarillo, su carne
huele a caballo y a sombra.
Yunques ahumados, sus pechos
gimen canciones redondas.
—Soledad: ¿por quién preguntas
10 sin compaña y a estas horas?
—Pregunte por quien pregunte,
dime: ¿a ti qué se te importa?
Vengo a buscar lo que busco,
mi alegría y mi persona.
—Soledad de mis pesares,
caballo que se desboca,
al fin encuentra la mar
y se lo tragan las olas.
—No me recuerdes el mar,
20 que la pena negra brota
en las tierras de aceituna
bajo el rumor de las hojas.
—¡Soledad, qué pena tienes!
¡Qué pena tan lastimosa!
Lloras zumo de limón
agrio de espera y de boca.
—¡Qué pena tan grande! Corro
mi casa como una loca,
mis dos trenzas por el suelo
30 de la cocina a la alcoba.
¡Qué pena! Me estoy poniendo
de azabache, carne y ropa.
¡Ay mis camisas de hilo!
¡Ay mis muslos de amapola!
—Soledad: lava tu cuerpo
con agua de las alondras,
y deja tu corazón
en paz, Soledad Montoya.

★

7

Ballad of Black Pain

To José Navarro Pardo

Roosters bury their picks
looking for the dawn,
when down the darkened hillside
Soledad Montoya comes.
She smells of horse and shadow,
her skin is yellow copper.
Her breasts like smoke-dark anvils
moan in circle songs.
"Soledad, who do you want,
10 so late and so alone?"
"I want the one I want,
so, what is it to you?
I came for what I came for:
my happiness, my person."
"Soledad of all my sorrows,
a bolting horse
always finds the sea
and is swallowed in the waves."
"Don't remind me of the sea,
20 for black pain thrusts its shoots
through the lands of olive trees,
beneath the rustling leaves."
"Soledad, what pain you bear!
What grievous pain!
You are crying lemon juice
of bitter waiting, bitter lips."
"What aching pain! All through
the house I race, insane.
I drag my braids across the floor
30 from the kitchen to the bedroom.
What pain! As black as jet
I turn, from dress to skin!
Ay, my linen underthings!
Ay, poppy of my thighs!"
Soledad, go bathe your body
in the water of the larks,
and give your heart
a rest, Soledad Montoya.

★

Por abajo canta el río:
volante de cielo y hojas.
Con flores de calabaza
la nueva luz se corona.
¡Oh pena de los gitanos!
Pena limpia y siempre sola.
¡Oh pena de cauce oculto
y madrugada remota!

8

San Miguel
(Granada)

A Diego Buigas de Dalmau

San Miguel

Se ven desde las barandas,
por el monte, monte, monte,
mulos y sombras de mulos
cargados de girasoles.

Sus ojos en las umbrías
se empañan de inmensa noche.
En los recodos del aire
cruje la aurora salobre.

Un cielo de mulos blancos
cierra sus ojos de azogue,
dando a la quieta penumbra
un final de corazones.
Y el agua se pone fría
para que nadie la toque.
Agua loca y descubierta
por el monte, monte, monte.

★

San Miguel, lleno de encajes
en la alcoba de su torre,
enseña sus bellos muslos
ceñidos por los faroles.

Arcángel domesticado
en el gesto de las doce,

The river sings below:
40 lace of leaves and sky.
New light crowns itself
with flowers of the pumpkin vine.
Oh gypsy pain!
Pain so clean and, always, so alone.
Oh pain from hidden streams
and the distant dark of dawn.

8

St. Michael
(Granada)

To Diego Buigas de Dalmau

St. Michael

They are seen from the balcony rails,
on the hill, the hill, the hill:
mules and shadows of mules
laden with sunflowers.

Their eyes in the cool shadows
fog up from huge night.
In the corners of the breeze,
snaps the salty dawn.

A sky of white mules
10 closes its mirrored eyes,
giving to the quiet light
a finale of hearts.
And the water turns cold
so no one will touch it.
The water, uncovered and wild,
on the hill, the hill, the hill.

★

St. Michael, covered in lace,
in the room of his tower
is showing his beautiful thighs
20 in a circle of lantern light.

Domesticated archangel,
in his pose of twelve,

finge una cólera dulce
de plumas y ruiseñores.
San Miguel canta en los vidrios,
efebo de tres mil noches,
fragante de agua colonia
y lejano de las flores.

★

El mar baila por la playa
30   un poema de balcones.
Las orillas de la luna
pierden juncos, ganan voces.
Vienen manolas comiendo
semillas de girasoles,
los culos grandes y ocultos
como planetas de cobre.
Vienen altos caballeros
y damas de triste porte,
morenas por la nostalgia
40   de un ayer de ruiseñores.
Y el obispo de Manila,
ciego de azafrán y pobre,
dice misa con dos filos
para mujeres y hombres.

★

San Miguel se estaba quieto
en la alcoba de su torre,
con las enaguas cuajadas
de espejitos y entredoses.

San Miguel, rey de los globos
50   y de los números nones,
en el primor berberisco
de gritos y miradores.

15

Romance de la Guardia Civil Española

A Juan Guerrero.
Cónsul general de la poesía

Los caballos negros son.
Las herraduras son negras.

186

he feigns a sweet anger
of feathers and nightingales.
St. Michael sings in the glass,
three thousand nights a pretty boy,
fragrant with cologne
and distant from the flowers.

★

The sea is dancing on the beach
30 a poem of balconies.
The banks of the moon
are gaining voices, losing reeds.
Manolas are coming,
eating sunflower seeds,
their bottoms large and dark
as copper planets.
Tall and thin come gentlemen
and ladies of sad bearing,
darkened by nostalgia
40 for a yesterday of nightingales.
And the Bishop of Manila,
saffron blind and poor,
says a two-edged Mass
for the men and women.

★

St. Michael hasn't moved
in the room inside his tower,
his petticoats encrusted
with spangles and brocade.

St. Michael, sovereign of balloons
50 and uneven numbers,
in the Berberesque delight
of shouts and miradors.

15

Ballad of the Spanish Civil Guard

To Juan Guerrero,
the Consul General of Poetry

Black are the horses,
the horseshoes are black.

Sobre las capas relucen
manchas de tinta y de cera.
Tienen, por eso no lloran,
de plomo las calaveras.
Con el alma de charol
vienen por la carretera.
Jorobados y nocturnos,
10 por donde animan ordenan
silencios de goma oscura
y miedos de fina arena.
Pasan, si quieren pasar,
y ocultan en la cabeza
una vaga astronomía
de pistolas inconcretas.

★

¡Oh ciudad de los gitanos!
En las esquinas banderas.
La luna y la calabaza
20 con las guindas en conserva.
¡Oh ciudad de los gitanos!
¿Quién te vio y no te recuerda?
Ciudad de dolor y almizcle,
con las torres de canela.

★

Cuando llegaba la noche,
noche que noche nochera,
los gitanos en sus fraguas
forjaban soles y flechas.
Un caballo malherido
30 llamaba a todas las puertas.
Gallos de vidrio cantaban
por Jerez de la Frontera.
El viento vuelve desnudo
la esquina de la sorpresa,
en la noche platinoche,
noche que noche nochera.

★

La Virgen y San José
perdieron sus castañuelas,
y buscan a los gitanos
40 para ver si las encuentran.
La Virgen viene vestida
con un traje de alcaldesa

Glistening on their capes
are stains of ink and wax.
Their skulls—and this is why
they do not cry—are cast in lead.
They ride the roads
with souls of patent leather.
Hunchbacked and nocturnal,
10   they command, where they appear,
the silence of dark rubber
and fears of fine sand.
They go as they will,
and hidden in their heads
is a vague astronomy
of phantasmagoric pistols.

★

Oh city of the gypsies!
Corners hung with banners.
The moon and pumpkins,
20   and cherries in preserve.
Oh city of the gypsies!
Who could see and not remember you?
City of musk and sorrow,
city of cinnamon towers.

★

As the night was coming,
the night so nightly night,
the gypsies at their forges
were shaping suns and arrows.
A badly wounded stallion
30   knocked at every door.
Glass roosters were singing
in Jerez de la Frontera.
The naked wind turns
the corner of surprise,
in the night silvernight,
the night so nightly night.

★

The Virgin and St. Joseph
have lost their castanets,
and are looking for the gypsies
40   to see if they can find them.
Here comes the Virgin, dressed
just like a mayor's wife,

de papel de chocolate
con los collares de almendras.
San José mueve los brazos
bajo una capa de seda.
Detrás va Pedro Domecq
con tres sultanes de Persia.
La media luna soñaba
50   un éxtasis de cigüeña.
Estandartes y faroles
invaden las azoteas.
Por los espejos sollozan
bailarinas sin caderas.
Agua y sombra, sombra y agua
por Jerez de la Frontera.

★

   ¡Oh ciudad de los gitanos!
En las esquinas banderas.
Apaga tus verdes luces
60   que viene la benemérita.
¡Oh ciudad de los gitanos!
¿Quién te vio y no te recuerda?
Dejadla lejos del mar
sin peines para sus crenchas.

★

   Avanzan de dos en fondo
a la ciudad de la fiesta.
Un rumor de siemprevivas,
invade las cartucheras.
Avanzan de dos en fondo.
70   Doble nocturno de tela.
El cielo, se les antoja,
una vitrina de espuelas.

★

   La ciudad libre de miedo,
multiplicaba sus puertas.
Cuarenta guardias civiles
entran a saco por ellas.
Los relojes se pararon,
y el coñac de las botellas
se disfrazó de noviembre
80   para no infundir sospechas.
Un vuelo de gritos largos
se levantó en las veletas.

in silver chocolate foil
with necklaces of almonds.
St. Joseph swings his arms
beneath a cape of silk.
Behind them comes Pedro Domecq
and three Persian sultans.
The half moon was dreaming
50   an ecstasy of storks.
And streamers and lamps
took over terraced roofs.
A dancer without hips
sobbed in every mirror.
Water and shadow, shadow and water
in Jerez de la Frontera.

★

Oh city of the gypsies!
Corners hung with banners.
Put your green lights out:
60   the Civil Guard is coming.
Oh city of the gypsies!
Who could see and not remember you?
Let her be, far from the sea,
with no combs to hold her hair.

★

They are riding two abreast
to the celebrating city.
The murmur of everlastings
invades their cartridge belts.
They are riding two abreast.
70   A night of doubled serge.
The sky, they like to fancy,
is a showcase full of spurs.

★

The city, free of fear,
was multiplying doors.
Forty Civil Guardsmen
pour through to sack and burn.
The clocks came to a stop
and the brandy bottles
masqueraded as November
80   so as not to stir suspicions.
A flight of long screams
rose from the weathercocks.

from THE GYPSY BALLADS 1924–1927

Los sables cortan las brisas
que los cascos atropellan.
Por las calles de penumbra
huyen las gitanas viejas
con los caballos dormidos
y las orzas de monedas.
Por las calles empinadas
90   suben las capas siniestras,
dejando detrás fugaces
remolinos de tijeras.

★

En el Portal de Belén
los gitanos se congregan.
San José, lleno de heridas,
amortaja a una doncella.
Tercos fusiles agudos
por toda la noche suenan.
La Virgen cura a los niños
100   con salivilla de estrella.
Pero la Guardia Civil
avanza sembrando hogueras,
donde joven y desnuda
la imaginación se quema.
Rosa la de los Camborios,
gime sentada en su puerta
con sus dos pechos cortados
puestos en una bandeja.
Y otras muchachas corrían
110   perseguidas por sus trenzas,
en un aire donde estallan
rosas de pólvora negra.
Cuando todos los tejados
eran surcos en la tierra,
el alba meció sus hombros
en largo perfil de piedra.

★

¡Oh ciudad de los gitanos!
La Guardia Civil se aleja
por un túnel de silencio
120   mientras las llamas te cercan.

¡Oh ciudad de los gitanos!
¿Quién te vio y no te recuerda?
Que te busquen en mi frente.
Juego de luna y arena.

Sabers slash at winds
trampled under hoof.
Through the half-lit streets
old gypsy women flee
with their sleepy horses
and enormous jars of coins.
Up the steep streets
90   climb the sinister capes,
leaving behind them
brief whirlwinds of shears.

★

    In the manger of Bethlehem
all the gypsies gather.
St. Joseph, badly wounded,
lays a shroud upon a girl.
Sharp and stubborn, rifles
crackle in the night.
The Virgin mends the children
100   with saliva from a star.
But the Civil Guard advances,
sowing giant fires,
where, young and naked,
imagination burns.
Rosa, the Camborio,
sits moaning at her door
with her severed breasts
before her on a tray.
Other girls were running
110   chased by their braids,
in a wind exploding
with roses of black powder.
When all the tiled roofs
were furrows in the earth,
dawn heaved its shoulders
in a silhouette of stone.

★

    Oh city of the gypsies!
The Civil Guardsmen ride away
through a tunnel of silence
120   while the flames encircle you.

    Oh city of the gypsies!
Who could see you and not remember you?
Let them find you on my brow:
play of sand and moon.

                from THE GYPSY BALLADS 1924–1927

18

Thamar y Amnón

Para Alfonso García Valdecasas

La luna gira en el cielo
sobre las tierras sin agua
mientras el verano siembra
rumores de tigre y llama.
Por encima de los techos
nervios de metal sonaban.
Aire rizado venía
con los balidos de lana.
La tierra se ofrece llena
10   de heridas cicatrizadas,
o estremecida de agudos
cauterios de luces blancas.

★

Thamar estaba soñando
pájaros en su garganta,
al son de panderos fríos
y cítaras enlunadas.
Su desnudo en el alero,
agudo norte de palma,
pide copos a su vientre
20   y granizo a sus espaldas.
Thamar estaba cantando
desnuda por la terraza.
Alrededor de sus pies,
cinco palomas heladas.
Amnón delgado y concreto,
en la torre la miraba,
llenas las ingles de espuma
y oscilaciones la barba.
Su desnudo iluminado
30   se tendía en la terraza,
con un rumor entre dientes
de flecha recién clavada.
Amnón estaba mirando
la luna redonda y baja,
y vio en la luna los pechos
durísimos de su hermana.

★

18

Thamar and Amnon

To Alfonso García Valdecasas

The moon circles the sky
over dry lands,
while the summer sows
rumbling of tiger and flame.
Above the rooftops
metal nerves were ringing.
A wind full of curls
came with woolly bleatings.
The earth offers itself
10   covered with scars
or shuddering from the sharp
and cauterizing light.

★

Thamar was dreaming
of birds in her throat
to a tune of cold tambourines
and half-moon zithers.
Her nakedness at roof edge,
sharp pole star of a palm,
asks snowflakes for her belly
20   and hailstones for her back.
Thamar was singing
naked on the terrace.
Circled round her feet,
five frozen doves.
Amnon, thin and hard,
watched her from the tower,
loins full of foam,
and beard, of small vibrations.
His gleaming nakedness
30   stretched out on the terrace,
biting back the murmur
of a just-struck arrow.
Amnon was looking
at the moon, low and round,
and saw in the moon
the hard breasts of his sister.

★

Amnón a las tres y media
se tendió sobre la cama.
Toda la alcoba sufría
con sus ojos llenos de alas.
La luz maciza, sepulta
pueblos en la arena parda,
o descubre transitorio
coral de rosas y dalias.
Linfa de pozo oprimida
brota silencio en las jarras.
En el musgo de los troncos
la cobra tendida canta.
Amnón gime por la tela
fresquísima de la cama.
Yedra del escalofrío
cubre su carne quemada.
Thamar entró silenciosa
en la alcoba silenciada,
color de vena y Danubio,
turbia de huellas lejanas.
—Thamar, bórrame los ojos
con tu fija madrugada.
Mis hilos de sangre tejen
volantes sobre tu falda.
—Déjame tranquila, hermano.
Son tus besos en mi espalda
avispas y vientecillos
en doble enjambre de flautas.
—Thamar, en tus pechos altos
hay dos peces que me llaman
y en las yemas de tus dedos
rumor de rosa encerrada.

★

Los cien caballos del rey
en el patio relinchaban.
Sol en cubos resistía
la delgadez de la parra.
Ya la coge del cabello,
ya la camisa le rasga.
Corales tibios dibujan
arroyos en rubio mapa.

★

¡Oh, qué gritos se sentían
por encima de las casas!

At half past three, Amnon
lay down on the bed.
The whole room was suffering
40 with its wing-filled eyes.
The solid light entombs
villages in ocher sand
or reveals the transitory
coral of dahlias and roses.
Pent-up lymph of wells
spurts silence in the jars.
In the moss of tree limbs
the uncoiled cobra sings.
Amnon is softly moaning
50 on the sheets' cool chill.
The ivy of a shiver
covers burning flesh.
Thamar enters silently
the silence of the room,
the color of vein and Danube,
dark from distant signs.
"Erase my eyes, Thamar,
with your stare of dawn.
The threads of my blood
60 weave ruffles on your dress."
"Brother, leave me. Please.
Your kisses on my back
are wasps and puffs of wind,
flutes in double swarms."
"From your high breasts, Thamar,
two fish are calling me,
and from your fingertips,
murmur of a cloistered rose."

★

The hundred horses of the king
70 whinnied in the courtyard.
Cubes of sun pressed hard
on the thinness of the vine.
Now he takes her by the hair,
now he tears her underthings.
Warm corals drawing little creeks
across a map of blonde.

★

Oh, what shouts were heard
over all the houses!

from THE GYPSY BALLADS 1924–1927

Qué espesura de puñales
y túnicas desgarradas.
Por las escaleras tristes
esclavos suben y bajan.
Émbolos y muslos juegan
bajo las nubes paradas.
Alrededor de Thamar
gritan vírgenes gitanas
y otras recogen las gotas
de su flor martirizada.
Paños blancos, enrojecen
en las alcobas cerradas.
Rumores de tibia aurora
pámpanos y peces cambian.

★

Violador enfurecido,
Amnón huye con su jaca.
Negros le dirigen flechas
en los muros y atalayas.
Y cuando los cuatro cascos
eran cuatro rosonancias,
David con unas tijeras
cortó las cuerdas del arpa.

What thickets of knives
and tunics torn.
On the stairways, saddened
slaves go up and down.
Thighs and pistons play
beneath the halted clouds.
Around Thamar
virgin gypsies shout,
and others gather up the drops
of her martyred flower.
White cloth turns to red
behind the bedroom doors.
Noises of warm sunshine
exchanged by fish and vines.

★

Ravisher enraged,
Amnon flees on his gelding.
Negroes loose their arrows on him
from parapets and towers.
And when the four hooves
had become four echoes,
King David took a scissors
and cut the strings of his harp.

De

POETA EN
NUEVA YORK

[Autorretrato en Nueva York, 1929–32]

From

POET IN

NEW YORK

Translated by

Greg Simon

and Steven F. White

[*Self-portrait in New York, 1929–32*]

Vuelta de paseo

Asesinado por el cielo.
Entre las formas que van hacia la sierpe
y las formas que buscan el cristal
dejaré crecer mis cabellos.

Con el árbol de muñones que no canta
y el niño con el blanco rostro de huevo.

Con los animalitos de cabeza rota
y el agua harapienta de los pies secos.

Con todo lo que tiene cansancio sordomudo
10   y mariposa ahogada en el tintero.

Tropezando con mi rostro distinto de cada día.
¡Asesinado por el cielo!

La aurora

La aurora de Nueva York tiene
cuatro columnas de cieno
y un huracán de negras palomas
que chapotean las aguas podridas.

La aurora de Nueva York gime
por las inmensas escaleras
buscando entre las aristas
nardos de angustia dibujada.

La aurora llega y nadie la recibe en su boca
10   porque allí no hay mañana ni esperanza posible:
a veces las monedas en enjambres furiosos
taladran y devoran abandonados niños.

Los pimeros que salen comprenden con sus huesos
que no habrá paraíso ni amores deshojados:
saben que van al cieno de números y leyes,
a los juegos sin arte, a sudores sin fruto.

La luz es sepultada por cadenas y ruidos
en impúdico reto de ciencia sin raíces.
Por los barrios hay gentes que vacilan insomnes
20   como recién salidas de un naufragio de sangre.

After a Walk

Cut down by the sky.
Between shapes moving toward the serpent
and crystal-craving shapes,
I'll let my hair grow.

With the amputated tree that doesn't sing
and the child with the blank face of an egg.

With the little animals whose skulls are cracked
and the water, dressed in rags but with dry feet.

With all the bone-tired, deaf-and-dumb things
10   and a butterfly drowned in the inkwell.

Bumping into my own face, different each day.
Cut down by the sky!

Dawn

Dawn in New York has
four columns of mire
and a hurricane of black pigeons
splashing in the putrid waters.

Dawn in New York groans
on enormous fire escapes
searching between the angles
for spikenards of drafted anguish.

Dawn arrives and no one receives it in his mouth
10   because morning and hope are impossible there:
sometimes the furious swarming coins
penetrate like drills and devour abandoned children.

Those who go out early know in their bones
there will be no paradise or loves that bloom and die:
they know they will be mired in numbers and laws,
in mindless games, in fruitless labors.

The light is buried under chains and noises
in the impudent challenge of rootless science.
And crowds stagger sleeplessly through the boroughs
20   as if they had just escaped a shipwreck of blood.

from POET IN NEW YORK

El rey de Harlem

Con una cuchara de palo
le arrancaba los ojos a los cocodrilos
y golpeaba el trasero de los monos.
Con una cuchara de palo.

Fuego de siempre dormía en los pedernales
y los escarabajos borrachos de anís
olvidaban el musgo de las aldeas.

Aquel viejo cubierto de setas
iba al sitio donde lloraban los negros
10   mientras crujía la cuchara del rey
y llegaban los tanques de agua podrida.

Las rosas huían por los filos
de las últimas curvas del aire
y en los montones de azafrán
los niños machacaban pequeñas ardillas
con un rubor de frenesí manchado.

Es preciso cruzar los puentes
y llegar al rumor negro
para que el perfume de pulmón
20   nos golpee las sienes con su vestido
de caliente piña.

Es preciso matar al rubio vendedor de aguardiente,
a todos los amigos de la manzana y la arena;
y es necesario dar con los puños cerrados
a las pequeñas judías que tiemblan llenas de burbujas,
para que el rey de Harlem cante con su muchedumbre,
para que los cocodrilos duerman en largas filas
bajo el amianto de la luna,
y para que nadie dude la infinita belleza
30   de los plumeros, los ralladores, los cobres y las cacerolas de las cocinas.

¡Ay, Harlem! ¡Ay Harlem! ¡Ay, Harlem!
No hay angustia comparable a tus rojos oprimidos,
a tu sangre estremecida dentro del eclipse oscuro,
a tu violencia granate, sordomuda en la penumbra,
a tu gran rey prisionero, con un traje de conserje.

★

Tenía la noche una hendidura y quietas salamandras de marfil.
Las muchachas americanas

The King of Harlem

With a wooden spoon
he dug out the crocodiles' eyes,
and swatted the monkeys on their asses.
With a wooden spoon.

Age-old fire slept in the flints
and the beetles drunk on anisette
forgot about the moss of the villages.

The old man covered with mushrooms
was on his way to the place where the blacks wept
10   while the king's spoon cracked
and the vats of putrid water arrived.

The roses fled along the blades
of the air's last curves,
and on the piles of saffron
the children flattened tiny squirrels
with faces flushed in their stained frenzy.

It's necessary to cross the bridges
and reach the murmuring blacks
so the perfume of their lungs
20   can buffet our temples with its covering
of hot pineapple.

It's necessary to kill the blond vendor of firewater
and every friend of apple and sand,
and it's necessary to use the fists
against the little Jewish women who tremble, filled with bubbles,
so the king of Harlem sings with his multitude,
so crocodiles sleep in long rows
beneath the moon's asbestos,
and so no one doubts the infinite beauty
30   of feather dusters, graters, copper pans, and kitchen casseroles.

Ay, Harlem! *Ay*, Harlem! *Ay*, Harlem!
There is no anguish like that of your oppressed reds,
or your blood shuddering with rage inside the dark eclipse,
or your garnet violence, deaf and dumb in the penumbra,
or your grand king a prisoner in the uniform of a doorman.

★

The night was cracked, and there were motionless ivory salamanders.
American girls

llevaban niños y monedas en el vientre
y los muchachos se desmayaban en la cruz del desperezo.

40   Ellos son.
Ellos son los que beben el whisky de plata junto a los volcanes
y tragan pedacitos de corazón por las heladas montañas del oso.

Aquella noche el rey de Harlem, con una durísima cuchara,
le arrancaba los ojos a los cocodrilos
y golpeaba el trasero de los monos.
Con una durísima cuchara.

Los negros lloraban confundidos
entre paraguas y soles de oro,
los mulatos estiraban gomas, ansiosos de llegar al torso blanco,
50   y el viento empañaba espejos
y quebraba las venas de los bailarines.

¡Negros! ¡Negros! ¡Negros! ¡Negros!
La sangre no tiene puertas en vuestra noche boca arriba.
No hay rubor. Sangre furiosa por debajo de las pieles,
viva en la espina del puñal y en el pecho de los paisajes,
bajo las pinzas y las retamas de la celeste luna de Cáncer.

Sangre que busca por mil caminos muertes enharinadas y ceniza de nardos,
cielos yertos en declive donde las colonias de planetas
rueden por las playas con los objetos abandonados.

60   Sangre que mira lenta con el rabo del ojo,
hecha de espartos exprimidos y néctares subterráneos.
Sangre que oxida al alisio descuidado en una huella
y disuelve a las mariposas en los cristales de la ventana.

Es la sangre que viene, que vendrá
por los tejados y azoteas, por todas partes,
para quemar la clorofila de las mujeres rubias,
para gemir al pie de las camas, ante el insomnio de los lavabos,
y estrellarse en una aurora de tabaco y bajo amarillo.

¡Hay que huir!,
70   huir por las esquinas y encerrarse en los últimos pisos,
porque el tuétano del bosque penetrará por las rendijas
para dejar en vuestra carne una leve huella de eclipse
y una falsa tristeza de guante desteñido y rosa química.

★

were carrying babies and coins in their wombs,
and the boys stretched their limbs and fainted on the cross.

40 They are the ones.
The ones who drink silver whisky near the volcanoes
and swallow pieces of heart by the bear's frozen mountains.

That night the king of Harlem, with an unbreakable spoon,
dug out the crocodiles' eyes
and swatted the monkeys on their asses.
With an unbreakable spoon.
The blacks cried in confusion
among umbrellas and gold suns,
the mulattoes stretched rubber, thinking anxiously of turning their torsos
    white,
50 and the wind tarnished mirrors
and shattered the veins of the dancers.

Blacks! Blacks! Blacks! Blacks!
The blood has no doors in your recumbent night.
No blush in your face. Blood rages beneath skin,
alive in the dagger's spine and the landscapes' breast,
under the pincers and Scotch broom of Cancer's heavenly moon.

Blood that searches a thousand roads for deaths dusted with flour and
    ashes of spikenards,
rigid, descending skies in which the colonies of planets
can wheel with the litter on the beaches.

60 Blood that looks slowly from the corner of an eye,
blood wrung from hemp and subway nectars.
Blood that rusts the careless trade wind in a footprint
and dissolves butterflies in windowpanes.

Blood flows, and will flow
on rooftops everywhere
and burn the blond women's chlorophyll,
and groan at the foot of the beds near the washstands' insomnia,
and burst into an aurora of tobacco and low yellow.

There must be some way out of here,
70 some street to flee down, some locked room on the top floor to hide in,
because the forest's marrow will slip through the cracks
to leave on your skin the faint trace of an eclipse
and the false sorrow of faded glove and chemical rose.

★

Es por el silencio sapientísimo
cuando los cocineros y los camareros y los que limpian con la lengua
las heridas de los millonarios
buscan al rey por las calles o en los ángulos del salitre.

Un viento sur de madera, oblicuo en el negro fango,
escupe a las barcas rotas y se clava puntillas en los hombros.
80 Un viento sur que lleva
colmillos, girasoles, alfabetos
y una pila de Volta con avispas ahogadas.

El olvido estaba expresado por tres gotas de tinta sobre el monóculo.
El amor, por un solo rostro invisible a flor de piedra.
Médulas y corolas componían sobre las nubes
un desierto de tallos, sin una sola rosa.

A la izquierda, a la derecha, por el Sur y por el Norte,
se levanta el muro impasible
para el topo y la aguja del agua.
90 No busquéis, negros, su grieta
para hallar la máscara infinita.
Buscad el gran sol del centro
hechos una piña zumbadora.
El sol que se desliza por los bosques
seguro de no encontrar una ninfa.
El sol que destruye números y no ha cruzado nunca un sueño,
el tatuado sol que baja por el río
y muge seguido de caimanes.

¡Negros! ¡Negros! ¡Negros! ¡Negros!
100 Jamás sierpe, ni cebra, ni mula
palidecieron al morir.
El leñador no sabe cuándo expiran
los clamorosos árboles que corta.
Aguardad bajo la sombra vegetal de vuestro rey
a que cicutas y cardos y ortigas turben postreras azoteas.

Entonces, negros, entonces, entonces,
podréis besar con frenesí las ruedas de las bicicletas,
poner parejas de microscopios en las cuevas de las ardillas
y danzar al fin sin duda, mientras las flores erizadas
110 asesinan a nuestro Moisés casi en los juncos del cielo.

¡Ay, Harlem disfrazada!
¡Ay, Harlem, amenazada por un gentío de trajes sin cabeza!
Me llega tu rumor,

Through the all-knowing silence,
cooks, waiters, and those whose tongues lick clean
the wounds of millionaires
seek the king in the streets or on the sharp angles of saltpeter.

A wooden wind from the south, slanting through the black mire,
spits on the broken boats and drives tacks into its shoulders.
80 A south wind that carries
tusks, sunflowers, alphabets,
and a battery with drowned wasps.

Oblivion was expressed by three drops of ink on the monocle.
Love, by a single, invisible, stone-deep face.
And above the clouds, bone marrow and corollas
composed a desert of stems without a single rose.

To the left and right, south and north,
the wall rises, impassable
for the mole and the needle made of water.
90 Blacks, don't look in its cracks
to find the infinite mask.
Look for the great central sun.
Turn into a swarm of buzzing pineapple.
The sun that slides through the forests,
sure that a nymph will not be there.
The sun that destroys numbers, and has never crossed a dream,
the tattooed sun that descends the river
and bellows just ahead of the crocodiles.

Blacks! Blacks! Blacks! Blacks!
100 No serpent, no zebra or mule
ever turned pale in the face of death.
The woodcutter doesn't know when the clamorous trees
that he cuts down expire.
Wait in your king's jungle shade
until hemlock, thistles, and nettles disturb the last rooftops.

Then, blacks, and only then
will you be able to frantically kiss bicycle wheels,
place pairs of microscopes in squirrel lairs,
and dance fearlessly at last while the bristling flowers
110 cut down our Moses in the bulrushes that border heaven.

Ay, Harlem in disguise!
Ay, Harlem, threatened by a mob of headless suits!
I hear your murmur,

me llega tu rumor atravesando troncos y ascensores,
a través de láminas grises,
donde flotan tus automóviles cubiertos de dientes,
a través de los caballos muertos y los crímenes diminutos,
a través de tu gran rey desesperado,
cuyas barbas llegan al mar.

Danza de la muerte

El mascarón. Mirad el mascarón
cómo viene del África a New York.

Se fueron los árboles de la pimienta,
los pequeños botones de fósforo.
Se fueron los camellos de carne desgarrada
y los valles de luz que el cisne levantaba con el pico.

Era el momento de las cosas secas:
de la espiga en el ojo y el gato laminado;
del óxido de hierro de los grandes puentes
10 y el definitivo silencio del corcho.

Era la gran reunión de los animales muertos
traspasados por las espadas de la luz.
La alegría eterna del hipopótamo con las pezuñas de ceniza
y de la gacela con una siempreviva en la garganta.

En la marchita soledad sin onda
el abollado mascarón danzaba.
Medio lado del mundo era de arena,
mercurio y sol dormido el otro medio.

El mascarón. ¡Mirad el mascarón!
20 *Arena, caimán y miedo sobre Nueva York.*

Defiladeros de cal aprisionaban un cielo vacío
donde sonaban las voces de los que mueren bajo el guano.
Un cielo mondado y puro, idéntico a sí mismo,
con el bozo y lirio agudo de sus montañas invisibles,

acabó con los más leves tallitos del canto
y se fue al diluvio empaquetado de la savia,
a través del descanso de los últimos perfiles
levantando con el rabo pedazos de espejo.

I hear it moving through tree trunks and elevator shafts,
through gray sheets
where your cars float covered with teeth,
through dead horses and petty crimes,
through your grand, despairing king
whose beard reaches the sea.

Dance of Death

The mask. Look how the mask
comes from Africa to New York.

They are gone, the pepper trees,
the tiny buds of phosphorus.
They are gone, the camels with torn flesh,
and the valleys of light the swan lifted in its beak.

It was the time of parched things,
the wheat spear in the eye, the laminated cat,
the time of tremendous, rusting bridges
10   and the deathly silence of cork.

It was the great gathering of dead animals
pierced by the swords of light.
The endless joy of the hippopotamus with cloven feet of ash
and of the gazelle with an immortelle in its throat.

On the withered, waveless solitude,
the dented mask was dancing.
Half of the world was sand,
the other half mercury and dormant sunlight.

The mask. Look at the mask!
20   *Sand, crocodile, and fear above New York.*

Canyons of lime imprisoned an empty sky,
where the voices of those who die under the guano were heard.
A pure and manicured sky, identical with itself,
with the down and the keen-edged iris of its invisible mountains—

it finished off the slender stems of song
and was swept away toward channels of sap,
through the stillness of the last profiles,
lifting pieces of mirror with its tail.

Cuando el chino lloraba en el tejado
30   sin encontrar el desnudo de su mujer,
y el director del banco observaba el manómetro
que mide el cruel silencio de la moneda,
el mascarón llegaba a Wall Street.

No es extraño para la danza
este columbario que pone los ojos amarillos.
De la esfinge a la caja de caudales hay un hilo tenso
que atraviesa el corazón de todos los niños pobres.
El ímpetu primitivo baila con el ímpetu mecánico,
ignorantes en su frenesí de la luz original.
40   Porque si la rueda olvida su fórmula,
ya puede cantar desnuda con las manadas de caballos;
y si una llama quema los helados proyectos
el cielo tendrá que huir ante el tumulto de las ventanas.

No es extraño este sitio para la danza. Yo lo digo.
El mascarón bailará entre columnas de sangre y de números,
entre huracanes de oro y gemidos de obreros parados
que aullarán, noche oscura, por tu tiempo sin luces.
¡Oh salvaje Norteamérica!, ¡oh impúdica!, ¡oh salvaje!
Tendida en la frontera de la nieve.

50   *El mascarón. ¡Mirad el mascarón!*
¡Qué ola de fango y luciérnagas sobre Nueva York!

★

Yo estaba en la terraza luchando con la luna.
Enjambres de ventanas acribillaban un muslo de la noche.
En mis ojos bebían las dulces vacas de los cielos
y las brisas de largos remos
golpeaban los cenicientos cristales del Broadway.

La gota de sangre buscaba la luz de la yema del astro
para fingir una muerta semilla de manzana.
El aire de la llanura, empujado por los pastores,
60   temblaba con un miedo de molusco sin concha.

Pero no son los muertos los que bailan.
Estoy seguro.
Los muertos están embebidos devorando sus propias manos.
Son los otros los que bailan con el mascarón y su vihuela.
Son los otros, los borrachos de plata, los hombres fríos,
los que duermen en el cruce de los muslos y llamas duras,
los que buscan la lombriz en el paisaje de las escaleras,

While the Chinaman wept on the roof
30 without finding the naked body of his wife,
and the bank director examined the manometer
that measures the cruel silence of money,
the mask arrived on Wall Street.

This isn't a strange place for the dance,
these cemetery niches that turn the eyes yellow.
Between the sphinx and the bank vault, there is a taut thread
that pierces the heart of all poor children.
The primitive impetus dances with the mechanical impetus,
unaware, in their frenzy, of the original light.
40 Because if the wheel forgets its formula,
it will sing naked with herds of horses;
and if a flame burns the frozen blueprints,
the sky will have to flee before the tumult of windows.

This isn't a strange place for the dance, I tell you.
The mask will dance among columns of blood and numbers,
among hurricanes of gold and groans of the unemployed,
who will howl, in the dead of night, for your dark time.
Oh, savage, shameless North America!
Stretched out on the frontier of snow.

50

The mask. Look at the mask!
Such a wave of mire and fireflies above New York!

★

I was on the terrace, wrestling with the moon.
Swarms of windows riddled one of the night's thighs.
Placid sky-cattle drank from my eyes
and the breezes on long oars
struck the ashen store windows on Broadway.

The drop of blood looked for light in the star's yolk
so as to seem a dead apple seed.
The prairie air, driven by the shepherds,
60 trembled in fear like a mollusk without its shell.

But I'm sure there are no dancers
among the dead.
The dead are engrossed in devouring their own hands.
It's the others who dance with the mask and its *vihuela*.
Others, drunk on silver, cold men,
who sleep where thighs and hard flames intersect,
who seek the earthworm in the landscape of fire escapes,

213   *from* POET IN NEW YORK

los que beben en el banco lágrimas de niña muerta
o los que comen por las esquinas diminutas pirámides del alba.

70 ¡Que no baile el Papa!
¡No, que no baile el Papa!
Ni el Rey,
ni el millonario de dientes azules,
ni las bailarinas secas de las catedrales,
ni constructores, ni esmeraldas, ni locos, ni sodomitas.
Sólo este mascarón.
Este mascarón de vieja escarlatina.
¡Sólo este mascarón!

Que ya las cobras silbarán por los últimos pisos.
80 Que ya las ortigas estremecerán patios y terrazas.
Que ya la Bolsa será una pirámide de musgo.
Que ya vendrán lianas después de los fusiles
y muy pronto, muy pronto, muy pronto.
¡Ay, Wall Street!

El mascarón. ¡Mirad el mascarón!
¡Cómo escupe veneno de bosque
por la angustia imperfecta de Nueva York!

Diciembre 1929

Paisaje de la multitud que vomita
(Anochecer de Coney Island)

La mujer gorda venía delante
arrancando las raíces y mojando el pergamino de los tambores.
La mujer gorda,
que vuelve del revés los pulpos agonizantes.
La mujer gorda, enemiga de la luna,
corría por las calles y los pisos deshabitados
y dejaba por los rincones pequeñas calaveras de paloma
y levantaba las furias de los banquetes de los siglos últimos
y llamaba al demonio del pan por las colinas del cielo barrido
10 y filtraba un ansia de luz en las circulaciones subterráneas.
Son los cementerios. Lo sé. Son los cementerios
y el dolor de las cocinas enterradas bajo la arena.
Son los muertos, los faisanes y las manzanas de otra hora
los que nos empujan en la garganta.

Llegaban los rumores de la selva del vómito
con las mujeres vacías, con niños de cera caliente,

who drink a dead girl's tears at the bank
or eat tiny pyramids of dawn on street corners.

70 But don't let the Pope dance!
No, don't let the Pope dance!
Nor the King,
nor the millionaires with blue teeth,
nor the barren dancers of the cathedrals,
nor builders, nor emeralds, nor madmen, nor sodomites.
Only this mask.
This mask of ancient scarlet fever.
Only this mask!

Cobras shall hiss on the top floors.
80 Nettle shall shake courtyards and terraces.
The Stock Exchange shall become a pyramid of moss.
Jungle vines shall come in behind the rifles
and all so quickly, so very, very quickly.
Ay, Wall Street!

The mask. Look at the mask!
And how it spits its forest poison
through New York's imperfect anguish!

December 1929

Landscape of a Vomiting Multitude
(Dusk at Coney Island)

The fat lady came first,
tearing out roots and moistening drumskins.
The fat lady
who turns dying octopuses inside out.
The fat lady, the moon's antagonist,
was running through the streets and deserted buildings
and leaving tiny skulls of pigeons in the corners
and stirring up the furies of the last centuries' feasts
and summoning the demon of bread through the sky's clean-swept hills
10 and filtering a longing for light into subterranean tunnels.
The graveyards, yes, the graveyards
and the sorrow of the kitchens buried in sand,
the dead, pheasants and apples of another era,
pushing into our throat.

There were murmurings from the jungle of vomit
with the empty women, with hot wax children,

con árboles fermentados y camareros incansables
que sirven platos de sal bajo las arpas de la saliva.
Sin remedio, hijo mío, ¡vomita! No hay remedio.

20 No es el vómito de los húsares sobre los pechos de la prostituta,
ni el vómito del gato que se tragó una rana por descuido.
Son los muertos que arañan con sus manos de tierra
las puertas de pedernal donde se pudren nublos y postres.

La mujer gorda venía delante
con las gentes de los barcos y de las tabernas y de los jardines.
El vómito agitaba delicadamente sus tambores
entre algunas niñas de sangre
que pedían protección a la luna.
¡Ay de mí! ¡Ay de mí! ¡Ay de mí!
30 Esta mirada mía fue mía, pero ya no es mía,
esta mirada que tiembla desnuda por el alcohol
y despide barcos increíbles
por las anémonas de los muelles.
Me defiendo con esta mirada
que mana de las ondas por donde el alba no se atreve,
yo, poeta sin brazos, perdido
entre la multitud que vomita,
sin caballo efusivo que corte
los espesos musgos de mis sienes.

40 Pero la mujer gorda seguía delante
y la gente buscaba las farmacias
donde el amargo trópico se fija.
Sólo cuando izaron la bandera y llegaron los primeros canes
la ciudad entera se agolpó en las barandillas del embarcadero.

Nueva York, 29 de diciembre 1929

Ciudad sin sueño
(Nocturno del Brooklyn Bridge)

No duerme nadie por el cielo. Nadie, nadie.
No duerme nadie.
Las criaturas de la luna huelen y rondan las cabañas.
Vendrán las iguanas vivas a morder a los hombres que no sueñan
y el que huye con el corazón roto encontrará por las esquinas
al increíble cocodrilo quieto bajo la tierna protesta de los astros.

No duerme nadie por el mundo. Nadie, nadie.
No duerme nadie.

with fermented trees and tireless waiters
who serve platters of salt beneath harps of saliva.
There's no other way, my son, vomit! There's no other way.
20   It's not the vomit of hussars on the breasts of their whores,
nor the vomit of cats that inadvertently swallowed frogs,
but the dead who scratch with clay hands
on flint gates where clouds and desserts decay.

The fat lady came first
with the crowds from the ships, taverns, and parks.
Vomit was delicately shaking its drums
among a few little girls of blood
who were begging the moon for protection.
Who could imagine my sadness?
30   The look on my face was mine, but now isn't me,
the naked look on my face, trembling for alcohol
and launching incredible ships
through the anemones of the piers.
I protect myself with this look
that flows from waves where no dawn would go,
I, poet without arms, lost
in the vomiting multitude,
with no effusive horse to shear
the thick moss from my temples.

40   But the fat lady went first
and the crowds kept looking for the pharmacies
where the bitter tropics could be found.
Only when a flag went up and the first dogs arrived
did the entire city rush to the railings of the boardwalk.

New York, December 29, 1929

Sleepless City
(*Brooklyn Bridge Nocturne*)

Out in the sky, no one sleeps. No one, no one.
No one sleeps.
Lunar creatures sniff and circle the dwellings.
Live iguanas will come to bite the men who don't dream,
and the brokenhearted fugitive will meet on street corners
an incredible crocodile resting beneath the tender protest of the stars.

Out in the world, no one sleeps. No one, no one.
No one sleeps.

from POET IN NEW YORK

Hay un muerto en el cementerio más lejano
que se queja tres años
porque tiene un paisaje seco en la rodilla;
y el niño que enterraron esta mañana lloraba tanto
que hubo necesidad de llamar a los perros para que callase.

No es sueño la vida. ¡Alerta! ¡Alerta! ¡Alerta!
Nos caemos por las escaleras para comer la tierra húmeda
o subimos al filo de la nieve con el coro de las dalias muertas.
Pero no hay olvido ni sueño:
carne viva. Los besos atan las bocas
en una maraña de venas recientes
y al que le duele su dolor le dolerá sin descanso
y el que teme la muerte la llevará sobre los hombros.

Un día
los caballos vivirán en las tabernas
y las hormigas furiosas
atacarán los cielos amarillos que se refugian en los ojos de las vacas.
Otro día
veremos la resurrección de las mariposas disecadas
y aun andando por un paisaje de esponjas grises y barcos mudos
veremos brillar nuestro anillo y manar rosas de nuestra lengua.

¡Alerta! ¡Alerta! ¡Alerta!
A los que guardan todavía huellas de zarpa y aguacero,
a aquel muchacho que llora porque no sabe la invención del puente
o a aquel muerto que ya no tiene más que la cabeza y un zapato,
hay que llevarlos al muro donde iguanas y sierpes esperan,
donde espera la dentadura del oso,
donde espera la mano momificada del niño
y la piel del camello se eriza con un violento escalofrío azul.

No duerme nadie por el cielo. Nadie, nadie.
No duerme nadie.
Pero si alguien cierra los ojos,
¡azotadlo, hijos míos, azotadlo!
Haya un panorama de ojos abiertos
y amargas llagas encendidas.
No duerme nadie por el mundo. Nadie, nadie.
Ya lo he dicho.
No duerme nadie.
Pero si alguien tiene por la noche exceso de musgo en las sienes,
abrid los escotillones para que vea bajo la luna
las copas falsas, el veneno y la calavera de los teatros.

There is a corpse in the farthest graveyard
10 complaining for three years
because of an arid landscape in his knee;
and a boy who was buried this morning cried so much
they had to call the dogs to quiet him.

Life is no dream. Watch out! Watch out! Watch out!
We fall down stairs and eat the moist earth,
or we climb to the snow's edge with the choir of dead dahlias.
But there is no oblivion, no dream:
raw flesh. Kisses tie mouths
in a tangle of new veins
20 and those who are hurt will hurt without rest
and those who are frightened by death will carry it on their shoulders.

One day
horses will live in the taverns
and furious ants
will attack the yellow skies that take refuge in the eyes of cattle.
Another day
we'll witness the resurrection of dried butterflies,
and still walking in a landscape of gray sponges and silent ships,
we'll see our ring shine and roses spill from our tongues.

30 Watch out! Watch out! Watch out!
Those still marked by claws and cloudburst,
that boy who cries because he doesn't know about the invention of bridges,
or that corpse that has nothing more than its head and one shoe—
they all must be led to the wall where iguanas and serpents wait,
where the bear's teeth wait,
where the mummified hand of a child waits
and the camel's fur bristles with a violent blue chill.

Out in the sky, no one sleeps. No one, no one.
No one sleeps.
40 But if someone closes his eyes,
whip him, my children, whip him!
Let there be a panorama of open eyes
and bitter inflamed wounds.
Out in the world, no one sleeps. No one. No one.
I've said it before.
No one sleeps.
But at night, if someone has too much moss on his temples,
open the trap doors so he can see in moonlight
the fake goblets, the venom, and the skull of the theaters.

Poema doble del Lago Eden

Nuestro ganado pace, el viento espira.
—Garcilaso

Era mi voz antigua
ignorante de los densos jugos amargos.
La adivino lamiendo mis pies
bajo los frágiles helechos mojados.

¡Ay, voz antigua de mi amor,
ay, voz de mi verdad,
ay, voz de mi abierto costado,
cuando todas las rosas manaban de mi lengua
y el césped no conocía la impasible dentadura del caballo!

10   Estás aquí bebiendo mi sangre,
bebiendo mi humor de niño pesado,
mientras mis ojos se quiebran en el viento
con el aluminio y las voces de los borrachos.

Dejarme pasar la puerta
donde Eva come hormigas
y Adán fecunda peces deslumbrados.
Dejarme pasar, hombrecillos de los cuernos,
al bosque de los desperezos
y los alegrísimos saltos.

20   Yo sé el uso más secreto
que tiene un viejo alfiler oxidado
y sé del horror de unos ojos despiertos
sobre la superficie concreta del plato.

Pero no quiero mundo ni sueño, voz divina,
quiero mi libertad, mi amor humano
en el rincón más oscuro de la brisa que nadie quiera.
¡Mi amor humano!

Esos perros marinos se persiguen
y el viento acecha troncos descuidados.
30   ¡Oh voz antigua, quema con tu lengua
esta voz de hojalata y de talco!

Quiero llorar porque me da la gana,
como lloran los niños del último banco,
porque yo no soy un hombre, ni un poeta, ni una hoja,
pero sí un pulso herido que ronda las cosas del otro lado.

Double Poem of Lake Eden

Our cattle graze, the wind sends forth its breath.
—Garcilaso

It was my ancient voice,
ignorant of the dense and bitter sap.
I can sense it lapping at my feet
beneath the moist and fragile ferns.

Ay, my love's ancient voice,
ay, voice of my truth,
ay, voice of my open side,
when all the roses spilled from my tongue
and the grass hadn't felt the horse's impassible teeth!

10 Here you are drinking my blood,
drinking the humor of the child I was,
while my eyes are battered by aluminum
and drunken voices in the wind.

Let me pass through the arch
where Eve devours ants
and Adam impregnates the dazzled fish.
Little men with horns, let me return
to the grove of leisure
and the somersaults of pure joy.

20 I know a ceremony so secret
it requires an old rusty pin,
and I know the horror of open eyes
on the concrete surface of a plate.

But I want neither world nor dream, divine voice,
I want my liberty, my human love
in the darkest corner of the breeze no one wants.
My human love!

Those sea-dogs chase each other
and the wind lies in ambush for careless tree trunks.
30 Oh, ancient voice, let your tongue burn
this voice of tin and talc!

I want to cry because I feel like it—
the way children cry in the last row of seats—
because I'm not a man, not a poet, not a leaf,
only a wounded pulse that circles the things of the other side.

Quiero llorar diciendo mi nombre,
rosa, niño y abeto a la orilla de este lago,
para decir mi verdad de hombre de sangre
matando en mí la burla y la sugestión del vocablo.

40 No, no. Yo no pregunto, yo deseo,
voz mía libertada que me lames las manos.
En el laberinto de biombos es mi desnudo el que recibe
la luna de castigo y el reloj encenizado.

Así hablaba yo.
Así hablaba yo cuando Saturno detuvo los trenes
y la bruma y el Sueño y la Muerte me estaban buscando.
Me estaban buscando
allí donde mugen las vacas que tienen patitas de paje
y allí donde flota mi cuerpo entre los equilibrios contrarios.

Vaca

A Luis Lacasa

Se tendió la vaca herida.
Árboles y arroyos trepaban por sus cuernos.
Su hocico sangraba en el cielo.

Su hocico de abejas
bajo el bigote lento de la baba.
Un alarido blanco puso en pie la mañana.

Las vacas muertas y las vivas,
rubor de luz o miel de establo,
balaban con los ojos entornados.

10 Que se enteren las raíces
y aquel niño que afila su navaja
de que ya se pueden comer la vaca.

Arriba palidecen
luces y yugulares.
Cuatro pezuñas tiemblan en el aire.

Que se entere la luna
y esa noche de rocas amarillas
que ya se fue la vaca de ceniza.

I want to cry saying my name,
rose, child, and fir on the shore of this lake,
to speak truly as a man of blood
killing in myself the mockery and the suggestive power of the word.

40 No, no, I'm not asking, I'm telling you what I want,
my liberated voice lapping at my hands.
In the labyrinth of folding screens it is my naked body that receives
the punishing moon and the clock covered with ash.

I was speaking that way.
I was speaking that way when Saturn stopped the trains
and the fog and Dream and Death were looking for me.
Looking for me
where cattle with the little feet of a page bellow
and my body floats between contrary equilibriums.

Cow

To Luis Lacasa

The wounded cow lay down,
trees and streams climbing over its horns.
Its muzzle bled in the sky.

Its muzzle of bees
under the slow mustache of slobber.
A white cry brought the morning to its feet.

Cows, dead and alive,
blushing light or honey from the stables,
bellowed with half-closed eyes.

10 Tell the roots
and that child sharpening his knife:
now they can eat the cow.

Above them, lights
and jugulars turn pale.
Four cloven hoofs tremble in the air.

Tell the moon
and that night of yellow rocks:
now the cow of ash has gone.

Que ya se fue balando
20   por el derribo de los cielos yertos,
donde meriendan muerte los borrachos.

Muerte

A Isidoro de Blas

¡Qué esfuerzo!
¡Qué esfuerzo del caballo
por ser perro!
¡Qué esfuerzo del perro por ser golondrina!
¡Qué esfuerzo de la golondrina por ser abeja!
¡Qué esfuerzo de la abeja por ser caballo!
Y el caballo,
¡qué flecha aguda exprime de la rosa!,
¡qué rosa gris levanta de su belfo!
10   Y la rosa,
¡qué rebaño de luces y alaridos
ata en el vivo azúcar de su tronco!
Y el azúcar,
¡qué puñalitos sueña en su vigilia!
Y los puñales diminutos,
¡qué luna sin establos, qué desnudos,
piel eterna y rubor, andan buscando!
Y yo, por los aleros,
¡qué serafín de llamas busco y soy!
20   Pero el arco de yeso,
¡qué grande, qué invisible, qué diminuto,
sin esfuerzo!

Nueva York
(Oficina y denuncia)

A Fernando Vela

Debajo de las multiplicaciones
hay una gota de sangre de pato;
debajo de las divisiones
hay una gota de sangre de marinero;
debajo de las sumas, un río de sangre tierna.
Un río que viene cantando
por los dormitorios de los arrabales,
y es plata, cemento o brisa

Now it has gone bellowing
20   through the wreckage of the rigid skies
where the drunks lunch on death.

Death

To Isidoro de Blas

How hard they try!
How hard the horse tries
to become a dog!
How hard the dog tries to become a swallow!
How hard the swallow tries to become a bee!
How hard the bee tries to become a horse!
And the horse,
what a sharp arrow it presses from the rose,
what a pale rose rising from its lips!
10   And the rose,
what a flock of lights and cries
knotted in the living sugar of its trunk!
And the sugar,
what daggers it dreams in its vigils!
And the daggers,
what a moon without stables, what nakedness,
eternal and blushing flesh they seek out!
And I, on the roof's edge,
what a burning angel I look for and am!
20   But the plaster arch,
how vast, how invisible, how minute,
without even trying!

New York
(Office and Denunciation)

To Fernando Vela

Under the multiplications,
a drop of duck's blood;
under the divisions,
a drop of sailor's blood;
under the additions, a river of tender blood.
A river that sings and flows
past bedrooms in the boroughs—
and it's silver, cement, or wind

en el alba mentida de New York.
Existen las montañas. Lo sé.
Y los anteojos para la sabiduría.
Lo sé. Pero yo no he venido a ver el cielo.
He venido para ver la turbia sangre,
la sangre que lleva las máquinas a las cataratas
y el espíritu a la lengua de la cobra.
Todos los días se matan en New York
cuatro millones de patos,
cinco millones de cerdos,
dos mil palomas para el gusto de los agonizantes,
un millón de vacas,
un millón de corderos,
y dos millones de gallos,
que dejan los cielos hechos añicos.

Más vale sollozar afilando la navaja
o asesinar a los perros en las alucinantes cacerías,
que resistir en la madrugada
los interminables trenes de leche,
los interminables trenes de sangre
y los trenes de rosas maniatadas
por los comerciantes de perfumes.
Los patos y las palomas,
y los cerdos y los corderos
ponen sus gotas de sangre
debajo de las multiplicaciones,
y los terribles alaridos de las vacas estrujadas
llenan de dolor el valle
donde el Hudson se emborracha con aceite.

Yo denuncio a toda la gente
que ignora la otra mitad,
la mitad irredimible
que levanta sus montes de cemento
donde laten los corazones
de los animalitos que se olvidan
y donde caeremos todos
en la última fiesta de los taladros.
Os escupo en la cara.
La otra mitad me escucha
devorando, orinando, volando en su pureza,
como los niños de las porterías
que llevan frágiles palitos
a los huecos donde se oxidan
las antenas de los insectos.

in New York's counterfeit dawn.
I know the mountains exist.
And wisdom's eyeglasses,
too. But I didn't come to see the sky.
I'm here to see the clouded blood,
the blood that sweeps machines over waterfalls
and the soul toward the cobra's tongue.
Every day in New York, they slaughter
four million ducks,
five million hogs,
two thousand pigeons to accommodate the tastes of the dying,
one million cows,
one million lambs,
and two million roosters
that smash the skies to pieces.

It's better to sob while honing the blade
or kill dogs on the delirious hunts
than to resist at dawn
the endless milk trains,
the endless blood trains
and the trains of roses, manacled
by the dealers in perfume.
The ducks and the pigeons,
and the hogs and the lambs
lay their drops of blood
under the multiplications,
and the terrified bellowing of the cows wrung dry
fills the valley with sorrow
where the Hudson gets drunk on oil.

I denounce everyone
who ignores the other half,
the half that can't be redeemed,
who lift their mountains of cement
where the hearts beat
inside forgotten little animals
and where all of us will fall
in the last feast of pneumatic drills.
I spit in all your faces.
The other half hears me,
devouring, pissing, flying in their purity,
like the supers' children in lobbies
who carry fragile twigs
to the emptied spaces where
the insect antennae are rusting.

No es el infierno, es la calle.
No es la muerte. Es la tienda de frutas.
Hay un mundo de ríos quebrados y distancias inasibles
en la patita de ese gato quebrada por un automóvil,
y yo oigo el canto de la lombriz
en el corazón de muchas niñas.
Óxido, fermento, tierra estremecida.
Tierra tú mismo que nadas por los números de la oficina.
¿Qué voy a hacer, ordenar los paisajes?
¿Ordenar los amores que luego son fotografías,
que luego son pedazos de madera y bocanadas de sangre?
No, no; yo denuncio.
Yo denuncio la conjura
de estas desiertas oficinas
que no radian las agonías,
que borran los programas de la selva,
y me ofrezco a ser comido por las vacas estrujadas
cuando sus gritos llenan el valle
donde el Hudson se emborracha con aceite.

Oda a Walt Whitman

Por el East River y el Bronx
los muchachos cantaban enseñando sus cinturas,
con la rueda, el aceite, el cuero y el martillo.
Noventa mil mineros sacaban la plata de las rocas
y los niños dibujaban escaleras y perspectivas.

Pero ninguno se dormía,
ninguno quería ser río,
ninguno amaba las hojas grandes,
ninguno la lengua azul de la playa.

Por el East River y el Queensboro
los muchachos luchaban con la industria,
y los judíos vendían al fauno del río
la rosa de la circuncisión
y el cielo desembocaba por los puentes y los tejados
manadas de bisontes empujadas por el viento.

Pero ninguno se detenía,
ninguno quería ser nube,
ninguno buscaba los helechos
ni la rueda amarilla del tamboril.

This is not hell, but the street.
Not death, but the fruit stand.
There is a world of tamed rivers and distances just beyond our grasp
in the cat's paw smashed by a car,
and I hear the earthworm's song
in the hearts of many girls.
Rust, fermentation, earth tremor.
60 You yourself are the earth as you drift in office numbers.
What shall I do now? Set the landscapes in order?
Order the loves that soon become photographs,
that soon become pieces of wood and mouthfuls of blood?
No, no: I denounce it all.
I denounce the conspiracy
of these deserted offices
that radiate no agony,
that erase the forest's plans,
and I offer myself as food for the cows wrung dry
70 when their bellowing fills the valley
where the Hudson gets drunk on oil.

Ode to Walt Whitman

By the East River and the Bronx
boys were singing, exposing their waists,
with the wheel, with oil, leather, and the hammer.
Ninety thousand miners taking silver from the rocks
and children drawing stairs and perspectives.

But none of them could sleep,
none of them wanted to be the river,
none of them loved the huge leaves
or the shoreline's blue tongue.

10 By the East River and the Queensboro
boys were battling with industry
and the Jews sold to the river faun
the rose of circumcision,
and over bridges and rooftops, the mouth of the sky emptied
herds of bison driven by the wind.

But none of them paused,
none of them wanted to be a cloud,
none of them looked for ferns
or the yellow wheel of the tambourine.

229   *from* POET IN NEW YORK

Cuando la luna salga
las poleas rodarán para turbar el cielo;
un límite de agujas cercará la memoria
y los ataúdes se llevarán a los que no trabajan.

Nueva York de cieno,
Nueva York de alambre y de muerte.
¿Qué ángel llevas oculto en la mejilla?
¿Qué voz perfecta dirá las verdades del trigo?
¿Quién el sueño terrible de tus anémonas manchadas?

Ni un solo momento, viejo hermoso Walt Whitman,
he dejado de ver tu barba llena de mariposas,
ni tus hombros de pana gastados por la luna,
ni tus muslos de Apolo virginal,
ni tu voz como una columna de ceniza;
anciano hermoso como la niebla,
que gemías igual que un pájaro
con el sexo atravesado por una aguja.
Enemigo del sátiro,
enemigo de la vid
y amante de los cuerpos bajo la burda tela.

Ni un solo momento, hermosura viril
que en montes de carbón, anuncios y ferrocarriles,
soñabas ser un río y dormir como un río
con aquel camarada que pondría en tu pecho
un pequeño dolor de ignorante leopardo.

Ni un solo momento, Adán de sangre, Macho,
hombre solo en el mar, viejo hermoso Walt Whitman,
porque por las azoteas,
agrupados en los bares,
saliendo en racimos de las alcantarillas,
temblando entre las piernas de los chauffeurs
o girando en las plataformas del ajenjo,
los maricas, Walt Whitman, te señalan.

¡También ése! ¡También! Y se despeñan
sobre tu barba luminosa y casta,
rubios del norte, negros de la arena,
muchedumbre de gritos y ademanes
como los gatos y como las serpientes,
los maricas, Walt Whitman, los maricas,
turbios de lágrimas, carne para fusta,
bota o mordisco de los domadores.

20 As soon as the moon rises
the pulleys will spin to alter the sky;
a border of needles will besiege memory
and the coffins will bear away those who don't work.

New York, mire,
New York, wire and death.
What angel is hidden in your cheek?
Whose perfect voice will sing the truths of wheat?
Who, the terrible dream of your stained anemones?

Not for a moment, Walt Whitman, lovely old man,
30 have I failed to see your beard full of butterflies,
nor your corduroy shoulders frayed by the moon,
nor your thighs as pure as Apollo's,
nor your voice like a column of ash;
old man, beautiful as the mist,
you moaned like a bird
with its sex pierced by a needle.
Enemy of the satyr,
enemy of the vine,
and lover of bodies beneath rough cloth . . .

40 Not for a moment, virile beauty,
who among mountains of coal, billboards, and railroads,
dreamed of becoming a river and sleeping like a river
with that comrade who would place in your breast
the small ache of an ignorant leopard.

Not for a moment, Adam of blood, Macho,
man alone at sea, Walt Whitman, lovely old man,
because on penthouse roofs,
gathered at bars,
emerging in bunches from the sewers,
50 trembling between the legs of chauffeurs,
or spinning on dance floors wet with absinthe,
the faggots, Walt Whitman, point you out.

He's one, too! That's right! And they land
on your luminous chaste beard,
blonds from the north, blacks from the sands,
crowds of howls and gestures,
like cats or like snakes,
the faggots, Walt Whitman, the faggots,
clouded with tears, flesh for the whip,
60 the boot, or the teeth of the lion tamers.

¡También ése! ¡También! Dedos teñidos
apuntan a la orilla de tu sueño,
cuando el amigo come tu manzana
con un leve sabor de gasolina
y el sol canta por los ombligos
de los muchachos que juegan bajo los puentes.

Pero tú no buscabas los ojos arañados,
ni el pantano oscurísimo donde sumergen a los niños,
ni la saliva helada,
ni las curvas heridas como panza de sapo
que llevan los maricas en coches y en terrazas
mientras la luna los azota por las esquinas del terror.

Tú buscabas un desnudo que fuera como un río.
Toro y sueño que junte la rueda con el alga,
padre de tu agonía, camelia de tu muerte,
y gimiera en las llamas de tu ecuador oculto.

Porque es justo que el hombre no busque su deleite
en la selva de sangre de la mañana próxima.
El cielo tiene playas donde evitar la vida
y hay cuerpos que no deben repetirse en la aurora.

Agonía, agonía, sueño, fermento y sueño.
Este es el mundo, amigo, agonía, agonía.
Los muertos se descomponen bajo el reloj de las ciudades,
la guerra pasa llorando con un millón de ratas grises,
los ricos dan a sus queridas
pequeños moribundos iluminados,
y la vida no es noble, ni buena, ni sagrada.

Puede el hombre, si quiere, conducir su deseo
por vena de coral o celeste desnudo.
Mañana los amores serán rocas y el Tiempo
una brisa que viene dormida por las ramas.

Por eso no levanto mi voz, viejo Walt Whitman,
contra el niño que escribe
nombre de niña en su almohada,
ni contra el muchacho que se viste de novia
en la oscuridad del ropero,
ni contra los solitarios de los casinos
que beben con asco el agua de la prostitución,
ni contra los hombres de mirada verde
que aman al hombre y queman sus labios en silencio.

He's one, too! That's right! Stained fingers
point to the shore of your dream
when a friend eats your apple
with a slight taste of gasoline
and the sun sings in the navels
of boys who play under bridges.

But you didn't look for scratched eyes,
nor the darkest swamp where someone submerges children,
nor frozen saliva,
70 nor the curves slit open like a toad's belly
that the faggots wear in cars and on terraces
while the moon lashes them on the street corners of terror.

You looked for a naked body like a river.
Bull and dream who would join wheel with seaweed,
father of your agony, camellia of your death,
who would groan in the blaze of your hidden equator.

Because it's all right if a man doesn't look for his delight
in tomorrow morning's jungle of blood.
The sky has shores where life is avoided
80 and there are bodies that shouldn't repeat themselves in the dawn.

Agony, agony, dream, ferment, and dream.
This is the world, my friend, agony, agony.
Bodies decompose beneath the city clocks,
war passes by in tears, followed by a million gray rats,
the rich give their mistresses
small illuminated dying things,
and life is neither noble, nor good, nor sacred.

Man is able, if he wishes, to guide his desire
through a vein of coral or a heavenly naked body.
90 Tomorrow, loves will become stones, and Time
a breeze that drowses in the branches.

That's why I don't raise my voice, old Walt Whitman,
against the little boy who writes
the name of a girl on his pillow,
nor against the boy who dresses as a bride
in the darkness of the wardrobe,
nor against the solitary men in casinos
who drink prostitution's water with revulsion,
nor against the men with that green look in their eyes
100 who love other men and burn their lips in silence.

233   *from* POET IN NEW YORK

Pero sí contra vosotros, maricas de las ciudades,
de carne tumefacta y pensamiento inmundo.
Madres de lodo. Arpías. Enemigos sin sueño
del Amor que reparte coronas de alegría.

Contra vosotros siempre, que dais a los muchachos
gotas de sucia muerte con amargo veneno.
Contra vosotros siempre,
Fairies de Norteamérica,
Pájaros de La Habana,
Jotos de Méjico,
Sarasas de Cádiz,
Apios de Sevilla,
Cancos de Madrid,
Floras de Alicante,
Adelaidas de Portugal.

¡Maricas de todo el mundo, asesinos de palomas!
Esclavos de la mujer. Perras de sus tocadores.
Abiertos en las plazas con fiebre de abanico
o emboscados en yertos paisajes de cicuta.

¡No haya cuartel! La muerte
mana de vuestros ojos
y agrupa flores grises en la orilla del cieno.
¡No haya cuartel! ¡¡Alerta!!
Que los confundidos, los puros,
los clásicos, los señalados, los suplicantes
os cierren las puertas de la bacanal!

Y tú, bello Walt Whitman, duerme a orillas del Hudson
con la barba hacia el polo y las manos abiertas.
Arcilla blanda o nieve, tu lengua está llamando
camaradas que velen tu gacela sin cuerpo.

Duerme: no queda nada.
Una danza de muros agita las praderas
y América se anega de máquinas y llanto.
Quiero que el aire fuerte de la noche más honda
quite flores y letras del arco donde duermes
y un niño negro anuncie a los blancos del oro
la llegada del reino de la espiga.

But yes against you, urban faggots,
tumescent flesh and unclean thoughts.
Mothers of mud. Harpies. Sleepless enemies
of the love that bestows crowns of joy.

Always against you, who give boys
drops of foul death with bitter poison.
Always against you,
Fairies of North America,
Pájaros of Havana,
110   *Jotos* of Mexico,
Sarasas of Cádiz,
Apios of Seville,
Cancos of Madrid,
Floras of Alicante,
Adelaidas of Portugal.

Faggots of the world, murderers of doves!
Slaves of women. Their bedroom bitches.
Opening in public squares like feverish fans
or ambushed in rigid hemlock landscapes.

120   No quarter given! Death
spills from your eyes
and gathers gray flowers at the mire's edge.
No quarter given! Attention!
Let the confused, the pure,
the classical, the celebrated, the supplicants
close the doors of the bacchanal to you.

And you, lovely Walt Whitman, stay asleep on the Hudson's banks
with your beard toward the pole, openhanded.
Soft clay or snow, your tongue calls for
130   comrades to keep watch over your unbodied gazelle.

Sleep on, nothing remains.
Dancing walls stir the prairies
and America drowns itself in machinery and lament.
I want the powerful air from the deepest night
to blow away flowers and inscriptions from the arch where you sleep,
and a black child to inform the gold-craving whites
that the kingdom of grain has arrived.

Son de negros en Cuba

Cuando llegue la luna llena iré a Santiago de Cuba,
iré a Santiago
en un coche de agua negra.
Iré a Santiago.
Cantarán los techos de palmera.
Iré a Santiago.
Cuando la palma quiere ser cigüeña,
iré a Santiago.
Y cuando quiere ser medusa el plátano,
iré a Santiago.
Iré a Santiago
con la rubia cabeza de Fonseca.
Iré a Santiago.
Y con el rosa de Romeo y Julieta
iré a Santiago.
Mar de papel y plata de monedas.
Iré a Santiago.
¡Oh Cuba! ¡Oh ritmo de semillas secas!
Iré a Santiago.
¡Oh cintura caliente y gota de madera!
Iré a Santiago.
Arpa de troncos vivos. Caimán. Flor de tabaco.
Iré a Santiago.
Siempre he dicho que yo iría a Santiago
en un coche de agua negra.
Iré a Santiago.
Brisa y alcohol en las ruedas,
iré a Santiago.
Mi coral en la tiniebla,
iré a Santiago.
El mar ahogado en la arena,
iré a Santiago.
Calor blanco, fruta muerta,
iré a Santiago.
¡Oh bovino frescor de cañavera!
¡Oh Cuba! ¡Oh curva de suspiro y barro!
Iré a Santiago.

La Habana, abril 1930

236

Blacks Dancing to Cuban Rhythms

As soon as the full moon rises, I'm going to Santiago, Cuba,
I'm going to Santiago
in a coach of black water.
I'm going to Santiago.
The palm trees will sing above the rooftops.
I'm going to Santiago.
When the palm wants to be a stork,
I'm going to Santiago.
When the banana tree wants to be a sea wasp,
I'm going to Santiago.
I'm going to Santiago
with Fonseca's blond head.
I'm going to Santiago.
And with Romeo and Juliet's rose
I'm going to Santiago.
Paper sea and silver coins.
I'm going to Santiago.
Oh, Cuba, oh, rhythm of dried seeds!
I'm going to Santiago.
Oh, fiery waist, oh, drop of wood!
I'm going to Santiago.
Harp of living tree trunks. Crocodile. Tobacco plant in bloom!
I'm going to Santiago.
I always said I'd go to Santiago
in a coach of black water.
I'm going to Santiago.
Wind and rum on the wheels,
I'm going to Santiago.
My coral in the darkness,
I'm going to Santiago.
The sea drowned in the sand,
I'm going to Santiago.
White heat, rotting fruit,
I'm going to Santiago.
Oh, the bovine coolness of sugar cane!
Oh, Cuba! Oh, curve of sigh and clay!
I'm going to Santiago.

Havana, April 1930

De

DIVÁN
DEL TAMARIT

[*Agua Sexual, 1934*]

From

THE TAMARIT
DIVAN

Translated by

Catherine Brown

[*Sexual Water, 1934*]

Gacelas

Gacela primera
Del amor imprevisto

Nadie comprendía el perfume
de la oscura magnolia de tu vientre.
Nadie sabía que martirizabas
un colibrí de amor entre los dientes.

Mil caballitos persas se dormían
en la plaza con luna de tu frente,
mientras que yo enlazaba cuatro noches
tu cintura, enemiga de la nieve.

Entre yeso y jazmines, tu mirada
10   era un pálido ramo de simientes.
Yo busqué, para darte, por mi pecho
las letras de marfil que dicen *siempre*.

Siempre, siempre: jardín de mi agonía,
tu cuerpo fugitivo para siempre,
la sangre de tus venas en mi boca,
tu boca ya sin luz para mi muerte.

Gacela II
De la terrible presencia

Yo quiero que el agua se quede sin cauce.
Yo quiero que el viento se quede sin valles.

Quiero que la noche se quede sin ojos
y mi corazón sin la flor del oro;

que los bueyes hablen con las grandes hojas
y que la lombriz se muera de sombra;

que brillen los dientes de la calavera
y los amarillos inunden la seda.

Puedo ver el duelo de la noche herida
10   luchando enroscada con el mediodía.

Resisto un ocaso de verde veneno
y los arcos rotos donde sufre el tiempo.

Ghazals

I
Ghazal of Love Unforeseen

No one understood the perfume, ever:
the dark magnolia of your belly.
No one ever knew you martyred
love's hummingbird between your teeth.

A thousand Persian ponies fell asleep
in the moonlit plaza of your brow,
while four nights through I bound
your waist, the enemy of snow.

Between plaster and jasmine
your glance, pale branch of seed.
I searched my breast to give you
the ivory letters saying: Ever.

Ever, ever, my agony's garden,
your elusive form forever:
blood of your veins in my mouth,
your mouth now lightless for my death.

II
Ghazal of the Terrible Presence

I want there to be no channel for the water.
I want there to be no valleys for the wind.

I want there to be no eyes for the night,
no flower of gold for my heart;

and I want the oxen to talk to the big leaves,
and the earthworm to die of the shadow,

and I want teeth in the skull to gleam,
and the yellows to wash over the silk.

I can see the struggle of wounded night
wrestling in coils with midday.

I can endure a sunset green with poison
and the broken arches where time suffers.

Pero no ilumines tu limpio desnudo
como un negro cactus abierto en los juncos.

Déjame en un ansia de oscuros planetas,
pero no me enseñes tu cintura fresca.

Gacela V
Del niño muerto

Todas las tardes en Granada,
todas las tardes se muere un niño.
Todas las tardes el agua se sienta
a conversar con sus amigos.

Los muertos llevan alas de musgo.
El viento nublado y el viento limpio
son dos faisanes que vuelan por las torres
y el día es un muchacho herido.

No quedaba en el aire ni una brizna de alondra
cuando yo te encontré por las grutas del vino.
No quedaba en la tierra ni una miga de nube
cuando te ahogabas por el río.

Un gigante de agua cayó sobre los montes
y el valle fue rodando con perros y con lirios.
Tu cuerpo, con la sombra violeta de mis manos,
era, muerto en la orilla, un arcángel de frío.

Gacela VI
De la raíz amarga

Hay una raíz amarga
y un mundo de mil terrazas.
Ni la mano más pequeña
quiebra la puerta del agua.

¿Dónde vas, adónde, dónde?
Hay un cielo de mil ventanas
—batalla de abejas lívidas—
y hay una raíz amarga.

Amarga.

But do not show me your immaculate nude
like a black cactus open in the reeds.

Leave me in longing for shadowy planets,
but do not show me the cool of your waist.

V
Ghazal of the Dead Child

Every afternoon in Granada
a child dies, every afternoon.
Every afternoon the water sits down
to talk things over with its friends.

The dead wear wings of moss.
The wind cloudy and the wind clean
are two pheasants that circle the towers
and the day is a wounded boy.

No blade of lark remained in the air
10   when I found you there in the wine caves.
No crumb of cloud remained on the land
when you were drowning in the river.

A giant of water fell down the mountains
and the valley rolled by with irises and dogs.
Your body, shadowed violet by my hands,
dead on the bank, was an archangel of cold.

VI
Ghazal of the Bitter Root

There is a bitter root
and a world of a thousand terraces.
Not even the tiniest hand
breaks down the door of the waters.

Where are you going, where?
There is a sky of one thousand windows
—a battle of livid bees—
and there is a bitter root.

Bitter.

Duele en la planta del pie,
el interior de la cara,
y duele en el tronco fresco
de noche recién cortada.

¡Amor, enemigo mío,
muerde tu raíz amarga!

Gacela VIII
De la muerte oscura

Quiero dormir el sueño de las manzanas,
alejarme del tumulto de los cementerios.
Quiero dormir el sueño de aquel niño
que quería cortarse el corazón en alta mar.

No quiero que me repitan que los muertos no
                                    pierden la sangre;
que la boca podrida sigue pidiendo agua.
No quiero enterarme de los martirios que da la hierba,
ni de la luna con boca de serpiente
que trabaja antes del amanecer.

10   Quiero dormir un rato,
un rato, un minuto, un siglo;
pero que todos sepan que no he muerto;
que hay un establo de oro en mis labios;
que soy el pequeño amigo del viento Oeste;
que soy la sombra inmensa de mis lágrimas.

Cúbreme por la aurora con un velo
porque me arrojará puñados de hormigas,
y moja con agua dura mis zapatos
para que resbale la pinza de su alacrán.

20   Porque quiero dormir el sueño de las manzanas
para aprender un llanto que me limpie de tierra;
porque quiero vivir con aquel niño oscuro
que quería cortarse el corazón en alta mar.

Gacela X
De la huida

Me he perdido muchas veces por el mar
con el oído lleno de flores recién cortadas,

It hurts in the sole of the foot,
on the inside of the face,
and it hurts in the cool trunk
of the new-cut night.

Love, my enemy,
bite your bitter root!

VIII
Ghazal of Dark Death

I want to sleep the sleep of apples,
far away from the uproar of cemeteries.
I want to sleep the sleep of that child
who wanted to cut his heart out on the sea.

I don't want to hear that the dead lose no blood,
that the decomposed mouth is still begging for water.
I don't want to find out about grass-given martyrdoms,
or the snake-mouthed moon that works before dawn.

I want to sleep just a moment,
a moment, a minute, a century.
But let it be known that I have not died:
that there is a stable of gold in my lips,
that I am the West Wind's little friend,
that I am the enormous shadow of my tears.

Wrap me at dawn in a veil,
for she will hurl fistfuls of ants;
sprinkle my shoes with hard water
so her scorpion's sting will slide off.

Because I want to sleep the sleep of apples
and learn a lament that will cleanse me of earth;
because I want to live with that dark child
who wanted to cut his heart out on the sea.

X
Ghazal of the Flight

I have often been lost on the sea
with my ear full of fresh-cut flowers,

con la lengua llena de amor y de agonía.
Muchas veces me he perdido por el mar,
como me pierdo en el corazón de algunos niños.

No hay nadie que, al dar un beso,
no sienta la sonrisa de la gente sin rostro,
ni hay nadie que, al tocar un recién nacido,
olvide las inmóviles calaveras de caballo.

10   Porque las rosas buscan en la frente
un duro paisaje de hueso
y las manos del hombre no tienen más sentido
que imitar a las raíces bajo tierra.

Como me pierdo en el corazón de algunos niños,
me he perdido muchas veces por el mar.
Ignorante del agua, voy buscando
una muerte de luz que me consuma.

Casida II
Del llanto

He cerrado mi balcón
porque no quiero oír el llanto,
pero por detrás de los grises muros
no se oye otra cosa que el llanto.

Hay muy pocos ángeles que canten,
hay muy pocos perros que ladren,
mil violines caben en la palma de mi mano.

Pero el llanto es un perro inmenso,
el llanto es un ángel inmenso,
10   el llanto es un violín inmenso,
las lágrimas amordazan al viento,
y no se oye otra cosa que el llanto.

Casida III
De los ramos

Por las arboledas del Tamarit
han venido los perros de plomo
a esperar que se caigan los ramos,
a esperar que se quiebren ellos solos.

with my tongue full of agony and love.
Often I have been lost on the sea,
as I am lost in the heart of certain children.

There is no one who can kiss
without feeling the smile of those without faces;
there is no one who can touch
an infant and forget the immobile skulls of horses.

10   Because roses search the forehead
for a hard landscape of bone,
and human hands have no more sense
than to mimic roots beneath the soil.

As I am lost in the heart of certain children,
I have often been lost on the sea.
Not knowing water, I keep looking
to be consumed in luminous death.

II
Qasida of the Weeping

I have closed off my balcony,
for I do not want to hear the weeping.
But out there, beyond gray walls,
nothing is heard but the weeping.

There are very few angels who sing.
There are very few dogs who bark.
A thousand violins fit in the palm of my hand.

But the weeping is an enormous dog,
the weeping is an enormous angel,
10   the weeping is an enormous violin,
tears have muzzled the wind,
and nothing is heard but the weeping.

III
Qasida of the Branches

Through the groves at Tamarit
the leaden dogs have come,
to wait for the branches to fall,
for the branches to break by themselves.

El Tamarit tiene un manzano
con una manzana de sollozos.
Un ruiseñor agrupa los suspiros
y un faisán los ahuyenta por el polvo.

Pero los ramos son alegres,
los ramos son como nosotros.
No piensan en la lluvia y se han dormido,
como si fueran árboles, de pronto.

Sentados con el agua en las rodillas
dos valles esperaban al Otoño.
La penumbra con paso de elefante
empujaba las ramas y los troncos.

Por las arboledas del Tamarit
hay muchos niños de velado rostro
a esperar que se caigan mis ramos,
a esperar que se quiebren ellos solos.

Casida VI
De la mano imposible

Yo no quiero más que una mano,
una mano herida, si es posible.
Yo no quiero más que una mano,
aunque pase mil noches sin lecho.

Sería un pálido lirio de cal,
sería una paloma amarrada a mi corazón,
sería el guardián que en la noche de mi tránsito
prohibiera en absoluto la entrada a la luna.

Yo no quiero más que esa mano
para los diarios aceites y la sábana blanca de mi agonía.
Yo no quiero más que esa mano
para tener un ala de mi muerte.

Lo demás todo pasa.
Rubor sin nombre ya. Astro perpetuo.
Lo demás es lo otro; viento triste,
mientras las hojas huyen en bandadas.

At Tamarit there's an apple tree
with an apple of sobs.
A nightingale gathers up sighs,
a pheasant drives them off through the dust.

But the branches are happy
10 the branches are like us.
They don't think of rain,
and they've dropped off to sleep,
as if they were trees, just like that.

Sitting with their knees in water
two valleys awaited the Fall.
The half-light with elephant step
was leaning on trunks and on branches.

Through the groves at Tamarit
are many children with faces veiled
20 to wait for my branches to fall,
for my branches to break by themselves.

VI
Qasida of the Impossible Hand

I want nothing else, only a hand,
a wounded hand, if possible.
I want nothing else, only a hand,
though I spend a thousand nights without a bed.

It would be a pale lily of lime,
a dove tethered fast to my heart.
It would be the guard who, on the night of my death,
would block entrance absolutely to the moon.

I want nothing else, only that hand,
10 for the daily unctions and my agony's white sheet.
I want nothing else, only that hand,
to carry a wing of my own death.

Everything else all passes away.
Now blush without name. Perpetual star.
Everything else is something else: sad wind,
while the leaves flee, whirling in flocks.

Casida VII
De la rosa

La rosa
no buscaba la aurora:
casi eterna en su ramo,
buscaba otra cosa.

La rosa
no buscaba ni ciencia ni sombra:
confín de carne y sueño,
buscaba otra cosa.

La rosa
10 no buscaba la rosa:
inmóvil por el cielo,
buscaba otra cosa.

Casida IX
De las palomas oscuras

Por las ramas del laurel
vi dos palomas oscuras.
La una era el sol,
la otra la luna.
Vecinitas, les dije,
¿dónde está mi sepultura?
En mi cola, dijo el sol.
En mi garganta, dijo la luna.
Y yo que estaba caminando
10 con la tierra por la cintura
vi dos águilas de nieve
y una muchacha desnuda.
La una era la otra
y la muchacha era ninguna.
Aguilitas, les dije,
¿dónde está mi sepultura?
En mi cola, dijo el sol.
En mi garganta, dijo la luna.
Por las ramas del laurel
20 vi dos palomas desnudas.
La una era la otra
y las dos eran ninguna.

VII
Qasida of the Rose

The rose
was not looking for the dawn:
almost eternal on its stem,
it looked for something else.

The rose
was not looking for science or shadow:
confine of flesh and dream
it looked for something else.

The rose
10   was not looking for the rose.
Through the sky, immobile,
it looked for something else.

IX
Qasida of the Dark Doves

Through the laurel's branches
I saw two dark doves.
One was the sun,
the other the moon.
Little neighbors, I called,
where is my tomb?
In my tail, said the sun.
In my throat, said the moon.
And I who was walking
10   with the earth at my waist,
saw two snowy eagles
and a naked girl.
The one was the other
and the girl was neither.
Little eagles, I called,
where is my tomb?
In my tail, said the sun.
In my throat, said the moon.
Through the laurel's branches
20   I saw two naked doves.
The one was the other
and both of them, neither.

De

SEIS POEMAS GALEGOS

[*Rua das Gaveas, 1934*]

From

SIX GALICIAN
POEMS

Translated by

Catherine Brown

[*Rua das Gaveas, 1934*]

Madrigal â cibdá de Santiago

Chove en Santiago
meu doce amor.
Camelia branca do ar
brila entebrecido o sol.

Chove en Santiago
na noite escura.
Herbas de prata e sono
cobren a valeira lúa.

Olla a choiva pol-a rúa,
laio de pedra e cristal.
Olla no vento esvaído
soma e cinza do teu mar.

Soma e cinza do teu mar,
Santiago, lonxe do sol;
ágoa de mañán anterga
trema no meu corazón.

Noiturnio do adoescente morto

Imos silandeiros orela do vado
pra ver ô adoescente afogado.

Imos silandeiros veiriña do ar,
antes que ise río o leve pr'o mar.

Súa i-alma choraba, ferida e pequena
embaixo os arumes de pinos e d'herbas.

Ágoa despenada baixaba da lúa
cobrindo de violas a montana núa.

O vento deixaba camelias de soma
na lumieira murcha da súa triste boca.

¡Vinde mozos loiros do monte e do prado
pra ver ô adoescente afogado!

¡Vinde xente escura do cume e do val
antes que ise río o leve pr'o mar!

254

Madrigal for the City of Santiago

Rain falls on Santiago,
my sweet love.
White camellia of the air,
the veiled sun shines.

Rain falls on Santiago
in the dark of night.
Grasses of silver and dream
cover the vacant moon.

Look at the rain in the street,
10 lament of stone and of glass.
See on the languishing wind
shadow and ash of your ocean.

Shadow and ash of your ocean,
Santiago, far from the sun;
water of ancient morning
trembles in my heart.

Nocturne of the Drowned Youth

Let us go down, silent, to the bank of the ford
to look at the youth who drowned there, in the water.

Let us go down, silent, to the shore of the air
before this river takes him down to the sea.

His soul was weeping, wounded and small,
under needles of pine and grasses.

Water descended, flung down from the moon,
and covered the naked mountain with violets.

The wind laid camellias of shadow
10 in the wilted light of his unhappy mouth.

Come, blind boys of the mountains and fields,
come look at the youth who drowned there, in the water.

Come, dark folk of the peaks and the valleys,
before this river takes him down to the sea.

O leve pr'o mar de curtiñas brancas
onde van e vên vellos bois de ágoa.

¡Ay, cómo cantaban os albres do Sil
sobre a verde lúa, coma un tamboril!

¡Mozos, imos, vinde, aixiña, chegar
20 *porque xa ise río o leva pr'o mar!*

Danza da lúa en Santiago

¡Fita aquel branco galán,
fita seu transido corpo!

É a lúa que baila
na Quintana dos mortos.

Fita seu corpo transido,
negro de somas e lobos.

Nai: A lúa está bailando
na Quintana dos mortos.

¿Quén fire poldro de pedra
10 na mesma porta do sono?

¡É a lúa! ¡É a lúa
na Quintana dos mortos!

¿Quén fita meus grises vidros
cheos de nubens seus ollos?

É a lúa, é a lúa
na Quintana dos mortos.

Déixame morrer no leito
soñando na frol d'ouro.

Nai: A lúa está bailando
20 na Quintana dos mortos.

¡Ai filla, c'o ar do ceo
vólvome branca de pronto!

Non é o ar, é a triste lúa
na Quintana dos mortos.

It takes him down to the white-curtained sea,
where old water-oxen come and go slowly.

Oh, how the trees by the river were singing
over the sunken green drum of the moon!

Boys, let us go; come, hurry, away!
20 *for now this river takes him down to the sea.*

Dance of the Moon in Santiago

Look at that white cavalier,
look at his wasted body!

It is the moon that dances
in the courtyard of the dead.

Look at his wasted body,
black with shadow and wolves.

Mother, the moon is dancing
in the courtyard of the dead.

Who wounds the stone colt
10 at the portals of sleep?

It's the moon! It's the moon
in the courtyard of the dead!

Who looks in my gray windows
with his eyes full of clouds?

It's the moon, it's the moon
in the courtyard of the dead.

Let me die here in bed,
the flower of gold in my dreams.

Mother, the moon is dancing
20 in the courtyard of the dead.

Oh, daughter, the air from the sky
has suddenly turned me white!

It isn't the air; it's the unhappy moon
in the courtyard of the dead.

¿Quén xime co-este xemido
d'inmenso boi malencónico?

Nai: É a lúa, é a lúa
na Quintana dos mortos.

¡Sí, a lúa, a lúa
coroada de toxo,
que baila, e baila, e baila
na Quintana dos mortos!

30

Who moans with that moan
of an ox, huge and sad?

Mother, it's the moon, it's the moon
in the courtyard of the dead.

Yes, it's the moon, the moon
30 with its crown of gorse
that dances, dances, dances
in the courtyard of the dead!

LLANTO POR
IGNACIO SÁNCHEZ MEJÍAS

A mi querida amiga

Encarnación López Júlvez

[*Imagen de la muerte, 1934*]

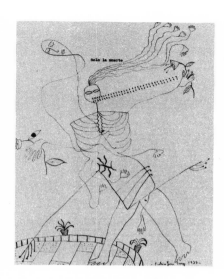

LAMENT FOR
IGNACIO SÁNCHEZ MEJÍAS

To my dear friend

Encarnación López Júlvez

Translated by Alan S. Trueblood

[Image of Death, 1934]

1. La cogida y la muerte

A las cinco de la tarde.
Eran las cinco en punto de la tarde.
Un niño trajo la blanca sábana
a las cinco de la tarde.
Una espuerta de cal ya prevenida
a las cinco de la tarde.
Lo demás era muerte y sólo muerte
a las cinco de la tarde.

El viento se llevó los algodones
10 *a las cinco de la tarde.*
Y el óxido sembró cristal y níquel
a las cinco de la tarde.
Ya luchan la paloma y el leopardo
a las cinco de la tarde.
Y un muslo con un asta desolada
a las cinco de la tarde.
Comenzaron los sones de bordón
a las cinco de la tarde.
Las campanas de arsénico y el humo
20 *a las cinco de la tarde.*
En las esquinas grupos de silencio
a las cinco de la tarde.
¡Y el toro solo corazón arriba!
a las cinco de la tarde.
Cuando el sudor de nieve fue llegando
a las cinco de la tarde,
cuando la plaza se cubrió de yodo
a las cinco de la tarde,
la muerte puso huevos en la herida
30 *a las cinco de la tarde.*
A las cinco de la tarde.
A las cinco en punto de la tarde.

Un ataúd con ruedas es la cama
a las cinco de la tarde.
Huesos y flautas suenan en su oído
a las cinco de la tarde.
El toro ya mugía por su frente
a las cinco de la tarde.
El cuarto se irisaba de agonía
40 *a las cinco de la tarde.*
A lo lejos ya viene la gangrena
a las cinco de la tarde.

1. The Goring and the Death

At five in the afternoon.
It was exactly five in the afternoon.
A boy brought the white sheet
at five in the afternoon.
A basketful of lime in readiness
at five in the afternoon.
Beyond that, death and death alone
at five in the afternoon.

The wind carried off wisps of cotton
at five in the afternoon.
And oxide dispersed glass and nickel
at five in the afternoon.
Dove locked in struggle with leopard
at five in the afternoon.
A thigh with a horn of desolation
at five in the afternoon.
The bass strings began to throb
at five in the afternoon.
The bells of arsenic, the smoke
at five in the afternoon.
At street corners silence clustering
at five in the afternoon.
Only the bull with upbeat heart
at five in the afternoon.
When snow-cold sweat began to form
at five in the afternoon,
when iodine had overspread the ring
at five in the afternoon,
death laid eggs in the wound
at five in the afternoon.
At five in the afternoon.
At exactly five in the afternoon.

A coffin on wheels is the bed
at five in the afternoon.
Bones and flutes resound in his ear
at five in the afternoon.
The bull was bellowing in his face
at five in the afternoon.
Death pangs turned the room iridescent
at five in the afternoon.
In the distance gangrene on the way
at five in the afternoon.

Trompa de lirio por las verdes ingles
a las cinco de la tarde.
Las heridas quemaban como soles
a las cinco de la tarde,
y el gentío rompía las ventanas
a las cinco de la tarde.
A las cinco de la tarde.
50   ¡Ay qué terribles cinco de la tarde!
¡Eran las cinco en todos los relojes!
¡Eran las cinco en sombra de la tarde!

2. La sangre derramada

¡Que no quiero verla!

Dile a la luna que venga,
que no quiero ver la sangre
de Ignacio sobre la arena.

¡Que no quiero verla!

La luna de par en par,
caballo de nubes quietas,
60   y la plaza gris del sueño
con sauces en las barreras.

¡Que no quiero verla!
Que mi recuerdo se quema.
¡Avisad a los jazmines
con su blancura pequeña!

¡Que no quiero verla!

La vaca del viejo mundo
pasaba su triste lengua
sobre un hocico de sangres
70   derramadas en la arena,
y los toros de Guisando,
casi muerte y casi piedra,
mugieron como dos siglos
hartos de pisar la tierra.
No.
¡Que no quiero verla!

Por las gradas sube Ignacio
con toda su muerte a cuestas.

Lily-trumpet in the verdant groin
at five in the afternoon.
The wounds burned with the heat of suns
at five in the afternoon,
and the throng burst through the windows
at five in the afternoon.
At five in the afternoon.
50 Horrifying five in the afternoon!
The stroke of five on every clock.
The dark of five in the afternoon.

2. The Spilled Blood

No, I refuse to see it!

Tell the moon to come—
I refuse to see the blood
of Ignacio on the sand.

No, I refuse to see it!

The moon opened wide
trotting through quiet clouds
60 and the gray bullring of a dream
with willows at the palings.

No, I refuse to see it!
The remembering burns.
Send word to the jasmine
to bring its tiny whiteness.

No, I refuse to see it.

The cow of this ancient world
was running her dreary tongue
over snoutfuls of blood
70 spilled across the sand,
and the bulls of Guisando,
almost death and nearly stone,
lowed like two centuries
tired of treading earth.
No.
I refuse to see it!

Ignacio mounts the steps,
shouldering his full death.

Buscaba el amanecer,
y el amanecer no era.
Busca su perfil seguro,
y el sueño lo desorienta.
Buscaba su hermoso cuerpo
y encontró su sangre abierta.
¡No me digáis que la vea!
No quiero sentir el chorro
cada vez con menos fuerza;
ese chorro que ilumina
los tendidos y se vuelca
sobre la pana y el cuero
de muchedumbre sedienta.
¿Quién me grita que me asome?
¡No me digáis que la vea!

No se cerraron sus ojos
cuando vio los cuernos cerca,
pero las madres terribles
levantaron la cabeza.
Y a través de las ganaderías
hubo un aire de voces secretas,
que gritaban a toros celestes
mayorales de pálida niebla.

No hubo príncipe en Sevilla
que comparársele pueda,
ni espada como su espada
ni corazón tan de veras.
Como un río de leones
su maravillosa fuerza,
y como un torso de mármol
su dibujada prudencia.
Aire de Roma andaluza
le doraba la cabeza
donde su risa era un nardo
de sal y de inteligencia.
¡Qué gran torero en la plaza!
¡Qué buen serrano en la sierra!
¡Qué blando con las espigas!
¡Qué duro con las espuelas!
¡Qué tierno con el rocío!
¡Qué deslumbrante en la feria!
¡Qué tremendo con las últimas
banderillas de tiniebla!

He looked for daybreak
80 and daybreak there was none.
He seeks the clean line of his profile
and sleep leads him astray.
He looked for his shapely body
and found his gaping blood.
Don't tell me I have to see it.
I don't want to feel the spurts
slowly subsiding,
the gushes glistening
on the bleachers, spilling
90 on the corduroy and leather
of bloodthirsty masses.
Who shouts for me to come look?
Don't tell me I have to see it.

His eyes did not shut
when he saw the horns close in
but the terrible mothers
lifted their heads to watch.
And sweeping the herds of cattle
came an air of secret voices
100 called out to bulls of heaven
by pale ranchers of mist.

No prince ever was in Seville
that could even approach him,
no sword like his sword,
no heart so truly a heart.
Like a river of lions
the marvel of his strength,
and like a marble torso
the contour of his prudence.
110 An air of Rome's Andalusia
hung golden about his head,
while his laughter was as spikenard—
all intelligence and wit.
What a great fighter in the ring!
What a good mountaineer on the heights!
How gentle toward ears of grain!
How harsh applying the spurs!
How tender toward the dew!
How dazzling at the fair!
120 How magnificent when he wielded
the last banderillas of the dark.

Pero ya duerme sin fin.
Ya los musgos y la hierba
abren con dedos seguros
la flor de su calavera.
Y su sangre ya viene cantando:
cantando por marismas y praderas,
resbalando por cuernos ateridos,
vacilando sin alma por la niebla,
130   tropezando con miles de pezuñas,
como una larga, oscura, triste lengua,
para formar un charco de agonía
junto al Guadalquivir de las estrellas.

¡Oh blanco muro de España!
¡Oh negro toro de pena!
¡Oh sangre dura de Ignacio!
¡Oh ruiseñor de sus venas!

No.
¡Que no quiero verla!
140   Que no hay cáliz que la contenga,
que no hay golondrinas que se la beban,
no hay escarcha de luz que la enfríe,
no hay canto ni diluvio de azucenas,
no hay cristal que la cubra de plata.
No.
¡¡Yo no quiero verla!!

3. Cuerpo presente

La piedra es una frente donde los sueños gimen
sin tener agua curva ni cipreses helados.
La piedra es una espalda para llevar al tiempo
150   con árboles de lágrimas y cintas y planetas.

Yo he visto lluvias grises correr hacia las olas
levantando sus tiernos brazos acribillados,
para no ser cazadas por la piedra tendida
que desata sus miembros sin empapar la sangre.

Porque la piedra coge simientes y nublados,
esqueletos de alondras y lobos de penumbra;
pero no da sonidos, ni cristales, ni fuego,
sino plazas y plazas y otras plazas sin muros.

But his sleep now is unending.
Now mosses and grass
pry open with practiced fingers
the flower of his skull.
And his blood now courses singing,
sings through salt marshes and meadows,
slides over stone-cold horns,
gropes soulless through the mist,
130 comes up against thousands of hooves
like some long, dark tongue of sadness,
to end in a pool gasping death
by the Guadalquivir of the stars.

Oh white wall of Spain!
Oh black bull of sorrow!
Oh hardened blood of Ignacio!
Oh nightingale of his veins!

No.
I refuse to see it!
140 There's no chalice to contain it,
no swallow to drink it up,
no glittering rime to chill it,
no chant, no outpouring of lilies,
no crystal to sheathe it in silver.
No.
I won't look at it, ever!

3. Presence of the Body

Stone is a forehead where dreams moan,
holding no curved water, no frozen cypress.
Stone is a shoulder meant to carry time,
150 with trees of tears and ribbons and planets.

I have watched gray rains running toward the waves,
lifting fragile, riddled arms
to avoid being snagged by outcrops of stone
which unknit their limbs without soaking in their blood.

Because stone gathers seeds and banks of cloud,
skeletons of larks, wolves dimming into shadow,
but yields no sound, no crystal, no fire—
yields only endless bullrings without walls.

Ya está sobre la piedra Ignacio el bien nacido.
160 Ya se acabó. ¡Qué pasa! ¡Contemplad su figura!
La muerte lo ha cubierto de pálidos azufres
y le ha puesto cabeza de oscuro minotauro.

Ya se acabó. La lluvia penetra por su boca.
El aire como loco deja su pecho hundido,
y el Amor, empapado con lágrimas de nieve,
se calienta en la cumbre de las ganaderías.

¿Qué dicen? Un silencio con hedores reposa.
Estamos con un cuerpo presente que se esfuma,
con una forma clara que tuvo ruiseñores
170 y la vemos llenarse de agujeros sin fondo.

¿Quién arruga el sudario? ¡No es verdad lo que dice!
Aquí no canta nadie, ni llora en el rincón,
ni pica las espuelas, ni espanta la serpiente:
aquí no quiero más que los ojos redondos
para ver ese cuerpo sin posible descanso.

Yo quiero ver aquí los hombres de voz dura.
Los que doman caballos y dominan los ríos:
los hombres que les suena el esqueleto y cantan
con una boca llena de sol y pedernales.

180 Aquí quiero yo verlos. Delante de la piedra.
Delante de este cuerpo con las riendas quebradas.
Yo quiero que me enseñen dónde está la salida
para este capitán atado por la muerte.

Yo quiero que me enseñen un llanto como un río
que tenga dulces nieblas y profundas orillas,
para llevar el cuerpo de Ignacio y que se pierda
sin escuchar el doble resuello de los toros.

Que se pierda en la plaza redonda de la luna
que finge cuando niña doliente res inmóvil;
190 que se pierda en la noche sin canto de los peces
y en la maleza blanca del humo congelado.

No quiero que le tapen la cara con pañuelos
para que se acostumbre con la muerte que lleva.
Vete, Ignacio: No sientas el caliente bramido.
Duerme, vuela, reposa: ¡También se muere el mar!

Ignacio the wellborn lies here on stone.
He is finished. What has happened? See his face.
Death has overlaid him with pale sulphur
and given him a minotaur's dark head.

He is finished. Rain seeps through his mouth.
Air rushes frenzied from his sunken chest
and Love, wet to the bone with tears of snow,
warms himself among the highland herds.

What are they saying? Here rests fetid silence.
The body here before us hazes over.
The luminous form that once held nightingales
we now see being punctured through and through.

Who is rumpling the shroud? What he says is not so.
No one is singing here or weeping in silence,
spurring horses, frightening off snakes;
here all I want is wide-open eyes
to see that body that can never rest.

I want to see here the men with harsh voices.
Tamers of horses, subduers of rivers,
whose bones you hear straining, who sing
with mouths full of sunlight and flint.

I want to see them here. Here at the stone.
By this body with the severed reins.
I want them to show me a way out
for this captain shackled by death;

have them teach me to weep like a river,
a river of soft mists and steep banks,
that will bear Ignacio's body out of sight
and still the double snorting of the bull.

Out of sight to the round bullring of the crescent
moon that's like a bull stock-still with pain;
out of sight into the fishes' songless night
and into the white scrub of smoke congealed.

I don't want them covering his face with kerchiefs
to break him in to the wearing of death.
Go now, Ignacio. Feel no more the hot bellows.
Sleep, soar, repose. The sea dies too!

4. Alma ausente

No te conoce el toro ni la higuera,
ni caballos ni hormigas de tu casa.
No te conoce el niño ni la tarde
porque te has muerto para siempre.

200   No te conoce el lomo de la piedra,
ni el raso negro donde te destrozas.
No te conoce tu recuerdo mudo
porque te has muerto para siempre.

El Otoño vendrá con caracolas,
uva de niebla y montes agrupados,
pero nadie querrá mirar tus ojos
porque te has muerto para siempre.

Porque te has muerto para siempre,
como todos los muertos de la Tierra,
210   como todos los muertos que se olvidan
en un montón de perros apagados.

No te conoce nadie. No. Pero yo te canto.
Yo canto para luego tu perfil y tu gracia.
La madurez insigne de tu conocimiento.
Tu apetencia de muerte y el gusto de su boca.
La tristeza que tuvo tu valiente alegría.

Tardará mucho tiempo en nacer, si es que nace,
un andaluz tan claro, tan rico de aventura.
Yo canto su elegancia con palabras que gimen
220   y recuerdo una brisa triste por los olivos.

4. Absence of the Soul

The bull does not know you, nor the fig tree,
nor horses, nor the ants on your floors.
The child does not know you, nor the evening,
because your death is forever.

200   The saddleback of rock does not know you,
nor the black satin where you tore apart.
Your silent recollection does not know you
because your death is forever.

Autumn will return bringing snails,
misted-over grapes, and clustered mountains,
but none will wish to gaze in your eyes
because your death is forever.

Because your death is forever,
like everyone's who ever died on Earth,
210   like all dead bodies discarded
on rubbish heaps with mongrels' corpses.

No one knows you. No one. But I sing you—
sing your profile and your grace, for later on.
The signal ripeness of your mastery.
The way you sought death out, savored its taste.
The sadness just beneath your gay valor.

Not soon, if ever, will Andalusia see
so towering a man, so venturesome.
I sing his elegance with words that moan
220   and remember a sad breeze in the olive groves.

De

[SONETOS DEL AMOR OSCURO]

[*Joven y marinero, 1934*]

From

[SONNETS OF
DARK LOVE]

Translated by

John K. Walsh and

Francisco Aragon

[*Young Man and Sailor, 1934*]

Soneto de la guirnalda de rosas

¡Esa guirnalda! ¡pronto! ¡que me muero!
¡Teje deprisa! ¡canta! ¡gime! ¡canta!,
que la sombra me enturbia la garganta
y otra vez viene y mil la luz de enero.

Entre lo que me quieres y te quiero,
aire de estrellas y temblor de planta,
espesura de anémonas levanta
con oscuro gemir un año entero.

Goza el fresco paisaje de mi herida,
quiebra juncos y arroyos delicados,
bebe en muslo de miel sangre vertida.

Pero ¡pronto!, que unidos, enlazados,
boca rota de amor y alma mordida,
el tiempo nos encuentre destrozados.

Soneto de la dulce queja

No me dejes perder la maravilla
de tus ojos de estatua, ni el acento
que de noche me pone en la mejilla
la solitaria rosa de tu aliento.

Tengo miedo de ser en esta orilla
tronco sin ramas; y lo que más siento
es no tener la flor, pulpa o arcilla
para el gusano de mi sufrimiento.

Si tú eres el tesoro oculto mío,
si eres mi cruz y mi dolor mojado,
si soy el perro de tu señorío,

no me dejes perder lo que he ganado
y decora las ramas de tu río
con hojas de mi otoño enajenado.

Llagas de amor

Esta luz, este fuego que devora,
este paisaje gris que me rodea,

Sonnet of the Garland of Roses

That garland! Hurry please! For I am dying!
Weave quickly now! And sing! And moan! And sing!
For the shadow is darkening my throat
and January light returns a thousand times.

Between your love for me and mine for you
lies star-filled air and the trembling of a plant.
A thicket of anemones is lifting
with dark moaning, an entire year.

So relish the fresh landscape of my wound,
10 break open delicate rivulets and reeds,
and sip the blood spilled on the honeyed thigh.

But hurry, so together, intertwined,
mouths bruised with love and souls bitten,
time will find us wasted.

Sonnet of the Sweet Complaint

Never let me lose the marvel
of your statue-like eyes, or the accent
the solitary rose of your breath
places on my cheek at night.

I am afraid of being, on this shore,
a branchless trunk, and what I most regret
is having no flower, pulp, or clay
for the worm of my despair.

If you are my hidden treasure,
10 if you are my cross, my dampened pain,
if I am a dog, and you alone my master,

never let me lose what I have gained,
and adorn the branches of your river
with leaves of my estranged Autumn.

Wounds of Love

This light, this fire that devours,
this gray landscape that surrounds me,

este dolor por una sola idea,
esta angustia de cielo, mundo y hora,

este llanto de sangre que decora
lira sin pulso ya, lúbrica tea,
este peso del mar que me golpea,
este alacrán que por mi pecho mora,

son guirnalda de amor, cama de herido,
10   donde sin sueño, sueño tu presencia
entre las ruinas de mi pecho hundido.

Y aunque busco la cumbre de prudencia
me da tu corazón valle tendido
con cicuta y pasión de amarga ciencia.

El poeta pide a su amor que le escriba

Amor de mis entrañas, viva muerte,
en vano espero tu palabra escrita
y pienso con la flor que se marchita
que si vivo sin mí, quiero perderte.

El aire es inmortal; la piedra inerte
ni conoce la sombra, ni la evita.
Corazón interior no necesita
la miel helada que la luna vierte.

Pero yo te sufrí; rasgué mis venas,
10   tigre y paloma sobre tu cintura
en duelo de mordiscos y azucenas.

Llena pues de palabras mi locura
o déjame vivir en mi serena
noche del alma para siempre oscura.

•

¡Ay voz secreta del amor oscuro!
¡Ay balido sin lanas! ¡Ay herida!
¡Ay aguja de hiel, camelia hundida!
¡Ay corriente sin mar, ciudad sin muro!

¡Ay noche inmensa de perfil seguro,
montaña celestial de angustia erguida!

this pain that comes from one idea,
this anguish of the sky, the earth, the hour,

   and this lament of blood that decorates
a pulseless lyre, a lascivious torch,
this burden of the sea that beats upon me,
this scorpion that dwells within my breast

   are all a wreath of love, bed of one wounded,
10 where, sleepless, I dream of your presence
amid the ruins of my fallen breast.

   And though I seek the summit of discretion,
your heart gives me a valley spread below
with hemlock and passion of bitter wisdom.

The Poet Asks His Love to Write Him

   O love of my heart, living death,
in vain I await your written word,
and think, with the withered flower: if I
must live without myself, I wish to lose you.

   Air is immortal. The lifeless stone
can neither know the shadow nor avoid it.
And the inner heart doesn't need
the frozen honey flowing from the moon.

   But I suffered you, tore open my veins,
10 tiger and dove on your waist,
caught in a duel of lilies and bites.

   Fill, then, with words my madness,
or let me live in the serene,
eternal dark night of the soul.

•

   O secret voice of dark love!
O bleating without fleece! O wound!
O needle of gall, sunken camellia!
O current without sea, city without walls!

   O immense night of sure profile,
celestial mountain tall with anguish!

¡Ay perro en corazón!, voz perseguida,
silencio sin confín, lirio maduro.

Huye de mí, caliente voz de hielo,
10   no me quieras perder en la maleza
donde sin fruto gimen carne y cielo.

Deja el duro marfil de mi cabeza,
apiádate de mí, ¡rompe mi duelo!,
¡que soy amor, que soy naturaleza!

El amor duerme en el pecho del poeta

Tú nunca entenderás lo que te quiero,
porque duermes en mí y estás dormido.
Yo te oculto llorando, perseguido
por una voz de penetrante acero.

Norma que agita igual carne y lucero
traspasa ya mi pecho dolorido,
y las turbias palabras han mordido
las alas de tu espíritu severo.

Grupo de gente salta en los jardines
10   esperando tu cuerpo y mi agonía
en caballos de luz y verdes crines.

Pero sigue durmiendo, vida mía.
¡Oye mi sangre rota en los violines!
¡Mira que nos acechan todavía!

Noche del amor insomne

Noche arriba los dos, con luna llena,
yo me puse a llorar y tú reías.
Tu desdén era un dios, las quejas mías
momentos y palomas en cadena.

Noche abajo los dos. Cristal de pena
llorabas tú por hondas lejanías.
Mi dolor era un grupo de agonías
sobre tu débil corazón de arena.

O dog in the heart, beleaguered voice,
borderless silence, ripened lily!

Away from me, simmering voice of ice,
10 and lose me not among the weeds
where flesh and heaven moan, leaving no fruit.

Forsake the hard ivory of my head,
take pity on me, break my pain!
For I am love, for I am nature!

His Beloved Sleeps on the Breast of the Poet

You cannot ever know how much I love you
because you sleep in me, asleep to all.
Weeping, I conceal you, persecuted
by a voice of penetrating steel.

A norm that unsettles both flesh and star
transfixes my afflicted breast,
and turbid words have bitten
the wings of your unflinching spirit.

A crowd of people leaps in the gardens
10 eager to glimpse your body and my agony,
on glowing horses with green manes.

But sleep, sleep on forever, my beloved.
Hear my broken blood in the violins!
Look out, for even now they lie in wait!

Night of Sleepless Love

We two, the night ahead, the full moon looming:
I began to weep while you laughed.
Your scorn became a god, and my complaints
were little doves and moments in a chain.

We two, the night behind, crystal of pain,
and you wept over deep and distant things.
My sorrow was a clump of agony
resting on your fragile heart of sand.

La aurora nos unió sobre la cama,
las bocas puestas sobre el chorro helado
de una sangre sin fin que se derrama.

Y el sol entró por el balcón cerrado
y el coral de la vida abrió su rama
sobre mi corazón amortajado.

The dawn drew us together on the bed.
10   Our mouths were waiting near the frozen spout
of blood that spilled forth in an endless flow.

The sun came through the shuttered balcony
and the coral of life opened its branch,
and settled here upon my shrouded heart.

POEMAS

SUELTOS

[*Pera y dado con puntos que se desprenden, 1930*]

UNCOLLECTED

POEMS

Translated by

Christopher Maurer

William Bryant Logan,

Greg Simon,

and Steven F. White

[Pear and Die with Falling Spots, 1930]

Cautiva

Por las ramas
indecisas
iba una doncella
que era la vida.
Por las ramas
indecisas.
Con un espejito
reflejaba el día
que era un resplandor
de su frente limpia.
Por las ramas
indecisas.
Sobre las tinieblas
andaba perdida,
llorando rocío,
del tiempo cautiva.
Por las ramas
indecisas.

Oda a Salvador Dalí

Una rosa en el alto jardín que tú deseas.
Una rueda en la pura sintaxis del acero.
Desnuda la montaña de niebla impresionista.
Los grises oteando sus balaustradas últimas.

Los pintores modernos en sus blancos estudios,
cortan la flor aséptica de la raíz cuadrada.
En las aguas del Sena un *ice-berg* de mármol
enfría las ventanas y disipa las yedras.

El hombre pisa fuerte las calles enlosadas.
Los cristales esquivan la magia del reflejo.
El Gobierno ha cerrado las tiendas de perfume.
La máquina eterniza sus compases binarios.

Una ausencia de bosques, biombos y entrecejos
yerra por los tejados de las casas antiguas.
El aire pulimenta su prisma sobre el mar
y el horizonte sube como un gran acueducto.

Marineros que ignoran el vino y la penumbra,
decapitan sirenas en los mares de plomo.

Captive

Through the branches
hesitant,
went a maiden
who was life,
Through the branches
hesitant.
she caught the day's reflection
in a little mirror:
the glow of her limpid brow.
10 Through the branches
hesitant.
Over the shadows
she went astray,
weeping dewdrops,
the captive of time.
Through the branches
hesitant.

[C.M.]

Ode to Salvador Dalí

A rose in the high garden you desire.
A wheel in the pure syntax of steel.
The mountain stripped bare of Impressionist fog.
The grays watching over the last balustrades.

The modern painters in their white ateliers
clip the square root's sterilized flower.
In the waters of the Seine a marble iceberg
chills the windows and scatters the ivy.

Man treads firmly on the cobbled streets.
10 Crystals hide from the magic of reflections.
The Government has closed the perfume stores.
The machine perpetuates its binary beat.

An absence of forests and screens and brows
roams across the roofs of the old houses.
The air polishes its prism on the sea
and the horizon rises like a great aqueduct.

Soldiers who know no wine and no penumbra
behead the sirens on the seas of lead.

La Noche, negra estatua de la prudencia, tiene
20   el espejo redondo de la luna en su mano.

Un deseo de formas y límites nos gana.
Viene el hombre que mira con el metro amarillo.
Venus es una blanca naturaleza muerta
y los coleccionistas de mariposas huyen.

★

Cadaqués, en el fiel del agua y la colina,
eleva escalinatas y oculta caracolas.
Las flautas de madera pacifican el aire.
Un viejo dios silvestre da frutas a los niños.

Sus pescadores duermen, sin ensueño, en la arena.
30   En alta mar les sirve de brújula una rosa.
El horizonte virgen de pañuelos heridos,
junta los grandes vidrios del pez y de la luna.

Una dura corona de blancos bergantines
ciñe frentes amargas y cabellos de arena.
Las sirenas convencen, pero no sugestionan,
y salen si mostramos un vaso de agua dulce.

★

¡Oh Salvador Dalí, de voz aceitunada!
No elogio tu imperfecto pincel adolescente
ni tu color que ronda la color de tu tiempo,
40   pero alabo tus ansias de eterno limitado.

Alma higiénica, vives sobre mármoles nuevos.
Huyes la oscura selva de formas increíbles.
Tu fantasía llega donde llegan tus manos,
y gozas el soneto del mar en tu ventana.

El mundo tiene sordas penumbras y desorden,
en los primeros términos que el humano frecuenta.
Pero ya las estrellas ocultando paisajes,
señalan el esquema perfecto de sus órbitas.

La corriente del tiempo se remansa y ordena
50   en las formas numéricas de un siglo y otro siglo.
Y la Muerte vencida se refugia temblando
en el círculo estrecho del minuto presente.

Al coger tu paleta, con un tiro en un ala,
pides la luz que anima la copa del olivo.

Night, black statue of prudence, holds
20 the moon's round mirror in her hand.

A desire for forms and limits overwhelms us.
Here comes the man who sees with a yellow ruler.
Venus is a white still life
and the butterfly collectors run away.

★

Cadaqués, at the fulcrum of water and hill,
lifts flights of stairs and hides seashells.
Wooden flutes pacify the air.
An ancient woodland god gives the children fruit.

Her fishermen sleep dreamless on the sand.
30 On the high seas a rose is their compass.
The horizon, virgin of wounded handkerchiefs,
links the great crystals of fish and moon.

A hard diadem of white brigantines
encircles bitter foreheads and hair of sand.
The sirens convince, but they don't beguile,
and they come if we show a glass of fresh water.

★

Oh Salvador Dalí, of the olive-colored voice!
I do not praise your halting adolescent brush
or your pigments that flirt with the pigment of your times,
40 but I laud your longing for eternity with limits.

Sanitary soul, you live upon new marble.
You run from the dark jungle of improbable forms.
Your fancy reaches only as far as your hands,
and you enjoy the sonnet of the sea in your window.

The world is dull penumbra and disorder
in the foreground where man is found.
But now the stars, concealing landscapes,
reveal the perfect schema of their courses.

The current of time pools and gains order
50 in the numbered forms of century after century.
And conquered Death takes refuge trembling
in the tight circle of the present instant.

When you take up your palette, a bullet hole in its wing,
you call on the light that brings the olive tree to life.

289

Ancha luz de Minerva, constructora de andamios,
donde no cabe el sueño ni su flora inexacta.

Pides la luz antigua que se queda en la frente,
sin bajar a la boca ni al corazón del hombre.
Luz que temen las vides entrañables de Baco
60   y la fuerza sin orden que lleva el agua curva.

Haces bien en poner banderines de aviso,
en el límite oscuro que relumbra de noche.
Como pintor no quieres que te ablande la forma
el algodón cambiante de una nube imprevista.

El pez en la pecera y el pájaro en la jaula.
No quieres inventarlos en el mar o en el viento.
Estilizas o copias después de haber mirado,
con honestas pupilas sus cuerpecillos ágiles.

Amas una materia definida y exacta
70   donde el hongo no pueda poner su campamento.
Amas la arquitectura que construye en lo ausente
y admites la bandera como una simple broma.

Dice el compás de acero su corto verso elástico.
Desconocidas islas desmiente ya la esfera.
Dice la línea recta su vertical esfuerzo
y los sabios cristales cantan sus geometrías.

★

Pero también la rosa del jardín donde vives.
¡Siempre la rosa, siempre, norte y sur de nosotros!
Tranquila y concentrada como una estatua ciega,
80   ignorante de esfuerzos soterrados que causa.

Rosa pura que limpia de artificios y croquis
y nos abre las alas tenues de la sonrisa.
(Mariposa clavada que medita su vuelo.)
Rosa del equilibrio sin dolores buscados.
¡Siempre la rosa!

★

¡Oh Salvador Dalí de voz aceitunada!
Digo lo que me dicen tu persona y tus cuadros.
No alabo tu imperfecto pincel adolescente,
pero canto la firme dirección de tus flechas.

The broad light of Minerva, builder of scaffolds,
where there is no room for dream or its hazy flower.

You call on the old light that stays on the brow,
not descending to the mouth or the heart of man.
A light feared by the loving vines of Bacchus
60   and the chaotic force of curving water.

You do well when you post warning flags
along the dark limit that shines in the night.
As a painter, you refuse to have your forms softened
by the shifting cotton of an unexpected cloud.

The fish in the fishbowl and the bird in the cage.
You refuse to invent them in the sea or the air.
You stylize or copy once you have seen
their small, agile bodies with your honest eyes.

You love a matter definite and exact,
70   where the toadstool cannot pitch its camp.
You love the architecture that builds on the absent
and admit the flag simply as a joke.

The steel compass tells its short, elastic verse.
Unknown islands rise to deny the sphere exists.
The straight line tells of its upward struggle
and the learned crystals sing their geometries.

★

But also the rose of the garden where you live.
Always the rose, always, our north and south!
Calm and ingathered like an eyeless statue,
80   not knowing the buried struggle it provokes.

Pure rose, clean of artifice and rough sketches,
opening for us the slender wings of the smile.
(Pinned butterfly that ponders its flight.)
Rose of balance, with no self-inflicted pains.
Always the rose!

★

Oh Salvador Dalí, of the olive-colored voice!
I speak of what your person and your paintings tell me.
I do not praise your halting adolescent brush,
but I sing the steady aim of your arrows.

90 Canto tu bello esfuerzo de luces catalanas,
tu amor a lo que tiene explicación posible.
Canto tu corazón astronómico y tierno,
de baraja francesa y sin ninguna herida.

Canto el ansia de estatua que persigues sin tregua,
el miedo a la emoción que te aguarda en la calle.
Canto la sirenita de la mar que te canta
montada en bicicleta de corales y conchas.

Pero ante todo canto un común pensamiento
que nos une en las horas oscuras y doradas.
100 No es el Arte la luz que nos ciega los ojos.
Es primero el amor, la amistad o la esgrima.

Es primero que el cuadro que paciente dibujas
el seno de Teresa, la de cutis insomne,
el apretado bucle de Matilde la ingrata,
nuestra amistad pintada como un juego de oca.

Huellas dactilográficas de sangre sobre el oro,
rayen el corazón de Cataluña eterna.
Estrellas como puños sin halcón te relumbren,
mientras que tu pintura y tu vida florecen.

110 No mires la clepsidra con alas membranosas,
ni la dura guadaña de las alegorías.
Viste y desnuda siempre tu pincel en el aire
frente a la mar poblada con barcos y marinos.

Adán

A José Barbeito

Árbol de sangre moja la mañana
por donde gime la recién parida.
Su voz deja cristales en la herida
y un gráfico de hueso en la ventana.

Mientras la luz que viene fija y gana
blancas metas de fábula que olvida
el tumulto de venas en la huida
hacia el turbio frescor de la manzana,

90   I sing your fair struggle of Catalan lights,
       your love of what might be made clear.
       I sing your astronomical and tender heart,
       a never-wounded deck of French cards.

       I sing your restless longing for the statue,
       your fear of the feelings that await you in the street.
       I sing the small sea siren who sings to you,
       riding her bicycle of corals and conches.

       But above all I sing a common thought
       that joins us in the dark and golden hours.
100   The light that blinds our eyes is not art.
       Rather it is love, friendship, crossed swords.

       Not the picture you patiently trace,
       but the breast of Theresa, she of sleepless skin,
       the tight-wound curls of Mathilde the ungrateful,
       our friendship, painted bright as a game board.

       May fingerprints of blood on gold
       streak the heart of eternal Catalunya.
       May stars like falconless fists shine on you,
       while your painting and your life break into flower.

110   Don't watch the water clock with its membraned wings
       or the hard scythe of the allegory.
       Always in the air, dress and undress your brush
       before the sea peopled with sailors and ships.

                                             [W.B.L.]

Adam

For José Barbeito

       A tree of blood soaks the morning
       where the newborn woman groans.
       Her voice leaves glass in the wound
       and on the panes, a diagram of bone.

       The coming light establishes and wins
       white limits of a fable that forgets
       the tumult of veins in flight
       toward the dim cool of the apple.

Adán sueña en la fiebre de la arcilla
un niño que se acerca galopando
por el doble latir de su mejilla.

Pero otro Adán oscuro está soñando
neutra luna de piedra sin semilla
donde el niño de luz se irá quemando.

Soneto

Yo sé que mi perfil será tranquilo
en el norte de un cielo sin reflejo,
mercurio de vigilia, casto espejo
donde se quiebre el pulso de mi estilo.

Que si la yedra y el frescor del hilo
fue la norma del cuerpo que yo dejo,
mi perfil en la arena será un viejo
silencio sin rubor de cocodrilo.

Y aunque nunca tendrá sabor de llama
mi lengua de palomas ateridas,
sino desierto gusto de retama,

libre signo de normas oprimidas
seré, en el cuello de la yerta rama
y en el sinfín de dalias doloridas.

Dos normas

[*Dibujo de la luna*]

Norma de ayer encontrada
sobre mi noche presente.
Resplandor adolescente
que se opone a la nevada.
No pueden darte posada
mis dos niñas de sigilo,
morenas de luna en vilo
con el corazón abierto;
pero mi amor busca el huerto
donde no muere tu estilo.

Adam dreams in the fever of the clay
10 of a child who comes galloping
through the double pulse of his cheek.

But a dark other Adam is dreaming
a neuter moon of seedless stone
where the child of light will burn.

[C.M.]

Sonnet

I know that my profile will be serene
in the north of an unreflecting sky.
Mercury of vigil, chaste mirror
to break the pulse of my style.

For if ivy and the cool of linen
are the norm of the body I leave behind,
my profile in the sand will be the old
unblushing silence of a crocodile.

And though my tongue of frozen doves
10 will never taste of flame,
only of empty broom,

I'll be a free sign of oppressed norms
on the neck of the stiff branch
and in an ache of dahlias without end.

[C.M.]

Two Norms

[*Sketch of the moon*]

Yesterday's norm encountered
on my present night.
Light of adolescence,
you oppose the snow.
The stealthy pupils of my eyes
do not want to take you in:
two brown girls of floating moon
and my open heart.
But my love looks for the orchard
10 where your style does not die.

[*Dibujo del sol*]

    Norma de seno y cadera
bajo la rama tendida,
antigua y recién nacida
virtud de la primavera.
Ya mi desnudo quisiera
ser dalia de tu destino,
abeja, rumor o vino
de tu número y locura;
pero mi amor busca pura
20 locura de brisa y trino.

•

Tan, tan.
¿Quién es?
El Otoño otra vez.
¿Qué quiere de mí?
El frescor de tu sien.
No te lo quiero dar.
Yo te lo quitaré.
Tan, tan.
¿Quién es?
10 El Otoño otra vez.

Pequeño poema infinito

Para Luis Cardoza y Aragón

Equivocar el camino
es llegar a la nieve
y llegar a la nieve
es pacer durante varios siglos las hierbas de los cementerios.

Equivocar el camino
es llegar a la mujer,
la mujer que no teme la luz,
la mujer que mata dos gallos en un segundo,
la luz que no teme a los gallos
10 y los gallos que no saben cantar sobre la nieve.

Pero si la nieve se equivoca de corazón
puede llegar el viento Austro,

[*Sketch of the sun*]

Norm of breast and hip
under the stretching bough;
old and newly born,
virtue of the Spring.
My naked body yearns to be
the dahlia of your destiny,
bee, murmur or wine
of your number and madness.
But my love goes on seeking
20 pure madness of breeze and trill.

                                  [C.M.]

•

Knock, knock!
Who's there?
Autumn again.
What do you want?
The coolness of your temple.
You can't have it.
I'll take it.
Knock, knock!
Who's there?
10 Autumn again.

                                    [C.M.]

Little Infinite Poem

For Luis Cardoza y Aragón

To take the wrong road
is to arrive at snow
and to arrive at snow
is to graze for several centuries on graveyard weeds.

To take the wrong road
is to arrive at woman,
woman unafraid of light,
woman killing two roosters a second,
light unafraid of roosters,
10 and roosters that can't sing on snow.

But if snow chooses the wrong heart,
the South Wind can come,

297   UNCOLLECTED POEMS

y como el aire no hace caso de los gemidos,
tendremos que pacer otra vez las hierbas de los cementerios.
Yo vi dos dolorosas espigas de cera
que enterraban un paisaje de volcanes
y vi dos niños locos
que empujaban llorando las pupilas de un asesino.

Pero el dos no ha sido nunca un número
20   porque es una angustia y su sombra,
porque es la demostración del otro infinito que no es suyo
y es las murallas del muerto
y el castigo de la nueva resurrección sin finales.

Los muertos odian el número dos,
pero el número dos adormece a las mujeres,
y como la mujer teme la luz,
la luz tiembla delante de los gallos
y los gallos sólo saben volar sobre la nieve,
30   tendremos que pacer sin descanso las hierbas de los cementerios.

Omega
(Poema para muertos)

Las hierbas.

Yo me cortaré la mano derecha.
Espera.

Las hierbas.

Tengo un guante de mercurio y otro de seda.
Espera.

¡Las hierbas!

No solloces. Silencio. Que no nos sientan.
Espera.

10   ¡Las hierbas!

Se cayeron las estatuas
al abrirse la gran puerta.

¡¡Las hierbaaas!!

and since air pays no attention to moaning,
we'll have to graze once more on graveyard weeds.
I saw two sad, waxen spikes of wheat
that buried a volcanic landscape,
and two crazy children
who wept as they pushed a murderer's eyeballs.

But two has never been a number.
20   It is anguish and its shadow,
it is the demonstration of something else's infinity,
and the dead man's walls,
and the punishment of the new, unending resurrection.

Dead men hate the number two,
but the number two lulls women to sleep
and since women fear light,
and light trembles before roosters,
and roosters only fly above the snow—
we'll have to graze on graveyard weeds.

                              [G.S. AND S.F.W.]

Omega
(Poem for the Dead)

The weeds.

I'll cut my right hand off.
Wait.

The weeds.

I have one glove of mercury and another of silk.
Wait.

The weeds!

No sobbing. Silence. They must not hear us.
Wait.

10   The weeds!

The statues fell down
as the great door swung open.

The weeeeds!!

                              [G.S. AND S.F.W.]

Notes to the Poems
by Christopher Maurer

Drawing on a long tradition of Lorca scholarship, these notes supply essential information about the texts (dates of composition, revision, and first publication) and clarify the least obvious of Lorca's literary and cultural allusions. I have also drawn attention to parallel passages in other poems, the poet's own comments on his work, and relevant biographical data.

The names of series of poems or of divisions within a book are given in uppercase; for example SIX SONGS AT NIGHTFALL. Names of poems published in this book are given in italics. Line numbers refer to the English text, except in direct quotations from the Spanish. Except as noted, all translations are my own. Works most frequently cited are abbreviated as follows:

AFGL   Archivo de la Fundación Federico García Lorca, Madrid.

B   Federico García Lorca. *Suites*. André Belamich, ed. Barcelona: Ariel, 1983.

C   ———. *Conferencias*. C. Maurer, ed. 2 vols. Madrid: Alianza Editorial, 1984.

CP   ———. *Collected Poems*. C. Maurer, ed. Translated by Francisco Aragon, Catherine Brown, et al. New York: Farrar, Straus and Giroux, 1991.

DS   ———. *Deep Song and Other Prose*. C. Maurer, tr. New York: New Directions, 1980.

E   ———. *Epistolario*. C. Maurer, ed. 2 vols. Madrid: Alianza Editorial, 1983.

GP1   ———. *Poesía, 1*. Miguel García-Posada, ed. 2nd ed. Madrid: Akal, 1982.

GP2   ———. *Poesía, 2*. Miguel García-Posada, ed. 2nd ed. Madrid: Akal, 1982.

IGM   Francisco García Lorca. *In the Green Morning*. C. Maurer, tr. New York: New Directions, 1986.

LLS   Mario Hernández, *Line of Light and Shadow. The Drawings of Federico García Lorca*. C. Maurer, tr. Durham: Duke University Press, 1991.

M   Federico García Lorca. *Canciones y Primeras canciones*. Piero Menarini, ed. Madrid: Espasa-Calpe, 1986.

OC   ———. *Obras completas*. Arturo del Hoyo, ed. 3 vols. Madrid: Aguilar, 1986.

PNY   ———. *Poet in New York*. C. Maurer, ed. Greg Simon and Steven F. White, tr. New York: Farrar, Straus and Giroux, 1988.

Other works mentioned are found in the Bibliography.

Libro de poemas / Book of Poems

Published in 1921 in an edition paid for by Lorca's parents, at the printshop of his friend Gabriel García Maroto, Madrid. The poet's brother, Francisco, had helped him select sixty-eight poems from several hundred written between 1918 and 1920. The Spanish text of the poems presented here follows Mario Hernández (1984), but the critical editions of Ian Gibson and Marco Massoli (both 1982) have also been consulted. Except for *Weathervane*, which serves as prologue, the poems are given here in the approximate order of their composition (the dates in the subtitles, not always accurate, were added at the suggestion of García Maroto).

By the time *Libro de poemas* was published, Lorca felt somewhat distant from this work. He had begun his *Suites* and was hoping to publish them immediately, to offset "my earliest poetical work, which is, at any rate, interesting and sincere" (letter to his parents, April 1921, ms. AFGL).

For detailed commentary on this book, see Candelas Newton, *Lorca: Libro de poemas*.

Veleta / Weathervane. Published in *La Pluma* (Madrid), January 1921. Line 34: The "gnome breezes" exist in Andalusian folklore (Gibson ed., 21). 38–39: the "rose / with pyramid petals" is the one which appears on mariners' wind charts; cf. notes to VIGNETTES OF THE WIND, *CP*, 805.

El camino / The Road. Line 17: Flammarion in the sense of "close observer of other worlds." Allusion to the popularizing French astronomer Nicolas-Camille Flammarion (1842–1925), known for his studies of double and multiple stars (the footprints). 49–50: Legendary bridge from a children's song: "Al pasar el puente / de Santa Clara / se me cayó el anillo / dentro del agua" (As I crossed the bridge / of St. Clara / my ring fell down / into the water).

Cantos nuevos / New Songs. The poet is sketching out the aesthetic of his next two books, *Poem of the Deep Song* and *Suites*. Like the Spanish *ultraístas* (see *CP*, introduction), Lorca seems to reject the "sadness," "anguish," and "reverie" of *fin de siècle* Spanish *modernismo*. Though Lorca was not an admirer of Futurism, which had been written about in Spanish literary journals for the previous ten years, lines 20–21 may allude to Marinetti's call for "parole in libertà."

Se ha puesto el sol / The Sun Has Set. Lines 20–21 are faintly reminiscent of a Spanish Christmas carol: "Ya se van los pastores / de Extremadura. / Ya se queda la sierra / triste y oscura" (The shepherds are leaving / Extremadura. / The mountain is growing / sad and dark).

El lagarto viejo / The Old Lizard. Lorca's interest in animals and insects, his rebellion against an anthropocentric universe, and his sense of the interconnectedness of all Nature are evident from his earliest works to his final ones. The characters of his first dramatic production, *The Butterfly's Evil Spell* (1920), are insects: a cockroach falls hopelessly in love with a wounded butterfly. See, also, his charming poem "Los encuentros de un caracol aventurero" (The Encounters of an Adventurous Snail in *OC*, I: 9–14). His devotion as a young man to St. Francis of Assisi and his interest in pantheism prompt him to insist, in an early essay: "In the forests there are gigantic loves, sublime sacrifices, and enormous souls. There are many men who are useless earth and animals with delicate souls . . . We can never understand animals, never know for sure if they possess a soul, just as they, in their indescribable conversations, will never understand *us* ("Mystic of Human Pain and the Horror of Society," *Prosa inédita*, 116). Line 34: Plateresque is an ornate style of Spanish Renaissance architecture (e.g., the façade of the University of Salamanca), so called because it evokes the delicate work of silversmiths. Lines 53–54 refer to a folk belief that the lizard protects man from the snake.

Poema del cante jondo / Poem of the Deep Song

Begun in August 1921. Over half the poems were written between November 11 and 21 of that year. Lorca read several of them in public in Granada in 1922, shortly before the amateur festival which he organized with Manuel de Falla to vindicate the aesthetic value of the Andalusian folk music known as *cante jondo*. Six poems were printed by Jorge Guillén in *Verso y prosa* (Murcia) in April 1927, and a longer selection was published by the Instituto de las Españas at Columbia University during Lorca's trip to New York, in 1930. The first edition appeared in Madrid in May 1931 (Ediciones Ulises). For a more detailed textual history, see Christian de Paepe's excellent critical edition, 7–100. Lorca's own lecture, "Deep Song" (1922), and the revised version (1930) entitled "Architecture of Deep Song"

(*DS* 23–41; *C* I:43–83) shed much light on these poems. The Spanish text given here is from the edition of Mario Hernández.

Lorca's earliest reference to this book occurs in a letter to his friend the musicologist Adolfo Salazar, ca. January 1, 1922: "I have gone back over the *Suites* for the last time, and am now putting the golden roof tiles on *Poem of the Deep Song*, which I am going to publish to coincide with the [*cante jondo*] festival. It is something different from the *Suites* and filled with suggestions of Andalusia. The rhythm is popular in a stylized way, and I bring out all the old *cantaores* [singers of *cante jondo*], all the fantastic flora and fauna that fill these sublime songs. Silverio, Juan Breva, Loco Mateo, La Parrala, El Fillo . . . and Death! It is a great carved altarpiece [*retablo*], it's . . . a jigsaw puzzle, if you know what I mean. The poem [i.e., book] begins with a motionless sunset, and then the *siguiriya*, the *soleá*, the *saeta*, and the *petenera* come filing across it. The poem is full of gypsies, tapers, forges, and it even contains allusions to Zoroaster. It is the first thing I've done with a *completely different orientation*, and I still don't know what I can say about it . . . but it *does* have novelty. The only person who knows it is Falla, and he is enthusiastic, which you will readily understand, knowing *Manué* and how crazy he is about these things. Spanish poets have never even *touched* this theme, and I deserve a smile, at least, for my daring. Send it to me right away" (*E* I:48–49).

POEMA DE LA SIGUIRIYA GITANA / POEM OF THE GYPSY *SIGUIRIYA*. The gypsy *siguiriya* (phonetic deformation of *seguidilla*) is one of the basic forms of *cante jondo*. The lyrics, which Lorca admired for their emotional intensity, usually contain four lines of verse with assonant rhyme and the following number of syllables: 6-6-11-6. On the *siguiriya*'s musical characteristics, see Katz, 627.

La guitarra / The Guitar. Lines 23–24: "[To me] the gypsy *siguiriya* had always evoked (I am an incurable lyricist) an endless road, a road without crossroads, ending at the pulsing fountain of the child Poetry, the road where the first bird died and the first arrow grew rusty" (*DS* 25). 27: The fingers? Allusion to Catholic images of the Virgin of Seven Sorrows with her heart transfixed by swords.

El grito / The Cry. Lorca refers to the "vocalized melisma" that typically precedes the singing (see Katz, 627). "The gypsy *siguiriya* begins with a terrible scream that divides the landscape into two ideal hemispheres. It is the scream of dead generations, a poignant elegy for lost centuries, the pathetic evocation of love under other moons and other winds. Then the melodic phrase begins to pry open the mystery of the tones and remove the precious stone of the sob, a resonant tear on the river of the voice. No Andalusian can help but shudder on hearing that scream [*grito*]" (*DS* 25).

El silencio / The Silence. "The voice pauses and gives way to an impressive measured silence. A silence glowing with the trace of the hot lily [or iris] which the voice has left in the sky" (*C* I:53).

El paso de la siguiriya / The Passage of the Siguiriya. "Then the melody begins, an undulant, endless melody, but not in the same sense as in Bach. Bach's infinite melody is round, the phrase could go on repeating itself in an eternal circular motion; but the melody of the *siguiriya* loses itself horizontally, escapes from our hands as we see it withdraw from us toward a point of common longing and perfect passion where the soul will never disembark" (*C* I:53).

Después de pasar / Afterwards. Literally, "After going by." The *cantaores* "sing as though fascinated by a point of light trembling on the horizon" (*C* I:82). Lines 6–7; Cf. lines 18–19 of *Madrigal* in *Book of Poems*; literally, "My pain, a spiral column, / bored through the moon" (*CP*, 85).

POEMA DE LA *SOLEÁ* / POEM OF THE *SOLEÁ*. The *soleá* (the word is a contraction of *soledad*, "solitude" or "loneliness") has three or four lines of verse, and is usually sung in 3/4 or 3/8 time.

Tierra seca . . . / Dry Land . . . Untitled in the first edition. Titled "Evocación" (Evocation) in two of the manuscripts.

Cueva / Cave. Probable allusion to the gypsy cave dwellers on the Sacromonte, Granada.

POEMA DE LA SAETA / POEM OF THE SAETA The *saeta* (the word also means dart or arrow) is a spontaneous, unaccompanied cry of devotion to the Virgin or to Christ, sung by those watching the all-night Holy Week processions, especially those of Seville. Lorca saw these for the first time in April 1922, together with his brother and Manuel de Falla. Lorca's sequence " 'takes place' in the streets of Seville and follows the progression from evocation of the 'landscape,' to the procession and religious floats, to the *saeta* itself sung from a balcony, and finally to the coming of dawn" (Loughran, 70).

Procesión / Procession. De Paepe (198) believes Lorca is recalling, besides Ariosto's poem, a scene from Chapter 23 of the second part of *Don Quijote* (Durandarte bewitched in the Cave of Montesinos); Durandarte and Christ are both "victims of love."

Saeta. The refrain is taken from popular *saetas* like "¡Miradlo por dónde viene, / el mejor de los nacidos!" (Look, he's coming by, / the best of men!) (Josephs and Caballero, 171). The *lirio* of line 2 (translated here as "lily" but also meaing "iris") probably alludes to the wounds of Christ or to his purple vestments (De Paepe, 201); a certain type of Spanish iris is known as *lirio nazareno* (iris of Nazareth).

Madrugada / Before Dawn. The singing of the *saeta* lasts into the early morning hours. The "archers" that Lorca is comparing to Cupid are those singing the *saeta* (literally, arrow). Lines 4–7: Lorca uses a similar image to describe the *siguiriya*. See *El silencio / The Silence*, above.

GRÁFICO DE LA PETENERA / GRAPHIC OF THE PETENERA. De Paepe (124) believes Lorca's emphasis shifts here from the pure *cante* (chant) of the first three sections to dance with guitar. The *petenera* is always accompanied by the guitar and is intended to be [danced]. It is a melancholy, sentimental song whose fundamental themes are similar to those of the *soleá* (Miller 37).

Campana / Bell. In the version which Lorca copied in New York, this poem is entitled "Clamor" (cf. *Death Knell*): mourning for the Petenera, the imaginary woman who personifies the lyrics called *peteneras*.

VIÑETAS FLAMENCAS / FLAMENCO VIGNETTES. The dedication was written after Lorca had heard the *cantaor* Manuel Torres (1878–1933?) remark: "In *cante jondo* what you must search for, and find, is the black torso of the Pharaoh" (Torres believed the *gypsies* to be of Egyptian origin). See *DS* 43. The corpulent Torres, who participated in the *cante jondo* festival of 1922, was one of the first *cantaores* to sing "from the torso," rather than in a shrill nasal voice.

Juan Breva. Professional name of Antonio Ortega (1835–1915), *cantaor* from Málaga, whom Lorca mentions in his lecture: "Juan Breva, who . . . sang *soleares* better than anyone else and called on the virgin Pain in the lemon groves of Málaga or beneath the maritime nights of Cádiz" (*DS* 40).

Café cantante / Cabaret. Lorca evokes the epoch of the flamenco "singing cabarets" in the second half of the nineteenth and early twentieth centuries; a period which threatened the purity of *cante jondo*, according to him and to Falla. Dolores Parrales (alias La Parrala), a singer of the *soleá*, was renowned for her beauty.

Malagueña. "The malagueña is never danced, and its lyrics, always of a serious, dramatic nature, frequently mention Málaga, its monuments and districts, or they relate events from the lives of mariners and others who make their living from the sea" (Miller, 34).

Barrio de Córdoba (Tópico nocturno) / Neighborhood in Córdoba (Nocturnal Theme). The word

Tópico carries the suggestion of "cliché" or "commonplace": of a theme already well developed in popular literature.

Adivinanza de la guitarra / Riddle of the Guitar. Lorca was aware of a long tradition of rhymed riddles in Spanish folklore.

Candil / Oil Lamp. Line 3: Lorca and Falla believed that the gypsies had come to Spain from India in the fifteenth century.

Chumbera / Prickly Pear. The shape of the plant reminds Lorca of the Laocoön (first century B.C.) in the Vatican Museum.

Suites

Written between early 1921 and August 1923. Published by the French Hispanist André Belamich in 1983, nearly half a century after Lorca's death. Neither the text nor the order of these poems can be considered definitive. Although Lorca spoke repeatedly between 1921 and 1936 of publishing *Suites* as a book, he did not leave a final, polished manuscript of the entire collection.

Two textual problems affect almost all the poems published here: it is not always clear which of these series Lorca considered "suites," and it is quite impossible to know how he would have ordered the sequences and, in some cases, the poems within each. Like Belamich, I have tried to present the series in the approximate order of their composition.

Two typographical matters: (1) For stylistic reasons, the stanza breaks and the use of italics in Jerome Rothenberg's English translation do not always correspond to those in the Spanish. (2) Missing lines are indicated by a line of dots between brackets. Three dots in brackets mark the lacunae left by missing poems.

SUITE DE LOS ESPEJOS / MIRROR SUITE. Ms. dated April 15, 1921, at the Residencia de Estudiantes. Aware that he had made a complete departure from the style of *Book of Poems*, Lorca writes excitedly to his parents, later that month, that he has composed a book (!) of "extraordinarily new things . . . the most perfect [work]" he has produced, "with the advantage of being the most advanced thing that is happening in poetry" (letter of April 1921, ms. AFGL). MIRROR SUITE was published by Juan Ramón Jiménez in *Indice* in early 1921. *Symbol*: Literally, "Christ / had a mirror / in each hand. / He used to multiply / his own specter. / He used to project his heart / in his black / looks (glances). / I believe!" *Rays*: Cf. *Floating Bridges* in IN THE GARDEN OF THE LUNAR GRAPEFRUITS (tr. Jerome Rothenberg): "And steadily our feet / keep walking & creating / —like enormous fans— / these roads in embryo." *Capriccio*, lines 5–6: Literally: "Behind each mirror / there is an eternal calm." *Eyes*: The "Castle of no return" is mentioned in numerous folktales (e.g., Espinosa, 321), and the strange traveler and Elenita appear in a ballad sung by children: "Estando una niña / bordando corbatas . . ." (A girl was sitting / embroidering neckties . . .), which Lorca once re-created and choreographed. The traveler carries Elena off to the mountains and cuts off her head (Llorca, 48, and Fuentes Vázquez, 98–99.).

NOCHE / NIGHT. The subtitle is literally "Suite for Piano and Emotional Voice" (AFGL). NOCHE, too, was written in 1921. It was published by Juan Ramón Jiménez in *Indice* in 1922 (the version followed here). This suite is probably the "tiny prayer book in honor of our immortal father Sirius" which Lorca mentions in a letter of August 2, 1921, to the musicologist Adolfo Salazar (see notes to FOUR BALLADS IN YELLOW, below). The end of *Swath* evokes a well-known Spanish children's song first recorded in the early seventeenth century, "La pájara pinta" (The Painted Bird), which Lorca also quotes in his puppet play *The Tragicomedy of Don Cristóbal and Mistress Rosita* (tr. Honig, 60). Much admired by modern Spanish poets, from Rafael Alberti to Gabriel Celaya, the song accompanies a circle game in which the child selects a girlfriend or boyfriend; thus Lorca's evocation of the "noche de mi amor." *One:* The meaning of lines 1–3 may be: "That star which appears [so] romantic / (to the magnolias / and to the roses)." *Memory:* The phrase *luna lunera* ("loony moon") occurs in many Spanish children's songs, including ones where the child makes some sort of wish (Newton, 281), and Rodriguez Marín, 59). *At the Poorhouse:* The ironical refrain appears in certain versions of the ballad "Mambrú se fue a la guerra . . ." (e.g., Celaya 195–96). The title of *Comet* is probably a pun: *cometa* is both "comet" and "kite." The kite would prove there are children on Sirius, the Dog Star, the brightest one in the sky, guard of the heavens in the cosmogony of Zoroaster. On the latter, cf. introductory note to *Poem of the Deep Song*, above.

REMANSOS / BACKWATERS. One ms. is dated June 12, 1921. Published by Jorge Guillén in *Verso y Prosa* (Murcia) in April 1927 with the subtitle (*Diferencias*), a term used for "variations" in sixteenth-century Spanish music. Published again in 1936 in *Primeras canciones*, with the poems in a different order and without the poem *Keep It Going*. Given here is a composite version: I have followed the contents and order of the *Verso y Prosa* version but have incorporated the textual changes made in poems 1–4 and 6 of *Primeras canciones*, with emendations suggested by Mario Hernández (219–20).

CUATRO BALADAS AMARILLAS / FOUR BALLADS IN YELLOW. July 1921? One of the ms. is dated August 20, 1922, but Lorca seems to allude to this poem in a letter of August 2, 1921, to Adolfo Salazar (*E* I:38): "I'm hard at work now, and think you'll like what I'm doing: much better, it seems to me, than the *suites* you already know. Would you like me to send you something? I call these pieces 'songs with reflections,' because that is all I want to do: allow my words to give the sublime feeling of the reflection, and take away from that which trembles the spiraling nature of a Baroque column [*quitando al temblor lo que tiene de salomónico*]. I'm also writing yellowing ballads [*baladas amarillentas*] and a tiny prayer book in honor of our immortal father Sirius . . . In a word, I'm working pretty hard." Revised again in 1926 and published ten years later in *Primeras canciones*, it is the version followed here, as edited by Hernández (*Primeras canciones*, 56–59). The first line of poem I is taken verbatim from a traditional ballad, "En lo alto de aquel monte / un gran palacio había" (High up on the mountain / was a great palace) (Menéndez Pelayo, 262); many ballads begin with similar phrases. In poem III, Lorca describes oxen, not bulls. In the autograph ms., Lorca crosses out two verses before lines 19–20 of poem IV: "Jacobus de Voragine, / take up your quill!" The *Golden Legend* was one of his favorite books.

EL REGRESO / THE RETURN. A ms. dated August 6, 1921, with a canceled dedication to the cinematographer Luis Buñuel, includes eleven poems. Revised in 1923; in October of that year Lorca copied out *The Return* and *Oxbow* for Fernández Almagro: "The suite 'The Return' is long, but I'm sending you its two most delicate little spangles" (*E* I:87). Published after elimination of five poems, in *La Verdad* (Murcia) in May 1924. The first poem was revised in 1931 for use in Act I of *Once Five Years Pass* (tr. Logan and Gil, 58–59).

SEIS CANCIONES DE ANOCHECER / SIX SONGS AT NIGHTFALL. Ms. dated August 14, 1921. Zujaira forms part of the Vega of Granada.

TRES CREPÚSCULOS / THREE CREPUSCULAR POEMS. Written on the same day—November 11, 1921—as *Poem of the Gypsy* Siguiriya from *Poem of the Deep Song*: an astonishing example of Lorca's poetic versatility. Revised in 1926.

MADRIGALES / MADRIGALS. Composed July–August 1922? I have restored several lines to the incomplete text presented by Menarini (315–16).

CASTILLO DE FUEGOS ARTIFICIALES . . . / BARRAGE OF FIREWORK POEMS . . . Ms. dated August 8, 1922, in Asquerosa, two months after Lorca's twenty-fourth birthday. Revised in 1926?

EN EL JARDÍN DE LAS TORONJAS DE LUNA / IN THE GARDEN OF THE LUNAR GRAPEFRUITS. Written summer 1923. The order of these poems is not always certain (see *CP*, 812). Two letters tell us of Lorca's progress on this series and on a slightly earlier one entitled "The Forest of Lunar Grapefruits." In the first letter he writes his friends Fernández Almagro and José de Ciria y Escalante: "I have finished a poem, 'The Garden of the Lunar Grapefruits,' and am willing to spend the whole summer working on it—I'm very anxious to get it exactly the way I've seen it. You could say that I have gone about it feverishly, for I've worked twenty days with their twenty nights . . . just to *pin it down*. The landscapes in this poem are absolutely motionless, with neither wind nor rhythm. I noticed that my verses were slipping out of my hands, and that my poetry was fleeting and *alive*. Reacting to that feeling, this poem is static [*extático*] and somnambulistic. My *garden* is the garden of possibilities, the garden of what is not, but could (and at times *should*) have been, the garden of theories that passed invisibly by and children who have not been born. Each word in the poem was a butterfly, and I have had to hunt them down one by one. / / Later I fought off my two worldly enemies (the enemies of all poets): Eloquence and Common Sense: terrifying hand-to-hand combat as in the battles of the *Poem of the Cid*.

"If you are true friends you'll write me quickly and I will send you a song from the garden, for example, the 'song of the seven-hearted boy' or the 'lament of the girl with no voice,' which seem to me to be pretty well *accomplished*" (*E* I:69–70).

In a second letter, mailed on July 30, 1923 (*E* I:73), Lorca tells Ciria y Escalante he is "polishing" his "extremely strange garden of lunar grapefruits": "I am going to send you several 'engravings' from this poem, on condition you not read them to anyone, for they are not yet finished . . . / / Now more than ever I find that words have a phosphorescent glow and are full of mysterious senses and sounds. I feel real panic when I sit down to write! And what joy I take in our old poets! [e.g., Fernando de Herrera and Lupercio Leonardo de Argensola]." He encloses a selection of seven poems, which he calls *estampitas* (little engravings), reiterating that the poems should not be shown to anyone, for "all of this will change." The poems are given in this order: *Song of the Seven-Hearted Boy*, *Portico*, *White Satyr*, *Engravings of the Garden (I)* (titled "Otra estampita": Another Engraving), *Frieze* (later transferred to *Songs*), *Little Song of the Unborn Child*, and *Wake Up/Ring Out* (identified as the final poem in the series).

Pórtico / Portico. For Lorca's fanciful drawing of the griffin vulture (which inhabits the salt marshes of Huelva in southern Spain), see *LLS*, no. 56.

Glorieta / Pergola. Circled in the manuscript, but not eliminated. Lorca is remembering a traditional ballad about an apparition ("Paseábase Marbella / de la sala al ventanal": Marbella was pacing / near the window of the room) which he believed to epitomize Spain's obsession with death. The poem continues: "If you are my pretty friend, / why don't you look at me? / The eyes I looked at you with / I have given to the dark. / If you are my pretty friend, / why don't you kiss me? / The lips I kissed you with / I have given to the earth. / If you are my pretty friend, / why don't you hold me tight? / The arms I hugged you with / I have covered with worms" (*DS* 48).

Avenida / Avenue. Lines 23–26, literally: "Maidens that leave an absent / mental fragrance of looks. / The breeze remains indifferent: / a white camellia with one hundred petals." The camellia is being compared to the compass rose on wind charts.

Canción del jardinero inmóvil / Song of the Motionless Gardener. Lines 3–4 say, literally: "You can hardly reach / the treasure of the day."

Sátiro blanco / White Satyr. Line 4, literally: "virginized his wide forehead." Lines 10–14 mean: ". . . aired itself with old storms. / / The syrinx on the ground was a fountain / with seven blue, crystalline spouts." Lorca is referring to the satyr's pan-pipe.

Puentes colgantes / Floating Bridges. Or "Suspension Bridges."

Estampas del jardín / Engravings of the Garden. There is no way to know for sure what poems were intended for this section. In his letter to Ciria y Escalante, Lorca uses the word *estampas* generically. On *Widow of the moon* . . . see *CP*, 813.

¿Qué quieres de mí . . . / *What do you want from me* . . . Fragment. The first part of the poem is missing.

Arco le lunas / Moonbow. Lorca wrote "No" in the margin of the manuscript, as though he had considered eliminating this poem, but seems to have changed his mind, for he made a fair copy.

Altas torres . . . / *Tall towers* . . . Published also in *Songs* (*CP*, 482–85)

Canción del muchacho de siete corazones / Song of the Seven-Hearted Boy. The "seven girls" are probably the seven colors mentioned in *Song of the Seven Maidens (Theory of the Rainbow)* in *Songs*. The phantom galley would remind Spanish readers of the ballad of Count Arnaldos (Smith, 208).

Duna / Dune. Lorca composed two endings for this poem, without crossing out either. The other reads (tr. Jerome Rothenberg): "Then the garden will follow / where time has its shore / will be beating like crazy / at the gateway of life."

Canciones / Songs

Published 1927. Although Lorca gave the years 1921–24 below the title, these poems were written between 1921 and 1926. Between December 1925 and February 1926, at a time when he felt disenchanted with his work in progress, Lorca went back over almost all the poems he had composed over the preceding five years. Three books emerged from his papers: the series he had written in 1921 (*Poem of the Deep Song*); an open-ended collection of poetic sequences (*Suites*); and a cumulus of short lyrical poems (*Songs*). The "deep song" poems had an obvious thematic and structural unity, but as Lorca winnowed his manuscripts, revised poems, added titles and dedications, and made fair copies, he agonized over which poems to include in *Suites* and which in *Songs*: the same themes run through both books, and poems were transferred back and forth between them.

In October 1926 the poet Emilio Prados, who was running a small press (Litoral) in Málaga with fellow poet Manuel Altolaguirre, visited Lorca in Granada and sequestered all his handwritten originals. *Songs* was published at Litoral in May of the following year (second edition, Madrid, 1929, at Revista de Occidente, directed by the essayist José Ortega y Gasset).

The final ordering and selection of *Songs* caused Lorca "genuine anguish": "I have omitted the rhythmic songs despite their success because I want everything to have the high air of the sierra" (*E* II:25). By the time *Songs* appeared, he felt himself "master" of the book, proud of his workmanship and editorial discernment. *Songs* represents a "sharp, serene lyrical effort, and to me it seems to contain great poetry (great in the sense of nobility and quality, not of worth [*valor*])" (*E* II:25). Even the long delay in publication seemed to have been beneficial. Fernández Almagro had warned Lorca that others were copying his unpublished poems. "Nothing could be further from the truth," he replies. "*They have come out without a scratch*, the poor things! But they have *a certain something*, and that something is what cannot be copied. I *don't think music is everything*, as do certain *young poets* [Rafael Alberti?]; I give my *love* to the word, and not to the sound. My songs are not of ash. How useful it was to have withheld them! God bless me! And now I've *retouched* them for the last time, and they're done!" (*E* I:134).

The Spanish text follows the edition of Mario Hernández. For chronological and textual information, I have made use of the edition of Piero Menarini and of mss. in AFGL and elsewhere.

Nocturno esquemático / Nocturne in Outline. Ms. dated July 21, 1924. Carlos Bousoño

(Alonso and Bousoño, 240) notices that the "outline" (or "scheme") is correlative: the *fennel* gives its aroma to the *air*, the *serpent* leaves its *trail* on the *earth*; the *rushes* are *apart* (or alone) in the *half-shadow*.

La canción del colegial / Schoolboy's Song. Fair copy dated February 1922.

El canto quiere ser luz . . . / Song would like to be light . . . Ms. dated 1925.

Tiovivo / Merry-go-round. Written in 1922.

Friso / Frieze. Sent to José de Ciria y Escalante on July 30, 1923, as a sample of IN THE GARDEN OF THE LUNAR GRAPEFRUITS (*E* I:78), but assigned, finally, to *Songs*.

Cazador / Hunter. A fair copy was sent to Jorge Guillén in mid-February 1927 and published by him in *Verso y Prosa* the following April.

Fábula / Fable. 1921?

Agosto . . . / August . . . Published in *Boletín del Centro Artístico de Granada* in September 1924, with the title "Cancioncilla" (Little Song). Menarini explains that *contraponientes* (line 2) is a neologism formed from *contra* (against) and *ponientes* (sunsets, western skies). Line 10: *Melón* (metaphorically, "tasty moon") is sometimes eaten in Spain with dark bread.

Arlequín / Harlequin. Ms. dated 1923. For Lorca's pen-and-ink drawings of harlequins, see *LLS*, nos. 122, 126–27, etc.

Cortaron tres árboles / Three Trees Were Cut Down. Originally entitled "Elegy for Three Trees." Ms. is undated. 1926?

Canción china en Europa / Song of China in Europe. Ms. dated November 17, 1926.

Cancioncilla sevillana / Sevillian Ditty. Both the *oro/moro* rhyme and the use of dialect (*naranjel*) are reminiscent of traditional poetry. Menarini (97) identifies a children's song echoed here: "Coche de oro / para el moro, / coche de plata / para la infanta": A golden carriage for the Moor, / A silver carriage / for the princess" (cf. Llorca, 101). Lorca is also imitating a well-known folksong glossed by Góngora (Cohen, 273–74) and Calderón de la Barca (Act II of *El alcalde de Zalamea*): "Las flores del romero, / niña Isabel, / *hoy son flores azules, / mañana serán miel*" (The flowers of the rosemary, / child Isabel, / *are blue flowers today; / tomorrow they will be honey*) (italics mine).

Caracola / Seashell. Ms. copy dated 1926.

El lagarto está llorando . . . / Mr. Lizard is crying . . . Ms. dated November 1925; revised and dedicated in 1926. Robertson (79) believes the poem "derive[s] from a circle game [Lorca] probably played as a child in Granada."

Canción cantada / Song Sung. Sent to Fernández Almagro in a letter of September 1924, with the title "Cancioncilla" (Little Song) (*E* I:100).

Canción tonta / Silly Song. This was the third poem in a ms. series of November 1925 entitled "Canciones tontas del niño y su mamá" (Silly Songs of the Child and His Mother). For the first time two poems, omitted from *Canciones*, see Menarini, 289–90. The poem *Mr. Lizard is crying . . .* seems to have formed part of the same series, and, in a note on the manuscript, Lorca reminds himself to write others, including one about "the boy who lays an egg."

Adelina de paseo / Adeline Out Walking. Dated July 19, 1924, and sent to José de Ciria y Escalante in a letter of that month (*E* I:79). According to the poet's brother, the song is based on a popular tune: "I went to sea to look for oranges, / but the sea has none, / and I came back soaked / by the waves that come and go" (Belamich, ed., *Oeuvres*, 1366).

Canción de jinete / Rider's Song. Ms. dated July 4, 1924. Published in the *Boletín del Centro Artístico de Granada*, September 1924, and reprinted in Gerardo Diego's anthologies of 1932 and 1934. Lorca associated this poem with the emotion expressed in *Ballad of Black Pain* from *The Gypsy Ballads*, written the same month. *Rider's Song*, he said, "seems to picture that prodigious Andalusian Omar ibn-Hafsun exiled forever from his fatherland" (*DS* 112), a reference to the Muslim rebel who threatened the Caliphate of Córdoba in the ninth century. In the first draft (reproduced in facsimile in *OC* I:lii–liii) the final stanza begins with the line (crossed out): "Mi niña! mi amor mi niña!," suggesting that the rider was trying to reach his beloved. The final version carefully avoids any explanation for his trip (see Introduction).

Galán, / galancillo . . . / Suitor, suitor of mine . . . Ms. dated August 22, 1924. The rhyme, structure, refrain, and the image of words written on a ribbon (lines 8–9) make this an elegant imitation of traditional children's songs.

Verlaine. The French poet had been a spiritual "traveling companion" of Lorca as an adolescent, and Sahuquillo, in examining this poem (243ff.), suggests that Lorca associated him with homosexuality. At age twenty Lorca describes himself to Adriano del Valle (*E* I:17): "I am a poor, passionate, silent lad who, almost like the marvelous Verlaine, has within him a lily that is impossible to water; and to the stupid eyes of those who look at me I present [the image] of a very red rose, with the sexual hue of an April peony, which is not the truth of my heart."

Baco / Bacchus. In small print in the first edition, as though this poem were the "shadow" of the preceding one. In his lecture on Góngora, Lorca explains: "In mythology, Bacchus suffers three passions and deaths. He is first a goat with twisting horns. For love of his dancer Cyssus, who dies and is turned into ivy, Bacchus changes into a vine. Lastly, he dies, and is turned into a fig tree" (see pp. 337–38). On Lorca's sources for this myth, see Martínez Nadal, *FGL*, 122–32.

Juan Ramón Jiménez. Ms. dated October 3, 1924, a few months after the great Spanish poet (1881–1958) had visited the Lorca family in Granada. Lorca had met him in Madrid five years earlier and had described him to his family as "lots of fun and very neurasthenic" (ms. letter, AFGL). García-Posada believes that the first three lines are "veiled criticism" of pure poetry and "of a poetics as unencumbered by reality as the one practiced by Juan Ramón" (*GP1* 158).

Venus. Probably written July 1924 (Menarini 132).

Debussy. Written July 1922. The title occurred to Lorca several years later, in homage to the composer of "Reflets dans l'eau" and of *Soirée dans Grenade*, where "one can find all the emotional themes of the Granadan night, the blue remoteness of the Vega, the Sierra greeting the tremulous Mediterranean, the enormous barbs of the clouds sunk into the distance, the admirable rubato of the city, the hallucinating play of its underground waters" (*DS* 29–30). Lorca was a fervent admirer of Debussy's piano music at least as early as the summer of 1917; see "Las reglas en la música" (The Rules of Music), *OC* III:270. This poem is followed by "Narcissus" (the "shadow" or "shading" of the third portrait), *CP*, 456–559.

Naranja y limón . . . / Orange and lemon . . . Entitled "Polos" (Poles) in the undated AFGL ms. Fair copy dated May 1922. Jorge Guillén (*OC* I:xxiii) writes of this poem: "The child that exists in the poet—and they are one—is combining [his] words in an [almost] arbitrary way . . . as though he were playing on the beach with pebbles and shells. That is the way that Federico played, using his imagination and his hands, with the world."

La calle de los mudos / The Street of the Mute. A language of fans and, presumably, of handkerchiefs, was a necessary part of courtship in a society where young women were closely chaperoned. Every Spanish woman carries a fan, writes Richard Ford (I:112) in the 1855 edition of his *Handbook*: "It is the index of her soul, the telegraph of her chameleon feelings, her signal to the initiated, which they understand for good or evil as the wagging of a dog's tail. She can express with her dumb fan more than Paganini could with his fiddlestick. A handbook might be written to explain the code of signals."

La luna asoma / The Moon Appears. There is an earlier version in the suite SUBLUNAR CANTOS (*CP*, 236–41), probably written in July 1921. The third stanza seems to hint at an old superstition. In his 1855 *Handbook* Ford remarks of Seville oranges: "The natives are not very fanciful about eating them: they do not think them good before March, and poison if eaten after sunset" (I:214).

Dos lunas de tarde / Two Evening Moons. Probably written in July 1921.

EROS CON BASTÓN / EROS WITH A CANE (1925). The poet's brother, Francisco, suggested the title (Belamich 1373). Toward the end of September 1925 Lorca confided to Fernández Almagro: "For the *first time in my life* I'm creating erotic poetry. An illustrious field of endeavor has suddenly opened up and is renewing me in an extraordinary way. I don't understand myself, Melchorito. My mother tells me, 'You're still growing . . .' And yet I'm just now *getting into problems* that I should have faced long ago . . . Am I a slow developer [*retrasado*]? . . . What *is* all this? It seems as though I've just reached adolescence. That's why when I'll be sixty I won't be old . . . I'm never going to be *old*" (*E* I:120). At least five of the poems in this section were written that summer.

Susto en el comedor / Fright in the Dining Room. First draft dated September 1925.

Lucía Martínez. September 1925?

La soltera en misa / The Unmarried Woman at Mass. Undated ms. (September 1925?) entitled "Prefacio" (Preface). This may have been meant as the first poem in the series.

Malestar y noche / Disquiet and Night. Ms. lost. Judging from the imagery, probably written in spring or summer 1925.

Desposorio / Marriage Vow. July 1923? Ms. undated, but like *Scene*, the poem once belonged to the LUNAR GRAPEFRUITS series in *Suites*, where the narrator is transformed into a hundred-year-old man. The title was added later.

Despedida / Leave-taking. Date of composition unknown. Jorge Guillén (lxxvii) notices that although this poem follows the parallelistic structure of the medieval Galician–Portuguese lyric, Lorca is also half remembering the "deep song" repertoire—e.g., *siguiriyas* like the one beginning "Cuando yo muera / mira que te encargo . . ." (When I die / I ask you . . .); see *Memento*.

Suicidio / Suicide. Ms. dated July 27, 1924.

Cancioncilla del primer deseo / Ditty of First Desire. 1922?

Preludio / Prelude. Composed, like *Debussy*, as part of a series or *suite* entitled DAYDREAMS OF A RIVER in 1922, but revised for inclusion in *Songs*.

Soneto / Sonnet. A ms. subtitled "Narciso" (Narcissus) is dated July 1924—a time when Lorca was discovering that "there is a certain eternal sentiment to the sonnet which fits in no other vessel than this apparently cold one" (*E* I:96). Line 7: A similar phrase occurs in Góngora's sonnet 66: "aunque con lengua muda / suave Filomena ya suspira . . ." (though with muted tongue, / gentle Philomela now sighs). Philomela was turned into a nightingale after Tereus raped her sister Procne and cut out Procne's tongue. In some versions of the myth, their roles are reversed.

Canción del naranjo seco / Song of the Dead Orange Tree. Composed in summer 1923 around the same time as the *suite* IN THE GARDEN OF THE LUNAR GRAPEFRUITS, whose narrator feels anguish over the children he might have engendered but never did.

Canción del día que se va / Song of Departing Day. Ms. dated August 9, 1923.

Primer romancero gitano / The Gypsy Ballads

Written between 1921 and 1927; published 1928 by Revista de Occidente, Madrid. The title is literally *First Gypsy Ballad Book*, but is commonly shortened to *The Gypsy Ballads*.

The idea for this collection seems to have occurred to Lorca in the summer of 1922 while he was still at work on *Suites* (*E* I:31). Unlike *Poem of the Deep Song*, the *Ballads* would be written slowly over several years, and it was not until early 1926, when Lorca was going over the manuscripts of almost all his poetry, that he decided to publish them as a book.

The Spanish text presented here follows the edition of Mario Hernández (1983), with a few differences of punctuation and spacing. The *Ballads* are Lorca's best-studied book. English-speaking readers will learn much from H. Ramsden, *Lorca's* Romancero gitano: *Eighteen commentaries*; Robert G. Havard, *Gypsy Ballads*; and Derek Harris, *Federico García Lorca, Romancero Gitano*. The most helpful discussions in Spanish are the editions of García-Posada, Josephs/Caballero, and Hernández and the monograph by Luis Beltrán Fernández de los Ríos.

Preciosa y el aire / Preciosa and the Wind. Ms. dated January 28, 1926. Published that November in *Litoral* (Málaga). Lorca was fascinated by the personification of the wind in the lyrics of *cante jondo*: "The wind is a character who emerges in the ultimate, most emotional moments. He comes into sight like a giant absorbed in pulling down stars and scattering nebulae; and in no popular poetry but ours have I heard him speak and console" (*DS* 34–35). Cummins (64–67) provides numerous examples of traditional lyrics where the wind "acts like a playful, unruly lover, lifting the young girl's skirts; the man prays for a wind to blow him into those skirts; to be burned by the wind is a frequent metaphor for love-making, particularly for the loss of virginity." Ramsden (8) quotes several traditional lyrics in which the wind is a sexual threat, e.g. (translation mine): "Don't go alone to the field / when the wind is blowing hard; / because girls are flowers / and even the wind strips their petals"; and "A bad little breeze / [is being] crazy with my skirts. / Away from me, bad wind! / Why lift my skirts?" The image of the wind as "suitor" occurs in "Arbolé arbolé" (*CP* 448–51). The name of the gypsy girl and some of the poem's imagery were borrowed from Cervantes's novella *La gitanilla* (*The Gypsy Girl*); e.g., the ballad which begins: "When Preciosa beats her tambourine . . ."; text in Cohen, 228–29; details in Ramsden. Jorge Guillén (1954) identifies another source: the Ovidian myth of Boreas, ravisher of Oreithyia. Forster believes that Lorca is superimposing *three* mythological figures: St. Christopher, Boreas, and Pan. Harris (19) points out that "St. Christopher was traditionally a giant of a man, but the priapic character of Lorca's San Cristobalón comes from the more immediate popular source of the puppet show. The Spanish Punch is called Cristóbal and carries the usual enormous cudgel with clear phallic intent." For Lorca's drawing of San Cristóbal, see *LLS*, no. 183. The exclamation of line 40 is borrowed from *cante jondo* lyrics (see note on *Saeta*).

Reyerta / The Dispute. Ms. dated August 6, 1926. Sent to Guillén the following month (*E* I:166–67) with the title "Reyerta de mozos" (Brawl [Feud, Dispute] between Young Men). Published in *La Verdad* (Murcia) in October 1926; and, with the title "Reyerta gitana" (Gypsy Brawl," in the Catalan literary magazine *L'Amic de les Arts*, June 1927. According to Lorca, this poem is an image of random violence, expressing "a silent, latent struggle all over Andalusia and Spain among groups that attack each other without knowing why, for mysterious reasons: because of a look, a rose, a love affair two centuries old, or because a man suddenly feels a bug on his cheek" (*DS* 110). Ford (II:804) marvels that "where an unarmed Englishman *closes* his fist, a Spaniard *opens* his knife. Man, again, in this hot climate, is very inflammable and combustible; a small spark explodes the dry powder, which ignites less readily in damp England." Harris (22) believes that the reference to playing cards in line 6 "indicates a reason for the fight while the quality of hardness from the knives is transferred to this synthesized 'luz de naipe.' " Havard (129) points out that "cards depict motifs in profile, and the equivalent of a jack in Spanish cards is a horse and rider. Lines 29–30 bring out the enduring nature of the violence, referring not only to the Punic Wars for the possession of Spain but also, ironically, to classroom competition among Spanish children. In some schools, particularly Jesuit ones, the class was divided into competing teams, the "Romans" and the "Carthaginians" (García-Posada, 118).

2: Albacete: town between Madrid and Valencia famed for its *navajas*, with long blades that fold back into a handle. 31: According to Harris (22), the word *loca*, applied to plants, means "growing wild"; literally, "the afternoon, with figs growing wild," or "grown wild with figs."

Romance sonámbulo / Sleepwalking Ballad. Ms. dated August 2, 1924. For Lorca's 1930 illustration of this ballad (showing the house with its *barandas*, or railings), see *LLS* no. 240.2. The poet's own commentary is willfully enigmatic: "It is one of the most mysterious [poems] in the book, and is thought by many to express Granada's longing for the sea and the anguish of a city that cannot hear the waves and seeks them in the play of her underground waters and in the undulous clouds with which she covers her mountains. That is true, but this poem is also something else. It is a pure poetic event, of Andalusian essence, and will always have changing lights, even for me, the man who communicated it. If you ask me why I wrote, 'A thousand crystal tambourines / were wounding dawn's dark sky' [lines 59–60], I will tell you that I saw them in the hands of angels and trees, but I will not be able to say more; certainly I cannot explain their meaning. And that is the way it should be. By means of poetry a man more rapidly approaches the cutting edge from which the philosopher and the mathematician turn away in silence" (*DS* 111–12). Dalí once remarked admiringly of this ballad, "It seems to have a story, but it doesn't" (Guillén, L). The thread of the narration seems to be this: a smuggler, badly wounded in a skirmish with the Civil Guard, returns shortly before dawn from the Passes of Cabra (mountain passes in the province of Córdoba, associated with smuggling and brigandry), in search of his beloved, a gypsy girl, and converses with the girl's father. But, tired of waiting for him, the girl has fallen (or thrown herself) from the terraced roof of the house into an *aljibe* (tank holding rainwater). Ramos-Gil (210) believes the girl is "the victim of the attraction, the spell cast by the dark water of the rain-tank": a reading that would coincide with Lorca's own (Granada's fascination with its underground waters, etc.). Line 1: Francisco García Lorca explores the ambiguity of this refrain, which can mean "I *want* you green," "I *love* you green," "I want you *green*," etc. He believes the "act of will" is more pronounced than the "act of love." "We can even suppose that the poet is anticipating not a particular green, but the very idea of green, not yet created. In this case, 'Verde que te quiero verde' would announce the creation of green . . . 'Let green exist, for I want it so.' This would be the *Fiat lux* of the entire poem. A green invoked, anticipated, still to be created. Green does not actually appear until the next verse: 'verde viento, verdes ramas.' . . . In [lines 3–4] the poet is ordering his poetic universe" (*De Garcilaso a Lorca*, 270). Envious of the opening line—all Spaniards recite it with admiration—Juan Ramón Jiménez pointed out that it was taken from a popular song: "Green, I love you green, / the color of an olive."

San Miguel (Granada) / St. Michael (Granada). The first of a tryptich of three characteristic Andalusian saints; the other two are St. Raphael (Córdoba) and St. Gabriel (Seville) (*CP* 542–49). Written in Lanjarón (a health spa south of Granada) in August 1926 and sent to Jorge Guillén on September 9 of that year (*E* I:164). Published in *Litoral* in November 1926. The poem describes the break of dawn on the feast of St. Michael (September 29), an occasion celebrated in Granada with a pilgrimage to the Church of San Miguel el Alto on the Sacromonte, the hill (lines 2, 16) over the gypsy quarter of the Albaicín. The mules are carrying sunflower seed, to be sold at the fair. In lines 17–24 and 45–48 Lorca describes a strange Baroque statue in the shrine. Ramsden (52) explains: "Behind the altar a glass screen (*vidrios*) separates the nave from the 'camarín' (*la alcoba de su torre*) where the boyish figure of the saint (*efebo de tres mil noches*), sumptuously attired in female dress, a degenerate form of the Roman military tunic (*lleno de encajes . . . enseña sus bellos muslos*), and with a fine plume of feathers on his head (*plumas*), is treading, somewhat delicately, on the prostrate figure of a demonic, tailed Satan, his right arm upraised, with three arrows in his hand (*el gesto de las doce*), threatening the demon beneath his feet." Drawing by Lorca in *LLS*, no. 244.4; photographs in García-Posada, between 156 and 157. Jorge Guillén's letter of September 13, 1926, to Juan Guerrero, editor of *La Verdad*, Murcia, suggests that this ballad raised at least a few eyebrows. Guillén writes humorously: "I had asked Federico, in return for the poems of mine that I sent him, for some of his own, with the crafty, treacherous intention of sending them to *La Verdad*. 'Good God, let them be publishable,' I said to myself. And sure enough, he has sent me two ballads. One of them, about St. Michael, is impossible (*enseña sus bellos muslos*, etc.). I'm sending you the other. You need his permission" (unpublished letter, Sala Zenobia y Juan Ramón Jiménez, University of Puerto Rico). Harris (44) believes that the images in lines 21–25 "point unerringly to [the] homosexual character [of Lorca's St. Michael]"; this is "confirmed beyond all doubt by the description of him as an 'efebo de tres mil noches'." Line 33: The *manolas* are city women of the lower classes, dressed up for the occasion. Bishop of Manila (line 41) was one of the titles held by the Bishop of Granada. 51–52: In a lecture on popular song, Lorca describes Granada, seen from the Cerro del Aceituno, on the feast of St. Michael. "The song one hears is chaotic. It is all Granada singing at once: rivers, voices, ropes, foliage, processions, an ocean of fruits, the music of the swing rides at the fairs" ("How a City Sings from November to November"). 49–50: "There is a local lottery on the saint's day for which the draw is made with numbered balls. This, together with the day itself, September 29, accounts for him being the 'rey de los globos / y de los números nones' . . . The archangel who in the calendar is the saint of the Church Militant has been turned by Lorca into the camp master of ceremonies of a local lottery" (Harris, 45).

Romance de la Guardia Civil Española / Ballad of the Spanish Civil Guard. The Guard is a paramilitary police force, founded to patrol the highways and beaches and control banditry and smuggling. By the end of the nineteenth century, it had become an organ of power for the *caciques*, the local despots who ruled the Spanish provinces. The first sixty-two lines of this poem were sent to Jorge Guillén on November 8, 1926, with the remark: "I began it two years ago—remember? . . . This is what I have done so far. Now the Civil Guard arrives and destroys the city. Later they go back to their barracks and drink anise, toasting to the death of the gypsies. The scenes of the sack [of the city] will be lovely. At times, the Guards will inexplicably turn into Roman centurions. This ballad will be extremely long, but it will be among the best. The final apotheosis of the Civil Guard is very moving. / / Once I have finished this ballad and the 'Ballad of the Martyrdom of the Gypsy St. Eulalia of Mérida' [*CP*, 570–75], I will consider the book finished. A good book, I think. And I will never again—*never! never!*—return to this theme" (*E* I:180–81).

In his lecture-reading of the *Ballads*, Lorca calls this "one of the most difficult" poems in the book, for the theme is "incredibly anti-poetic" (*DS* 122). In a letter of 1926 to his brother, Francisco, he describes the cruelty of the Civil Guard in a remote mountainous district of Granada, the Alpujarras: "The countryside is ruled by the Civil Guard. A lieutenant from Carataunas, who was much annoyed by the gypsies, and who wanted to make them disappear, called them into the barracks, took the tongs from the fireplace and pulled a tooth out of each one's mouth, saying, 'If you're not out of here by tomorrow, another tooth will *fall out*' . . . This Easter in Cáñar, a fourteen-year-old gypsy boy stole five hens from the mayor. The Civil Guard tied his arms to a piece of wood and paraded him through the village, whipping him and forcing him to sing. I was told this by a little boy who saw the procession passing as he sat at his desk in school . . . All this has a cruelty I had never suspected" (*E* I:145).

Line 8: The uniforms include black patent-leather tricorn hats and belts. 12: In 1927 Lorca explained the expression *miedos de fina arena* to a literary critic: "When the Civil

Guards draw near to simple people who have heard of their terrifying reputation, their fear slips coldly, roughly down their backs, like a fine, slippery sand between their shirts and their skin" (Harris, 153). 18, 100: As in other ballads, imagery borrowed from traditional poems (e.g., the "corners hung with banners") mingles with borrowings from learned poets; e.g., the expression *salivilla de estrella*, an allusion to Góngora (*DS* 71, *CP* 831–32). 26: Reminiscent of expressions like "luna lunera" in traditional Christmas songs (Harris, 153). 47: Owner of the great sherry house; the poem alludes to Christmas celebrations in Jerez de la Frontera. 65: Civil Guards always patrol in pairs and are often referred to as *parejas* (couples). 67: Lorca often associates the siempreviva (helichrysum) with death; it is used in cemetery wreaths. Lines 77–80 have long puzzled readers of this ballad. García-Posada believes Lorca is referring to a "sweet, purplish syrup, a children's medicinal, called 'noviembre.' " Another critic believes "the disguise of November may be explained as an image of the coldness of fear causing the bottles to be covered with a mist of condensation" (Harris, 68).

Thamar y Amnón / Thamar and Amnon. The third in a series of "Three Historical Ballads" (the first two are "Martyrdom of St. Eulalia," about a saint immortalized by the Hispano-Roman poet Prudentius, and "A Joke about Don Pedro on Horseback . . . ," which alludes to the death of a fourteenth-century Castilian king (*CP* 571–79, 832). Written 1926–27? Based on the story of incest in II Samuel 13:1–22, but Lorca's immediate sources were the numerous traditional ballads on this subject, and plays by Tirso de Molina and Calderón. "The gypsies and all the Andalusian people sing the ballad of Thamar and Amnon, calling Thamar *Altas Mares* ("high seas")" (*DS* 122). Lines 23–24: The dove is associated with Venus; Góngora calls it "lascivious bird of the Cyprian goddess" (García-Posada, 213). 64: Elsewhere Lorca speaks of the "needling" sound of the flute (e.g., *CP* 595). 68: Allusion to the deflowering of Thamar, seen as a gypsy rite. Lines 73–74 have a distinctly vulgar tone: Lorca is imitating the *romances de ciego*, the lurid ballads about crimes, sung by blind men in public squares. Salvador Dalí, who wrote Lorca a letter sharply criticizing *The Gypsy Ballads* (see *Poet in New York*, xiv), found this poem "the best of the lot . . . chunks of incest" (Santos Torroella, 88). 80: The torn tunics are "a conventional symbol of Jewish mourning" (Harris, 81).

Poeta en Nueva York / Poet in New York

Begun during Lorca's visit to New York, Vermont, and Cuba (June 1929–March 1930), a trip undertaken for the purpose of studying English at Columbia University. Published in 1940, four years after Lorca's death. There were two "first" editions: a bilingual one, with translations by Rolfe Humphries, published by W. W. Norton & Co. (New York) on May 1, 1940; and an edition in Spanish brought out by Lorca's friend, the writer José Bergamín, at Editorial Séneca, Mexico, approximately one month later. Both the manuscript used by Bergamín and all but a few pages of the typescript followed by Humphries are lost. For the detailed textual history of this book, see *PNY*, 259–76. In a series of letters to his family (*PNY*, 201–56), Lorca describes his life in America and alludes to the writing of some of these poems. A lecture-reading, given for the first time in 1932 (*PNY*, 183–98), presents the book autobiographically as the narration of a spiritual voyage. Until mid-1933, Lorca considered dividing these poems into two separate books. One, entitled *Poeta en Nueva York*, and illustrated with photographs and drawings, would have contained the more clearly autobiographical and anecdotal poems, as well as poems of social protest like "Dance of Death." The other collection, *Tierra y luna* (*Earth and Moon*), would have had a more rural setting (inspired by the trip to Vermont) and would have contained more metaphysical poems about love and death (see *PNY* 261–62). The text followed here is from *PNY*.

Vuelta de paseo / After a Walk. Unpublished during Lorca's lifetime.

La aurora / Dawn. Unpublished during Lorca's lifetime. In the manuscript, Lorca has rejected two titles: "Obrero parado" ("Unemployed Worker") and "Amanecer" ("Daybreak").

El rey de Harlem / The King of Harlem. First published in *Los cuatro vientos* (Madrid) in February 1933 as "Oda al Rey de Harlem." Lorca, who visited Harlem frequently during his stay at Columbia University, and who must have discussed racism and miscegenation with his friend the African-American novelist Nella Larsen, remarks in his 1932 lecture that he wanted "to write *the* poem of the black race in North America, and to show the pain the blacks feel to be black in a contrary world. They are slaves of all the white man's inventions and machines . . . And yet any visitor can easily see that . . . they long to be a nation." He characterizes this poem as capturing "the spirit of the black race, a cry of encouragement to those who tremble and search, cautiously and clumsily, for the flesh of the white woman" (*PNY*, 187–89).

Danza de la muerte / Dance of Death. First published in *Revista de Avance* (Havana) in April 1930. Lorca was on Wall Street the very day—October 24, 1929—that the stock market collapsed, and describes that "inferno," which modified his vision of the United States, in a letter to his parents, as well as in his lecture-reading of *PNY*. In the poem, he says, he has imagined "the typical African mask, death which is truly dead, without angels or 'Resurrexit'; death totally alien to the spirit, barbarous and primitive as the United States, a country which has never fought, and never will fight, for heaven" (*PNY* 190).

Paisaje de la multitud que vomita / Landscape of a Vomiting Multitude. Inspired by a trip to Coney Island, probably on Sunday, July 4, 1929. Published in *Poesía* (Buenos Aires) in November 1933 and in *Noreste* (Zaragoza) in 1935. The earliest extant manuscript is dated December 29, 1929. In a fine analysis, C. Brian Morris (50) points out: "The complexity, the gravity and the physiological directness of the poem offer a disturbing contrast to the transparency, even naivety, of the impressions of his visit [Lorca] recorded in a letter to his parents" (for the letter, see *PNY*, 209–11). A third account is given in the lecture-reading: "Coney Island is a great fair attended on Sundays in the summer by more than a million people. They drink, shout, eat, wallow, and leave the ocean strewn with newspapers and the streets covered with tin cans, cigarette butts, bites of food, and shoes with broken heels. On its way home from the fair, the crowd sings and vomits in groups of a hundred over the railings of the boardwalk. In groups of a thousand it urinates in the corners, on abandoned boats, or on the monument to Garibaldi or to the unknown soldier. You cannot imagine the loneliness a Spaniard feels there, especially an Andalusian . . ." (*PNY* 191).

Ciudad sin sueño / Sleepless City. Published in Gerardo Diego's anthology of 1932. The manuscript is dated October 9, 1929, and bears the title (crossed out by Lorca) "Vigilia" ("Vigil").

Poema doble del Lago Eden / Double Poem of Lake Eden. First published in *Poesía* (Buenos Aires) in November 1933. The epigraph is from the Second Eclogue of the Spanish Renaissance poet Garcilaso de la Vega. The poem was inspired by Lorca's visit to his friend Philip Cummings in Eden Mills, northern Vermont, where the Cummings family had a summer cabin: an atmosphere that filled Lorca with nostalgia, reminding him of the rural surroundings of his Andalusian childhood. The words "Double Poem" may be an allusion to the reflection of the woodlands in the unmoving surface of the lake. In a letter to his parents from Eden Mills, Lorca writes: "The ferns, toadstools and moss come spilling down from the mountains to the lake, and the birds (very few of them) sing delicately and distantly above the tangled thickets of wild raspberries. It is cold, and the water is dark and leaden. It is impossible to distinguish the reflection from the things reflected, and at night we see and speak to one another by the light of oil lamps . . . The poignant romantic atmosphere . . . seems to chime with the sort of poetry I'm now writing" (C. Maurer, "A Letter from García Lorca," *Encounters*, 5–6 [1992], 13).

Vaca / Cow. Published in *Revista de Occidente* (Madrid) in January 1931.

Muerte / Death. Published in *Revista de Occidente* (Madrid) in January 1931.

Nueva York (Oficina y denuncia) / New York (Office and Denunciation). Published in *Revista de Occidente* (Madrid) in January 1931.

Oda a Walt Whitman / Ode to Walt Whitman. Published in an edition of fifty copies by Ediciones Alcancía, Mexico, in August 1933. A fragment was reprinted in Gerardo Diego's anthology of 1934. The manuscript is dated June 15, [1930], and must, therefore, have been finished on board the ship which took Lorca from Havana back to New York and thence to Cádiz.

Son de negros en Cuba / Blacks Dancing to Cuban Rhythms. Written in Havana, this *son* (an Afro-Cuban chant) was first published in *Musicalia* (Havana) in April or May 1930. The poem alludes to a rail trip which Lorca took to Santiago de Cuba. The images in lines 12–16 refer to the cigar boxes Lorca had seen as a child: thus Romeo and Juliet, the blond hair of Fonseca, the paper sea and silver coins on the lids. Two of the labels are reproduced in Auclair, p. 216.

Diván del Tamarit / The Tamarit Divan

Written 1931–34. Five poems were written April 4–5, 1934, aboard the *Conte Biancamano* as Lorca returned to Spain from Buenos Aires. The *Diván* was revised and finished by September of that year. Published posthumously in 1940 in a special issue of *Revista Hispánica Moderna*, Columbia University. The book was to have been published by the University of Granada, and the page proofs had already been pulled when the project was interrupted, probably by the outbreak of the Civil War in 1936.

The Spanish text follows the critical edition of Andrew A. Anderson. For a detailed and helpful commentary, see Anderson, *Lorca's Late Poetry*.

In a prologue written for the Granada edition, the Arabist Emilio García Gómez explains: "In Arabic the word *qasida* refers to a fairly long poem of a certain internal architecture (the details are not important here), with a single rhyme. The *ghazal*—employed principally in Persian lyric poetry—is a short poem, preferably with an erotic theme . . . with more than four verses and less than 15. *Diván* is the poet's collected verse, generally arranged in the alphabetical order of the rhymes" (Anderson, 183–84). Lorca's interest in Oriental poetry dates from his early youth: in his 1922 lecture on *cante jondo*, he had pondered the similarities between Andalusian folk music and "the magnificent verses of Arabian and Persian poets" (*DS* 36). His main sources of knowledge were two anthologies: *Poesías asiáticas*, ed. and tr. Gaspar María de Nava, Conde de Noroña (1833), and *Poemas arábigo-andaluces*, tr. and ed. by Emilio García Gómez (1930). For an excellent translation of the latter, see Cola Franzen, *Poems of Arab Andalusia*, 1989.

The "Tamarit" was a *huerta* (or small farm) "which belonged to the father of one of [Lorca's] favorite cousins . . . The word Tamarit means 'abundant in dates' in Arabic, and the poet used to say that he loved [this] *huerta*, with its wonderful views of the Sierra Nevada and the poplar groves of the Vega" (Gibson, 386). The title might also be translated *The Divan of the Tamarit*.

Gacela II. De la terrible presencia / Ghazal of the Terrible Presence. Probably written between

April and September 1934 (Anderson, 193); published in *Quaderns de Poesía* (Barcelona) in October 1935.

Gacela IV. Del amor que no se deja ver / Ghazel of Love That Hides from Sight. Lines 1–2 are from the lyrics of a flamenco piece, a *tanguillo:* "I want to live in Granada / only to hear / the bell of the Vela / when I go to sleep" (Anderson, 198). In his *Handbook for Travellers in Spain*, Richard Ford explains (I:303) that the "*torre de la Vela* is so called, because on this watchtower hangs a silver-tongued bell, which, struck by the warder at certain times, is the primitive clock that gives notice to irrigators below. It is heard on a still night even at Loja, 30 m. off, and tender and touching are the feelings which the silver sound awakens. This bell is also rung every January 2, the anniversary of the surrender of Granada; on that day the Alhambra is visited by crowds of peasantry. Few maidens pass by without striking the bell, which ensures a husband, and a good one in proportion as the noise made, which it need not be said is continuous and considerable. The fete is altogether most national and picturesque." The crown of vervain (*verbena*) in line 3 would be appropriate for a future husband (or wife). The rhyme *verbena / Cartagena* was suggested by a children's song alluded to also in *Book of Poems*: "Ay! Ay! Ay! / When will my love come? / Verbena, verbena, / garden of Cartagena" (Anderson, 199). Line 8 could also be translated: "I tore out my garden of Cartagena."

Gacela VI. De la raíz amarga / Ghazal of the Bitter Root. Published in *Héroe* (Madrid), 1933. Anderson (205) explains that the image of the "bitter root" occurs in the Epistle of St. Paul to the Hebrews 12:14–16: "Follow peace with all men . . . / / Looking diligently lest any man fail of the grace of God; lest any root of bitterness springing up trouble you, and thereby many be defiled . . ." Lines 6–7: García-Posada (*GP1* 63) asks: "What can these 'thousand windows' be but the stars?" 16: Or "your bitter root is biting."

Gacela VIII. De la muerte oscura / Ghazal of Dark Death. Published in *Floresta de Verso y Prosa* (Madrid) in February 1936.

Gacela X. De la huida / Ghazal of the Flight. Published in *Almanaque Literario* (Madrid), January 1935.

Casida II. Del llanto / Qasida of the Weeping. Published in Gerardo Diego's anthology of 1934.

Casida III. De los ramos / Qasida of the Branches. In his lecture on *duende* Lorca had written of artistic inspiration: "The duende does not come at all unless he sees that death is possible. The duende must know beforehand that he can serenade death's house and rock those branches we all wear, branches that do not have, will never have, any consolation" (*DS*, 49, 50). Lines 14–15: Literally: "Seated with the water on their knees / two valleys were waiting for Autumn."

Casida VI. De la mano imposible / Qasida of the Impossible Hand. Ms. dated April 4, 1934. The image of the hand occurs in two other compositions of the same period. In his "Elegy" for the painter María Blanchard, who was physically deformed, Lorca writes: "No one caressed her monstrous waist, except that great hand, just unnailed from the cross and still spurting blood. This was the arm that . . . helped her in terrible 'childbirth' [i.e., death] when the huge dove of her soul could hardly squeeze through her sunken mouth" (*DS* 6). In *Once Five Years Pass*, the hand comes onstage to guide a dead child to the other world. Line 16: Cf. the final line of *Lament for Ignacio Sánchez Mejías*.

Casida VII. De la rosa / Qasida of the Rose. In his lecture on Góngora, Lorca writes: "The greatness of a poem does not depend on the magnitude of its theme . . . [T]he form and fragrance of just one rose can be made to render an impression of infinity" (*DS*, 69).

Casida IX. De las palomas oscuras / Qasida of the Dark Doves. Published in *Héroe* (Madrid) in 1932, in *La Nación* (Buenos Aires) in October 1933, and in *Primeras canciones* (*First Songs*), 1936. The *qasida* contains reminiscences of at least two folk songs. Daniel Devoto (*Intro-*

ducción, 114) has written that lines 3–4 recall "De tu cara sale el sol, / de tu garganta la luna; / morenas he visto yo; / pero como tú, ninguna" (The sun shines from your face, / from your throat, the moon; / I have seen dark women, / but none like you). Brenan (119) quotes and translates a traditional song from Granada province: "Pajarito de la nieve, / dime, ¿dónde tienes el nido? / Lo tengo en un pino verde / en una rama escondido" (Little bird of snow, / Tell me where have you built your nest? / I have made it in a green pine tree / on a safely hidden branch." See also Fuentes Vázquez, p. 193.

Seis poemas galegos / Six Galician Poems

Written 1932–34. Published in Santiago de Compostela by Editorial Nós toward the end of 1935. Lorca traveled on four occasions—first (1916) as a student and years later as lecturer and as director of the amateur theater troupe La Barraca—to Galicia, the rainy, hilly farming region that forms the northwestern angle of the Iberian Peninsula. Home of an important school of lyric poetry in the fourteenth century (the so-called Galician–Portuguese lyric), Galicia enjoyed a literary renaissance in the nineteenth and early twentieth centuries.

How these poems came to be "produced" in Galician is a matter of some dispute. Andrew Anderson, whose critical edition is followed here, argues convincingly that they were "composed originally, in written or oral form, in Castilian or defective Galician. Thereafter, they were translated or copied out, certainly with linguistic and possibly also aesthetic corrections by [Lorca's close friend] Ernesto Guerra da Cal and possibly another. Finally, they were transcribed again with further orthographic, linguistic, and aesthetic revisions by [the noted Galician author] Eduardo Blanco Amor. The received text is the result of an accretion of several redactions and versions, and certainly not all of these were supervised, corrected, or directly checked and approved by Lorca himself" ("Who Wrote *Seis poemas galegos* . . . ?" 139). For a detailed commentary, see Anderson, *Lorca's Late Poetry*.

Madrigal â cibdá de Santiago / Madrigal to the City of Santiago. Published at least seven times during Lorca's lifetime.

Noiturnio do adoescente morto / Nocturne of the Drowned Youth. Line 15: The image is from Góngora; Lorca had admired lines 417–18 of the *First Solitude*, where the West "draws round the Sun, on the blue couch of the sea, / turquoise curtains." Lorca took these curtains to refer to the wind (*DS*, 66). 16: On the expression "water-oxen," see Lorca's lecture on Góngora (*DS*, 60).

Llanto por Ignacio Sánchez Mejías / Lament for Ignacio Sánchez Mejías

Written 1934, published 1935 by Cruz y Raya, Madrid. The *Lament* commemorates Lorca's friend the bullfighter Ignacio Sánchez Mejías (Seville, 1891–Madrid, 1934), who was gored in a provincial ring at Manzanares and died two days later of gangrene poisoning, on August 13, 1934. Sánchez Mejías had retired from the ring in 1927 to pursue a career as a playwright and to manage the dancer Encarnación López Júlvez, La Argentinita, to whom the poem is dedicated. His return to the ring in 1934, at age forty-three, surprised and dismayed his friends. A connoisseur of poetry and of *cante jondo* (the poet Jorge Guillén called him one of the most lucid and intelligent people he had ever met), Sánchez Mejías had invited Lorca, Guillén, and other writers to Seville in December 1927 to celebrate the three hundredth anniversary of the death of Góngora. Of Sánchez Mejías's death Lorca remarked to a friend: "It is like my own death, an apprenticeship for my own death. I feel an astonishing sense of calm . . . There are moments when I see the dead Ignacio so vividly that I can imagine his body, destroyed, pulled apart by the worms and the brambles, and I find only a silence which is not nothingness, but mystery" (Auclair, 28–29).

The *Llanto* (the title, from the Latin *planctus*, suggests a "lament" or "lamentation" more visceral and intense than an "elegy") was composed in October 1934 and published in a small edition (two thousand copies) by the poet's friend the writer José Bergamín (publisher of *Poet in New York*) at Cruz y Raya, Madrid, in April of the following year. The Spanish text reproduced here is from the annotated critical edition of Andrew A. Anderson.

1. *La cogida y la muerte / The Goring and the Death.* In the *Llanto*, the poet officiates over a liturgical form (with elements of the Holy Mass and of the litany) of his own invention. Of section 1, Francisco García Lorca writes: "I believe that this is the first time in the history of Spanish meter that the [hendecasyllabic] line, of learned, Renaissance tradition, is joined to the older octosyllable" (*Federico y su mundo*, 207). Line 5: Quicklime was used as a disinfectant in the infirmaries of bullrings (García-Posada, *Primer Romancero*, 223) and was often used at burial (Anderson, 285). 15: Sánchez Mejías was deeply gored in the right thigh; cf. 43, where the horn has left a wound in the shape of a lily. 23: Presumably the bull is rejoicing in his triumph; Lorca's expression recalls the latin, *sursum corda* ("Lift up your hearts"), from the Mass. 43: Anderson (1986) believes Lorca may also be alluding to Adonis, who died after being wounded in the groin by the tusks of a boar. On the cult of Adonis in Roman Spain, see Josephs, 108 ff. 47: José Bergamín, who was with Sánchez Mejías in the infirmary at Manzanares, writes that "the little room . . . had a tiny barred window, like a jail cell, which barely let in the dusty, burning air on that hottest of August afternoons. I opened the shutters from time to time; and outside the window there was always a sunburnt peasant face asking the same anxious question: 'Has he died yet?' " (García-Posada, *Primer Romancero*, 225).

2. *La sangre derramada / The Spilled Blood.* Lines 58–61: "The moon—'wide open': either at the full or brightly gleaming—is like a horse amidst the quiet clouds. In what sense? Probably in that the clouds are scudding before the wind and so creating the common optical illusion that while *they* are still the moon is racing" (Jones and Scanlon, 101). 67: An allusion to the moon, associated, in mythology and in primitive religious beliefs, with the bull and the cow. In a prose poem on the bullfight, Lorca had written: "Man makes his sacrifice to the fighting bull, the offspring of the sweet cow, goddess of the dawn, who lives in the dew. The enormous sky-cow, a mother continuously shedding her blood, asks that man be sacrificed, and, naturally, her wish is granted" (Anderson, 291). Lorca's allusion to the dawn and the dew makes it clear he is referring, in the prose passage just quoted, to the Sevillian "Virgin of the Dew," celebrated in a pilgrimage to the edge of the great marsh of the Guadalquivir delta at Pentecost (see Josephs, 120). On the moon's "absorption" of blood, see Álvarez de Miranda (90). 71: Crudely carved granite figures of bulls, from the second century B.C., in what is now the province of Ávila. 77: An allusion to Calvary. The term "gradas" (steps) would be appropriate for those leading to the altar. 91: The "bloodthirsty masses" are reminiscent of those who call for the crucifixion of Christ in Luke 23:13–25 (Anderson). Christological imagery too obvious to require annotation is found throughout the *Llanto*. 96: The "terrible mothers" (or "terrifying mothers") are probably the Fates, the Moirai or Parcae, whose influence is exerted at birth. Martínez Nadal (*Cuatro lecciones*, 82) believes Lorca is remembering *Faust*, Part II, Act I, Scene V. 100: The zodiacal constellation Taurus? The *niebla* (mist) would be the white starshine (cf. *Night*), and the *mayorales* (ranchers) probably allude to the constellation Boötes, called *Boyero* (ox driver) in Spanish. 110: The Roman Baetica. The emperor Trajan was born at Italica, near modern Seville. 114–21: lines reminiscent of Jorge Manrique's "Verses on the Death of His Father" (Cohen, 48–75), a poem Lorca emulates throughout the *Llanto*. 127: The *marismas* (salt marshes) near the mouth of the Guadalquivir, in the

Andalusian province of Huelva, produce some of the finest fighting bulls in Spain. 133: "The Milky Way, near which Ignacio's blood comes to rest, as if—like other heroes who die a violent death (Hercules, Orion)—he finds his place in the heavens as a constellation" (Jones and Scanlon, 105). 141: The swallows are thought to have removed the crown of thorns and to have drunk up the blood of the crucified Christ: both legends are alluded to in *saetas* sung during Holy Week processions (Aguilar y Tejera, 125). Line 144 alludes to the monstrance where the consecrated Host is displayed for veneration.

3. *Cuerpo presente / Presence of the Body.* Lorca's meter changes to the fourteen-syllable alexandrines he had used in his *Odes* and, very often, in *Book of Poems.* The title also signifies the laying out of a cadaver, or lying in state. Lorca told his friend the painter José Caballero that he was thinking in this section not only of the slabs found in morgues but also of "the long, rough slab of stone that serves as an operating table in the infirmaries of the oldest bullrings" (Auclair, 26). 159: The epithet is reminiscent of the Spanish epic *Poem of the Cid.* Anderson observes that lines 172–73 can also be taken as an imperative: "Here let no one sing . . ." 188–89: Literally: ". . . the moon, which imitates, when she is a girl, a motionless, suffering bull" (an image, in the manner of Góngora, of the bright, slender "horns" of the moon).

4. *Alma ausente / Absence of the Soul.* The title plays antithetically upon that of the preceding section. 211: Literally: "on a heap of extinguished [snuffed-out] dogs."

[*Sonnets of Dark Love*]

García Lorca wrote many sonnets between 1917 and 1936 and, in an interview near the end of his life, mentions a book entitled *Sonetos* as among four he is preparing for publication. Days before he was assassinated, while in hiding at the home of fellow poet Luis Rosales, Lorca was working on a collection entitled *Jardín de los sonetos (Garden of Sonnets).* No table of contents has survived, but the book would probably have included eleven love sonnets written in 1935, inspired by Rafael Rodríguez Rapún, a young engineering student with whom Lorca had fallen in love in 1933. These eleven poems constitute a cycle to which Lorca referred, in conversations with friends, as the *Sonetos del amor oscuro (Sonnets of Dark Love).* Many of them remained unpublished in Spanish until December 1983, when they appeared in an anonymous limited edition, unauthorized by the poet's family (for further information, see *CP,* 849–52; Hernández, "Jardín . . ."; Eisenberg; and Infantes, 71–82). An "authorized" version of these texts was published in a special supplement to the Madrid daily *A.B.C.* on March 17, 1984.

The text given here is taken from Andrew Anderson's edition and commentary, based on the mss. in the AFGL (San Francisco: Cadmus Editions, in press). For a more detailed commentary, see Anderson, *Lorca's Late Poetry,* 275–399.

Soneto de la guirnalda de rosas / Sonnet of the Garland of Roses. The Anderson edition explains a web of allusion to the myth of Venus and Adonis: "Venus was accidentally struck by one of Cupid's darts and became infatuated with Adonis. Adonis, on the other hand, was not so overwhelmed by Venus' charms as to forgo the pleasure of the hunt, but one day, while after a wild boar, he was fatally wounded by its tusks in the thigh or groin [cf. line 9] and bled to death [cf. line 11]. As Venus hastened to his side, a rose thorn pierced her foot and the drops of her blood stained the previously white roses red . . . [F]rom the drops of blood which fell to the ground from Adonis' mortal wound sprang red anemones [cf. line 7]." Adonis personifies, "in his annual death and resurrection, the yearly cycle of decay and revival of life, especially vegetable life." Line 7: Lorca often associates the anemone with sleep and dream (it is the flower of Morpheus). John K. Walsh suggests: "The breaking of delicate reeds and rivulets in line 10 might refer to interior veins broken in furious lovemaking. In the poem, then, the poet would be placing himself in a passive role."

Soneto de la dulce queja / Sonnet of the Sweet Complaint. Spanish text from Hernández, *Antología*, 125. 11: Literally, "if I am the dog of your dominion."

Llagas de amor / Wounds of Love. Title: Anderson observes that the word *llagas* (rather than *heridas*) brings to mind the wounds of Christ. Lines 1–9: "All the items enumerated . . . are either causes of the wounds or expressions of the effects the wounds have" (Anderson edition). The definition of love through an enumeration of its symptoms and effects is common in the sixteenth- and seventeenth-century Spanish and Portuguese sonnet. 14: Or "passion of bitter knowledge."

El poeta pide a su amor que le escriba / The Poet Asks His Love to Write Him. 4: Lorca alludes to a well-known poem glossed by both St. Theresa of Avila and St. John of the Cross: "Vivo sin vivir en mí, / y tan alta vida espero / que muero porque no muero" (I live without living in myself / and hope for such a high life / that I am dying of not dying). 4: Regarding the "lifeless" (literally, "inert") stone, cf. the opening of section 3 of the *Lament for Ignacio Sánchez Mejías*. 13–14: The expression "noche serena" recalls verse 189 of St. John's *Spiritual Canticle*. 14: Allusion to the *noche oscura del alma*, or "dark night of the soul," of St. John of the Cross: a state preliminary to union with God, in which the senses are blind to what surrounds them. See "Song of the Ascent of Mount Carmel": "In a dark night, inflamed by love's desires—oh, lucky chance—I went out unnoticed, all being then quiet in my house" (Cohen, 218).

Ay voz secreta del amor oscuro . . . / O secret voice of dark love . . . The series of exclamations opening this sonnet recalls St. John of the Cross's "Song of the Living Flame of Love" (Cohen, 222–23): "Oh, gentle cautery! oh, delicate wound! oh, soft hand! oh, gentle touch that tastes of eternal life . . . !" Line 8: As happens often in Lorca's poetry, *lirio* might mean either iris or lily. 9: Lorca's habit of not using accent marks has led to two readings of the ms.: (1) *Huye de mi . . . voz* (Flee from my . . . voice) and (2) *Huye de mí, . . . voz* (Flee from me, . . . voice). See Hernández, "Jardín . . . ," 196–97, who prefers the first of these readings. I understand the voice mentioned in line 9 to be the same as the one in line 1. 13: Anderson notes that "the other senses of *duelo*—mourning and duel—may well be relevant here."

El amor duerme en el pecho del poeta / His Beloved Sleeps on the Breast of the Poet. The title alludes to a stanza from St. John of the Cross's "Dark Night of the Soul" wherein the soul remarks of Christ: "En mi pecho florido, / que entero para él sólo se guardaba, / allí quedó dormido" (In my burgeoning heart, which kept itself wholly for Him alone, there He fell asleep" (Cohen, 220–21). Line 2: Anderson notes that the adjective *dormido* is "one of the very rare instances in these sonnets where the gender of the past participle in Spanish defines the beloved as male." 9–11: An allusion to Christ's agony in the Garden of Gethsemane, where his disciples slept (cf. line 2) and where he was accosted by "a great multitude with swords and staves" (Mark 14:43).

Noche del amor insomne / Night of Sleepless Love. In lines 1 and 5 Lorca has created neologisms (*noche arriba, noche abajo*) that play on colloquial expressions like *calle arriba, calle abajo* (up the street, down the street), *monte arriba, monte abajo* (up or down the hill), *boca arriba, boca abajo* (face up, face down), etc. The sense of these lines can only be guessed at. Perhaps: The night face up . . . The night face down . . .

Poemas sueltos / Uncollected Poems

Cautiva / Captive. Undated. Published in *Primeras canciones*, 1936. Text from Hernández, 65.

Oda a Salvador Dalí / Ode to Salvador Dalí. From an unfinished book entitled *Odes*, which Lorca referred to in interviews and letters between 1928 and 1936. García-Posada (*GP2* 703) believes the book would have included *Ode to Salvador Dalí*, "Ode to the Most Holy Sacrament of the Altar" (*CP* 258–609), "Solitude (In Homage to Fray Luis de León)" (*CP* 594–97), and "Oda y burla de Sesostris y Sardanápalo" (Ode and Jest of Sesostris and Sardanapalus, devoted to an Assyrian king notorious for his effeminacy and corruption). The latter poem was never completed.

Ode to Salvador Dalí was begun in summer 1925, finished in March 1926, published in *Revista de Occidente* (Madrid) the following month. Lorca refers to this poem in a letter as "Didactic Ode to Salvador Dalí" (*E* I:149), a good description of its intent. He had met Dalí at the Residencia de Estudiantes in 1922 and had spent Holy Week of 1925 with the Dalí family in Cadaqués and Barcelona: his first taste of the cultural diversity and ebullience of Catalunya.

The reader should remember that the Dalí of 1925 and early 1926 was neither a Cubist nor the Surrealist of later years, but was at work on more or less "realistic" paintings in the spirit of what he called (borrowing a phrase from the Catalan writer Eugenio D'Ors) "Holy Objectivity": *Basket of Bread, Girl Sewing, Port of Cadaqués*, and the early portraits of his father and sister. To Lorca, his style, like that of Jorge Guillén and of Góngora (the lecture on the great Baroque poet was written around the same time), had come to symbolize an aesthetic of unsentimental clarity. "To me [Dalí] seems unique," the poet wrote several years later to the art critic Sebastià Gasch. "He possesses a *clarity* of judgment that is truly moving. He makes a mistake and it doesn't matter: *he is alive*. His razor-sharp intelligence combines with a disconcerting childishness in an astoundingly original, captivating way. What moves me most about him right now is his *delirious* yearning to construct (that is, to create) . . . Nothing more dramatic than this objectivity, this search for joy for its own sake. Remember that this has always been the Mediterranean canon. 'I believe in the Resurrection of the flesh,' says Rome. Dalí is the man who fights phantasms with a hatchet of gold" (*E* II:92). Line 3: For Lorca's negative judgments on Impressionism, see "Sketch de la nueva pintura" (A Sketch of the New Painting) (*OC* III:272–81). 6: Manuel de Falla praised Lorca for this image of Cubism (Maurer, "Epistolario," 264), less an allusion to the art of Dalí than to the spirit of modern painting. 9: Dalí wrote to Lorca in 1925: "There is nothing so marvelous as feet pressed to earth under the 'weight' of the body; more than in Poussin, in Egypt we find feet planted firmly on the ground . . . When I paint, I paint without shoes. I like to feel the earth very close to my 'two' feet" (Santos Torroella, 15). 16: Lorca uses the same phrase to evoke Cadaqués in a letter to Ana María Dalí, shortly after his visit in 1925: "I think of Cadaqués. To me it seems a perfect landscape, both present and eternal. The horizon rises up like a great aqueduct . . ." (*E* I:112). Dalí had told Lorca in 1925 of his concern for "the construction, the architecture of the landscape: I believe that painting is still a long way from Cézanne's ambition, 'faire du Poussin d'après nature' " (Santos Torroella, 13). 27: During his first visit to Dalí, Lorca writes to a friend: "Witches from the Pyrenees come down to beg the sirens for a little light. In this landscape I have heard, for the first time in my life, the true, classic shepherd's flute" (*E* I:110). 31: Handkerchiefs of farewell?

Line 39: With the advent of Cubism, "dark grays, white, sienna, tobacco, and other muted, austere colors . . . conquer the greens, reds, many-shaded yellows, and mauve-colored deliquescences" of the Impressionists. "At last the orgy of color has been put to an end" ("Sketch," *OC* III:275). 41: Hygiene—both literally and figuratively, as a defense against the "virus" of sentimentality—was one of Dalí's obsessions in his rebellion against bohemian, neo-Romantic visions of art. His "Manifest Groc" of 1928 would call for an "estricta asepsia espiritual." 44: Eutimio Martín (*Antología* 81) points out that in September

1926 Dalí had written to Lorca: "I have painted the whole afternoon: 7 waves, hard and cold as are the waves of the sea . . . tomorrow I will paint 7 more . . . How fondly I paint my windows open to the sea!" The fourteen parallel waves would suggest a sonnet. 49 ff: The first draft had read: "The current of time pools and orders itself / in the parallelograms dreamt by the centuries . . . / / You are afraid of flowers and the water of the river, / because they are fleeting and they pass like the breeze. / You love definite, exact matter, / indifferent to mysteries and deathly to the worm. / / (Your palette, timid as a foolish bird / pulses in your hands with the seven colors.)"

Line 71: Dalí writes to Lorca in 1925: "I am experimenting with the construction of the atmosphere, better said, the construction of the void; I am fascinated by the plasticity of empty spaces, a matter which never seems to have concerned anyone . . ." (Santos Torroella, 15). 90: Crossed out in the ms.: "I sing your beautiful struggle for Latin clarity" (see preliminary note). 93: Crossed out: "adorned with straight lines and without a single wound." The playing cards suggest harsh light without shadow, as in *The Dispute*. 93: Martín (*Antología* 83) observes that certain figures in the French deck of cards are shown with their hearts exposed. 98–101: Lorca censored himself in line 103; the first draft read: "el culo [the behind] of Theresa," alluding, perhaps, to a well-known canvas of Dalí's sister, Ana María, standing at a window. 105: Crossed out: "our friendship, radiant with heart and with laughter." The line means, literally: "our friendship painted like a game of snakes and ladders." *Oca* is played with dice, and the brightly colored game board shows geese, rivers, wells, etc. 107: An allusion to the Catalan flag (Martín, *Antología* 84). Its four red bars on a field of gold are said to have been traced by the fingers, bloodied in battle, of a Catalan conqueror.

Adán / Adam. Ms. dated "December 1, 1929. New York." Published in *Héroe* (Madrid) in 1932, in *Poesía* (Buenos Aires) in 1933 (with the dedication "For Pablo Neruda, surrounded by phantasms"), and again in the chapbook *Primeras canciones*, 1936. Spanish text from GP2 433. Line 2: The "newborn woman," obviously, is Eve. José Angel Valente (196) explains this sonnet in relation to the "non-germinative nature of homosexuality," a frequent theme in Lorca's poems and plays. 9: *Adán sueña*: "And the Lord God *caused a deep sleep to fall upon Adam, and he slept*; and he took out one of his ribs, and closed up the flesh instead thereof" (Genesis 2:21).

Soneto / Sonnet. First draft dated "New York. 1929. December." Published in *Revista de Avance* (Havana) in April 1930, and, with variants, in *Cristal* (Pontevedra) in 1932. In the manuscript, line 2 reads: "en el musgo de un norte sin reflejo" (in the moss of an unreflecting north). Lines 9–11: Cf. Lorca's image of childhood in *Double Poem of Lake Eden*: "When all the roses spilled from my tongue . . ." 11: Literally, "the deserted taste of broom." 12–14: Cf. *Two Norms*. Spanish text from Anderson, *Antología poética*, 199, but I have followed García-Posada and others in substituting *rama* for *llama* in line 13.

Dos normas / Two Norms. Written March 1928, published in *Parábola* (Burgos) several months later with the dedication: "To the great poet Jorge Guillén." Another version (the one followed here) appeared posthumously in *Revista Hispánica Moderna* (New York), July–October 1940. Written in a metrical form, the *décima*, which Guillén had cultivated with much success. In the manuscript, the first norm begins with a sketch of the moon, and the second with a sketch of the sun (Martín, *FGL*, 77).

Tan, tan . . . / Knock, knock! . . . Written 1933? Lorca includes this poem in his lecture "How a City Sings from November to November." Based on a children's rhyme (Llorca, 16). Several versions of the rhyme and of Lorca's poem are studied by Hernández (1992) and Fuentes Vázquez, p. 159.

Pequeño poema infinito / Little Infinite Poem. Ms. dated January 10, 1930. Written in New

York. Spanish text from Hernández (*Manuscritos neoyorquinos*, 218–19). In the ms., the title "Pequeña narración china" (Little Chinese Tale) is crossed out.

Omega (Poema para muertos) / Omega (Poem for the Dead). Probably written summer 1931, when Lorca tells his friend Regino Sainz de la Maza: "I have written a book of poems, *Poems for the Dead*, one of the most intense that has ever come from my hand. I have been like a fountain, writing morning, noon and night. Sometimes I have run a fever, like the old Romantics, but without ever ceasing to feel the intense conscious joy of creation" (*E* II:142). Plans for this book were abandoned. *Omega* was first published in 1935 in the poetry magazine *1616* (London). Text from Martín, *Poeta en Nueva York*, 290.

Bibliography

Complete Works
Belamich, André, *Oeuvres complètes.* Vol. I. Paris: Gallimard (Pléiade), 1981.

García-Posada, Miguel. *Poesía, 1.* 2nd ed. Madrid: Akal, 1982. (1st ed., 1980.)

————. *Poesía, 2.* Madrid: Akal, 1982.

Hernández, Mario. *Obras.* Madrid: Alianza, 1981–present. See under individual works.

Hoyo, Arturo del. *Obras completas.* 3 vols. Madrid: Aguilar, 1986.

Anthologies
Anderson, Andrew A. *Antología poética.* Granada: Edición del Cincuentenario, 1986.

Hernández, Mario. *Antología poética.* Madrid: Ediciones Alce, 1978.

Martín, Eutimio. *Antología comentada, I, Poesía.* Madrid: Ediciones de la Torre, 1988.

Letters
Maurer, Christopher. *Epistolario.* 2 vols. Madrid: Alianza Editorial, 1983.

Lectures
Maurer, Christopher. *Conferencias.* 2 vols. Madrid: Alianza Editorial, 1984.

Drawings
Hernández, Mario. *Dibujos.* Madrid: Museo Español del Arte Contemporáneo, 1986.

————. *Line of Light and Shadow: The Drawings of Federico García Lorca.* Christopher Maurer, tr. Durham: Duke University Press, 1991.

Book of Poems
Gibson, Ian. *Libro de poemas (1921).* Barcelona: Ariel, 1982.

Hernández, Mario. *Libro de poemas [1918–1920].* Madrid: Alianza Editorial, 1984.

Massoli, Marco. *F.G.L. e il suo "Libro de poemas": un poeta alla ricerca della propria voce.* (Introduzione. Testo critico. Commento.) Pisa: C. Curso Editore, 1982.

Poem of the Deep Song
De Paepe, Christian. *Poema del cante jondo.* Madrid: Espasa-Calpe, 1986.

Hernández, Mario. *Poema del cante jondo 1921 seguido de tres textos teóricos de F.G.L. y Manuel de Falla.* Madrid: Alianza Editorial, 1982.

Josephs, Allen, and Juan Caballero. *Poema del cante jondo. Romancero gitano.* 7th ed. Madrid: Cátedra, 1981.

Suites
Belamich, André. *Suites.* Barcelona: Ariel, 1983.

Hernández, Mario. *Primeras canciones. Seis poemas galegos. Poemas sueltos. Colección de canciones populares antiguas.* Madrid: Alianza Editorial, 1981.

Rogers, Paul. *Surtidores. Algunas poesías inéditas de Federico García Lorca.* Mexico: Editorial Patria, 1957.

Songs
Hernández, Mario. *Canciones 1921–1924.* Madrid: Alianza Editorial, 1982.

Menarini, Piero. *Canciones y primeras canciones.* Madrid: Espasa-Calpe, 1986.

Gypsy Ballads

García–Posada, Miguel. *Primer romancero gitano. Llanto por Ignacio Sánchez Mejias. Romance de la corrida de toros en Ronda y otros textos taurinos.* Madrid: Castalia, 1988.

Harris, Derek. *Romancero Gitano.* London: Grant & Cutler Ltd., 1991.

Hernández, Mario. *Primer romancero gitano 1924–1927.* 2nd ed. Madrid: Alianza Editorial, 1983.

Josephs, Allen, and Juan Caballero. See *Poem of the Deep Song.*

Poet in New York

Bergamín, José. *Poeta en Nueva York.* México: Editorial Séneca, 1940.

Hernández, Mario. *Manuscritos neoyorquinos. Poeta en Nueva York y otras hojas y poemas.* Madrid: Tabapress / Fundación Federico García Lorca, 1990.

———. *Poeta en Nueva York.* Madrid: Fundación Banco Exterior, 1987.

Martín, Eutimio. *Poeta en Nueva York. Tierra y luna.* Barcelona: Ariel, 1981.

The Tamarit Divan, Six Galician Poems, Lament for Ignacio Sánchez Mejías

Anderson, Andrew A. *Diván del Tamarit. Seis poemas galegos. Llanto por Ignacio Sánchez Mejías. Poemas sueltos.* Madrid: Espasa-Calpe, 1988.

Hernández, Mario. *Diván del Tamarit. Llanto por Ignacio Sánchez Mejías. Sonetos.* Madrid: Alianza, 1981.

Sonnets of Dark Love

Anderson, Andrew A. *Sonnets.* San Francisco: Cadmus Editions, in press.

Juvenilia

De Paepe, Christian. *Poesía inédita de la juventud.* Madrid: Cátedra, 1994.

Maurer, Christopher. *Prosa inédita de la juventud.* Madrid: Cátedra, 1994.

Soria Olmedo, Andrés. *Teatro inédito de la juventud.* Madrid: Cátedra, 1994.

Bibliography

Anderson, Andrew A. Ongoing bibliography in *FGL. Boletín de la Fundación Federico García Lorca*, 1987–present.

Colecchia, Francesca. *García Lorca. An Annotated Primary Bibliography.* New York and London: Garland Publishing, 1982.

Selected Poetry, Drama, and Prose in English

Bauer, Carlos, tr. *Ode to Walt Whitman & Other Poems.* San Francisco: City Lights Books, 1988.

———, tr. *Poem of the Deep Song / Poema del cante jondo.* San Francisco: City Lights Books, 1987.

———, tr. *The Public and Play Without a Title: Two Posthumous Plays.* New York: New Directions, 1983.

Belitt, Ben. *The Audience* (excerpts). *Evergreen Review* II, 6 (Autumn, 1958), 93–107.

———. "Fourteen Lyrics." *Quarterly Review of Literature* IV, 1, 5–13.

———. *Poet in New York.* New York: Grove Press, 1955.

Blackburn, Paul, tr. *Blackburn / Lorca.* Momo's Press, 1979.

———. "Ode to Salvador Dalí." *Caterpillar* 5 (1968), 9–13.

Bly, Robert. Lorca and Jiménez. *Selected Poems.* Boston: Beacon Press, 1973.

Brilliant, Alan. *Tree of Song.* Santa Barbara: Unicorn Press, 1971.

Campbell, Roy. *Lament for the Death of a Matador*. Seville, 1954.

———. *Lorca. An Appreciation of His Poetry*. New Haven: Yale University Press, 1952.

Cobb, Carl W. *Lorca's Romancero gitano: A Ballad Translation and Critical Study*. Jackson: University Press of Mississippi, 1983.

Cummings, Philip. Daniel Eisenberg, ed. *Songs*. Pittsburgh: Duquesne University Press, 1976.

Dewell, Michael, and Carmen Zapata, trs. *Three Plays: Blood Wedding, Yerma, and The House of Bernarda Alba*. New York: Farrar Straus and Giroux, 1993.

Edwards, Gwynne. *Plays*. London: Methuen, 1990.

———, and Peter Luke. *Three Plays. Blood Wedding, Doña Rosita the Spinster, Yerma*. London: Methuen, 1987.

———, and Henry Livings. *Plays: Three. Mariana Pineda, The Public, Play Without a Title*. London: Methuen, 1994.

Forman, Sandra, and Allen Josephs. *Only Mystery: Federico García Lorca's Poetry in Word and Image*. Gainesville: University Press of Florida, 1992.

García Lorca, Francisco, and Donald M. Allen, eds. *The Selected Poems*. New York: New Directions, 1961.

Gershator, David, ed. and tr. *Selected Letters*. New York: New Directions, 1983.

Graham-Lujan, James, and Richard L. O'Connell, tr. *Five Plays: Comedies and Tragicomedies*. New York: New Directions, 1963.

———. Prologue by Francisco García Lorca. *Three Tragedies: Blood Wedding, Yerma, Bernarda Alba*. New York: New Directions, 1947.

Havard, Robert G. *Mariana Pineda*. Warminster: Arits and Phillips, 1987.

———. *Gypsy Ballads*. Warminster: Aris and Phillips, 1990.

Heller, Michael. "Deep Song: Some Provocations." Ironwood, #21, pp. 27–34.

Honig, Edwin. *Four Puppet Plays. Divan Poems and Other Poems. Prose Poems and Dramatic Pieces. Play Without a Title*. Riverdale on Hudson: The Sheep Meadow Press, 1990.

———. *García Lorca*. New York: New Directions, 1963.

Hughes, Langston, tr. *Gypsy Ballads. The Beloit Poetry Journal* II, Chapbook no. 1 (Fall, 1951).

Humphries, Rolfe, tr. *The Gypsy Ballads of Federico García Lorca*. Bloomington and London: Indiana University Press of America, 1953.

———. *The Poet in New York and Other Poems of Federico García Lorca*. New York: W. W. Norton, 1940.

Johnston, David. *Blood Wedding*. London: Hodder and Stoughton Educational, 1989.

———. *The Love of Don Perlimplín for Belisa in the Garden and Yerma*. London: Hodder and Stoughton, 1990.

Kirkland, Will, tr. *The Cricket Sings. Poems and Songs for Children*. New York: New Directions, 1980.

Klibbe, Lawrence. *Impressions and Landscapes*. Lanham, Md.: University Press of America, 1987.

Lewis, Richard. *Still Waters of the Air. Poems by Three Modern Spanish Poets*. New York: Dial Press, 1970.

Lloyd, A. L. *Lament for the Death of a Bullfighter, and Other Poems in the Original Spanish with English Translation*. New York: Oxford University Press, 1937. Reprint, Westport: Greenwood Pres, 1977.

Logan, William Bryant, and Angel Gil Orrios. *Once Five Years Pass and Other Dramatic Works*. Barrytown, N.Y.: Station Hill Press, 1989.

Loughran, David K. *Gypsy Ballads and Songs*. Hanover: Ediciones del Norte, 1994.

———. *Sonnets of Love Forbidden*. Missoula, Mont.: Windsong Press, 1989.

Maurer, Christopher. *Deep Song and Other Prose*. New York: New Directions, 1980.
———. *How a City Sings from November to November*. San Francisco: Cadmus Editions, 1984.
———. "Poem of the Bull" and "Correspondence Federico García Lorca–Salvador Dalí," *Northwest Review* (Eugene, Oregon), XXX, 1 (1992) 53–64.
———. "A Letter from García Lorca." *Encounters* 5–6 (1991), 13–15.
Raine, Kathleen, and Rafael Martínez Nadal. *Sun and Shadow*. London: Enitharmon, 1972.
Rexroth, Kenneth. *Thirty Spanish Poems of Love and Exile*. San Francisco: City Lights Books, 1968.
Sawyer-Lauçanno, Christopher. *Barbarous Nights. Legends and Plays from the Little Theater*. San Francisco: City Lights Books, 1991.
Simon, Greg, and Steven F. White. *Poet in New York*. New York: Farrar, Straus and Giroux, 1988.
Simont, Marc. *The Lieutenant Colonel and the Gypsy*. New York: Doubleday, 1971.
Skelton, Robin. *Songs and Ballads*. Montreal: Guernica, 1992.
Spender, Stephen, and J. L. Gili, tr. *Poems*. London: Dolphin, 1939.
Spicer, Jack. *After Lorca* (1957). Reprinted in *The Collected Books of Jack Spicer*, Robin Blaser, ed. Los Angeles: Black Sparrow Press, 1975.
Stafford, William, and Herbert Baird, "Quarrel." *Kenyon Review* 29 (1967), 662–63.
Wright, James. "Afternoon." *Sixties* 4 (1960), 18–19.
———. "Gacela of the Remembrance of Love." *Poetry* 96, 3 (June 1960), 151–52.

Other Works Cited

Aguilar y Tejera, Agustín. *Saetas populares*. Madrid: CIAP, 1930.
Alonso, Dámaso, and Carlos Bousoño. *Seis calas en la expresión literaria española (Prosa-Poesía-Teatro)*. Madrid: Gredos, 1963.
Alvarez de Miranda, Angel. *Obras*. Vol. II. Madrid: Ediciones Cultura Hispánica, 1959.
Anderson, Andrew A. "Who Wrote *Seis poemas galegos* and in What Language?" In C. Brian Morris, ed., *"Cuando yo me muera . . ." Essays in Memory of Federico García Lorca*. Lanham, Md.: Univesity Press of America, 1988. Pp. 129–46.
———. *Lorca's Late Poetry: A Critical Study*. Leeds: Francis Cairns, 1990.
Auclair, Marcelle. *Enfances et mort de García Lorca*. Paris: Seuil, 1968.
Barea, Arturo. *Lorca: The Poet and His People*. Ilsa Barea, tr. New York: Cooper Square Publishers, 1973.
Brenan, Gerald. *South from Granada*. New York: Octagon Books, 1976. (1st ed., 1957.)
Celaya, Gabriel. *La voz de los niños*. Barcelona: Editorial Laia, 1972.
Cohen, J. M. *The Penguin Book of Spanish Verse*. London: Penguin, 1988.
Cummins, J. G. *The Spanish Traditional Lyric*. New York: Pergamon Press, 1977.
Devoto, Daniel. *Introducción a "Diván del Tamarit" de Federico García Lorca*. Paris: Ediciones Hispanoamericanas, 1976.
———. "Lecturas de García Lorca." *Revue de Littérature Comparée*, XXXIII, 4 (October–December 1959), 518–28.
Diego, Gerardo. *Poesía española. Antología (Contemporáneos)*. Madrid: Signo, 1934. (1st ed., 1932.)
Eisenberg, Daniel. "Reaction to the Publication of the Sonetos del amor oscuro." *Bulletin of Hispanic Studies* LXV (1988), 261–71.
Espinosa, Aurelio M. *Cuentos populares españoles recogidos de la tradición oral de España*. Vol. I. Madrid: Consejo Superior de Investigaciones Científicas, 1946.
Fernández de los Ríos, Luis Beltrán. *La arquitectura del humo: Una reconstrucción del "Romancero gitano" de Federico García Lorca*. London: Tamesis Books, 1986.

Ford, Richard A. *A Handbook for Travelers in Spain*. 2 vols. 3rd ed. London: John Murray, 1855.

Forster, Jeremy C. "Aspects of Lorca's St. Christopher." *Bulletin of Hispanic Studies* XLIII (1966), 109–16.

Fuentes Vázquez, Tadea. *El folklore infantil en la obra de Federico García Lorca*. Granada: Universidad de Granada, 1991.

García Lorca, Francisco. *De Garcilaso a Lorca*. Claudio Guillén, ed. Madrid: Istmo, 1984.

———. *Federico y su mundo*. Mario Hernández, ed. 2nd ed. Madrid: Alianza, 1981.

———. *In the Green Morning: Memories of Federico*. Christopher Maurer, tr. New York: New Directions, 1986.

Gibson, Ian. *Federico García Lorca: A Life*. New York: Pantheon, 1989.

Guillén, Jorge. "Federico en persona." In Arturo del Hoyo, ed., *Obras completas*. Madrid: Aguilar, 1986. I:xvii–xxxiv.

Hernández, Mario. "Jardín deshecho: los 'sonetos' de García Lorca." *El Crotalón. Anuario de Filología Española* I (1984), 193–228.

———. "Federico García Lorca: rueda y juego de la tradición popular." *El legado cultural de España al siglo xxi. 2. La literatura: clásicos contemporáneos*. Madrid: Círculo de Lectores, 1992. Pp. 261–92.

Herrera, Fernando de. *Poesía castellana original completa*. Cristóbal Cuevas, ed. Madrid: Cátedra, 1985.

Infantes, Victor. "Lo 'oscuro' de los 'Sonetos del amor oscuro' de Federico García Lorca. In Gabriele Morelli, ed., *Federico García Lorca: Saggi critici nel cinquantenario della morte*. Fasano: Schena Editore, 1988. Pp. 59–88.

Jones, R. O., and G. M. Scanlon. "Ignacio Sánchez Mejías: The 'Mythic Hero.' " In Nigel Glendenning, ed., *Studies in Modern Spanish Literature and Art Presented to Helen F. Grant*. London: Tamesis Books, 1972. Pp. 97–108.

Josephs, Allen. *White Wall of Spain: The Mysteries of Andalusian Culture*. Ames: Iowa State University Press, 1983.

Juan de la Cruz. *Vida y Obras*. Crisógono de Jesús, Matías del Niño Jesús, and Lucinio Ruano, eds. 6th ed. Madrid: Biblioteca de Autores Cristianos, 1972.

Katz, Israel J. "Flamenco." In Stanley Sadie, ed., *The New Grove Dictionary of Music and Musicians*. Vol. VI. London: Macmillan, 1980. Pp. 625–30.

Llorca, Fernando. *Lo que cantan los niños*. Madrid: Editorial Llorca, n.d.

Loughran, David K. *Federico García Lorca: The Poetry of Limits*. London: Tamesis Books, 1978.

Mandestam, Nadezhda. *Hope Abandoned*. Max Hayward, tr. London: Collins and Harvill Press, 1974.

Martín, Eutimio. *Federico García Lorca, heterodoxo y mártir. Análisis y proyección de la obra juvenil inédita*. Madrid: Siglo XXI, 1986.

Martínez Nadal, Rafael. *Cuatro lecciones sobre Federico García Lorca*. Madrid: Fundación Juan March / Cátedra, 1980.

———. *Federico García Lorca. Mi penúltimo libro sobre el hombre y el poeta*. Madrid: Editorial Casariego, 1992.

Maurer, Christopher. "Epistolario: Federico García Lorca y Manuel de Falla." In Laura Dolfi, ed., *L'imposible / posible di Federico García Lorca. Atti del convegno di studi, Salerno, 9–10 maggio 1988*. Naples: Edizioni Scientifiche Italiane, 1989. Pp. 251–66.

———. "De la correspondencia de García Lorca: Datos inéditos sobre la transmisión de su obra." *FGL. Boletín de la Fundación Federico García Lorca* 1 (1987), 58–85.

Menéndez Pelayo, Marcelino. *Antología de poetas líricos castellanos*. Vol. IX. Santander:

Aldus, 1945. (Vol. XXV. Edición Nacional de las *Obras completas* de Menéndez Pelayo. Madrid: CSIC, 1945.)

Miller, Norman C. *García Lorca's Poema del cante jondo*. London: Tamesis Books, 1978.

Morris, C. B. "Fat Body, Thin Soul: Lorca's Landscape of Coney Island." In *Lorca Poet and Playwright. Essays in Honour of J. M. Aguirre*. Robert Havard, ed. Cardiff/New York: University of Wales Press/St. Martin's Press, 1992. Pp. 49–70.

———. *This Loving Darkness: The Cinema and Spanish Writers, 1920–36*. Oxford: Oxford University Press, 1980.

Newton, Candelas M. *Lorca: Libro de poemas o las aventuras de una búsqueda*. Salamanca: Acta Salmanticensia, 1986.

Ramos-Gil, Carlos. *Claves líricas de García Lorca. Ensayos sobre la expresión y los climas poéticos lorquianos*. Madrid: Aguilar, 1967.

Ramsden, H. *Lorca's Romancero gitano: Eighteen Commentaries*. Manchester: Manchester University Press, 1988.

Robertson, Sandra. *Lorca, Alberti and the Theater of Popular Poetry*. New York: Peter Lang, 1991.

Rodríguez Marín, Francisco. *Cantos populares españoles*. Vol. I. Sevilla: Francisco Alvarez, 1882.

Sahuquillo, Angel. *Federico García Lorca y la cultura de la homosexualidad: Lorca, Dalí, Cernuda, Gil-Albert, Prados y la voz silenciada del amor homosexual*. Stockholm: University of Stockholm (Akademisk avhandling for filosofie doktorsexamen), 1986. (Spanish edition: Alicante, Instituto de Cultura "Juan Gil-Albert" / Diputación de Alicante, 1991.)

Santos Torroella, Rafael. *Salvador Dalí escribe a Federico García Lorca [1925–1936]*. Special issue of *Poesía. Revista Ilustrada de Información Poética* 27–28 (1987).

Smith, C. Colin. *Spanish Ballads*. Oxford, New York: Pergamon Press, 1964.

Ucelay, Margarita. "La problemática teatral: Testimonios directos de Federico García Lorca." *FGL. Boletín de la Fundación Federico García Lorca*, 6 (1989), 27–58.

Valente, José Angel. "Pez luna." *Trece de Nieve* (Madrid) 1–2 (1976), 191–201.

Verlaine, Paul. *Oeuvres poétiques complètes*. Y.-G. Le Dantec and Jacques Borel, also Paris: Gallimard, 1962.

Walsh, John K. Unpublished notes on Lorca's Sonetos and Diván.

Zambrano, María. "El viaje: Infancia y muerte." *Trece de Nieve* (Madrid) 1–2 (1976), 181–90.

The Translators

FRANCISCO ARAGON, formerly a co-editor of the *Berkeley Poetry Review*, has translated Gerardo Diego's *Manuel de espumas*. His translation of *Cuerpo en llamas / Body in Flames* by Francisco X. Alarcón was published by Chronicle Books in 1990.

CATHERINE BROWN is an assistant professor of Spanish at the University of Michigan, Ann Arbor.

COLA FRANZEN is the translator of Alicia Borinski, Saúl Yurkievich, Marjorie Agosín, and other Latin American and Spanish poets, novelists, and critics.

WILL KIRKLAND, a poet, is the translator of *The Cricket Sings*, an anthology of children's poems by Lorca, and of contemporary Spanish poets.

WILLIAM BRYANT LOGAN, a writer and teacher, is the translator of Lorca's *Once Five Years Pass*.

JEROME ROTHENBERG is the author of over fifty books of poetry and translations, including *Geometría and the Lorca Variations*, and the editor of a number of anthologies of experimental and traditional poetry. He is a member of the Department of Visual Arts and the Department of Literature at the University of California, San Diego.

GREG SIMON, with Steven F. White, is the translator of Lorca's *Poet in New York*. He lives and works in Portland, Oregon.

ALAN S. TRUEBLOOD is professor emeritus of Hispanic Studies and Comparative Literature at Brown University. He is the translator of Góngora, Sor Juana Inés de la Cruz, Lope de Vega, Alexander von Humboldt, and Antonio Machado.

JOHN K. WALSH, professor of Spanish at the University of California, Berkeley (*d.* 1990), was the author of numerous studies on García Lorca and on Spanish medieval literature.

STEVEN F. WHITE teaches Spanish at St. Lawrence University. His most recent book of poems is *From the Country of Thunder*.

CHRISTOPHER MAURER, professor of Spanish and Portuguese at Vanderbilt University, has also edited Lorca's lectures and correspondence. His scholarly work centers on Spanish poetry of the sixteenth, seventeenth, and twentieth centuries.

Index of Titles

Indice de Títulos